Loving Midlife Marriage

Loving Midlife Marriage

A Guide to Keeping Romance Alive from the Empty Nest through Retirement

Betty L. Polston, Ph.D.

with

Susan K. Golant, M.A.

John Wiley & Sons, Inc.

New York ◆ Chichester ◆ Weinheim ◆ Brisbane ◆ Singapore ◆ Toronto

Published by John Wiley & Sons, Inc.
Published simultaneously in Canada

Design and production by Navta Associates, Inc.

Library of Congress Cataloging-in-Publication Data:
Polston, Betty L.
    Loving midlife marriage : a guide to keeping romance alive from the empty nest through retirement / Betty L. Polston, with Susan K. Golant.
        p.   cm.
    Includes bibliographical references and index.
    ISBN 0-471-31453-6 (alk. paper)
    1. Married people—United States—Psychology.   2. Spouses—United States—Psychology.   3. Middle aged persons—United States—Psychology.   4. Empty nesters—United States—Psychology.
    I. Golant, Susan K.   II. Title.
HQ1059.5.U5P66   1999
306.872—dc21   99-17025

Printed in the United States of America
10 9 8 7 6 5 4 3 2 1

This book is dedicated with love and
unbounded appreciation to my husband, Bernie;
my children, Selena and Josh;
and the memory of my mother, Marion Levin

Contents

Acknowledgments

I found few guideposts when I started my research into what comprises a successful marriage after the empty nest and retirement. In addition to my research, I relied on many individuals along the way to offer their insights, experiences, wisdom, and inspiration. I am grateful to all of you.

To the over one hundred individuals and couples in retirement and empty-nest marriages whom I interviewed for this book—thank you. You shared your very personal, joyful, sometimes painful, experiences. You did this, you told me, for a multitude of reasons, among which were the desire to help others and to talk about and celebrate your marriages' successful survival. Your wisdom and experience have been an invaluable addition to this book.

I thank my clients who have shared their struggles with me.

My thanks to our agent, Robert E. Tabian, who believed almost before the idea behind this book left my lips that it was a subject worthy of investigation.

Tom Miller, our editor at John Wiley & Sons, was very positive and supportive in making creative suggestions. It has been a pleasure working with him.

To my dear friends, all wives and mothers in midlife—Jan Cooper, Dottie Polakow, Carolyn Katz, Sheila Warner, and Madeline Linick—you have listened and shared. Jeanne Trudeau, whose ideas and loving support I cherish, and Selma Kaufer, my husband's sister, who in thought and deed is more a true sister than an in-law—you are a major part of my life. Thank you for being so supportive, kind, and caring.

I am grateful to my dear cousin Barbara Burbank and her friend Dorothy Clark, who introduced Susan and me. Susan Golant, my co-author, I admire and respect you. Without your work, support, and belief in this subject, this book would not have been possible. We laughed and cried and struggled giving birth to it. Your ability to stay with this project even though it entailed more than we both anticipated is admirable. I am grateful for your expertise, focus, intelligence, and empathy. You are the consummate professional.

As an inspiration to keep learning, growing, and questioning, I thank Selena and Josh, two of the most wonderful gifts a parent could realize, and also, my new son-in-law, Steve. Not only am I blessed with you, dear children, but the world is a better place because of your empathy and concern for your fellow man and woman. Am I grateful—are you kidding?

To my husband, Bernie, I give the final nod of appreciation. You endured so many interruptions when I needed a word or an idea at a moment's notice. You helped me knock down some of my occasional writer's blocks. You acted as a knowledgeable sounding board when trying out new ideas and exercises. And, you were part of the reason this book was written. Without our reactions to the empty nest and your retirement there would be no book. You have provided an oasis in our lives for growth and change to take place. I feel safe, secure, and accepted by you, and I love you for it.

—Betty L. Polston, Ph.D.

◆ ◆ ◆

I would like to thank Tom Miller, our editor at John Wiley & Sons, whose good humor and attentiveness brought our book to the light of day, and our agent, Robert E. Tabian, whose steadfast guidance I truly value. I would also like to thank my dear friend Dorothy Clark, who referred Betty Polston to me so many years ago, and Betty, herself, for bringing so much color and laughter into my life. This has truly been an adventure in publishing for both of us.

As always, I am indebted to my husband and soul mate, Dr. Mitch Golant, whose enduring love and support make ours a vital and exciting marriage. Sometimes it's hard to believe that we're still crazy about each other after all these years—but we are! Without him and our daughters, Cherie and Aimee, I would have lacked the emotional stores from which to draw inspiration for this book. And I will be forever grateful to my parents, whose marriage has spanned nearly six decades (including the chasm of the Holocaust) and, despite unimaginable hardships, continues to be a model of devotion, selflessness, and love.

—Susan K. Golant, M.A.

I've Been There, Done That, and It Works!

I F YOU ARE MARRIED WITH CHILDREN and over 45, this book is for you. Based on one hundred interviews with empty-nest and happily retired couples, my twenty-five years of clinical experience as a psychotherapist, and my own painful but growth-producing experiences, it is for individuals and couples in long-term, committed relationships.

Addressing two major changes in married life—the empty nest and one or both spouses' retirement—*Loving Midlife Marriage* casts a wide net. Nearly everyone passes through these major life transitions. For you, the empty nest or retirement may not occur for ten to fifteen years—or you may be in the middle of experiencing one or both, and want to know what to do.

This book grew out of two crises in my personal life. First, my husband retired, bringing on a multitude of changes in our marriage. Seven years later, our daughter married, leaving me with a sense of loss and confusion about my role as mother. I found myself wondering, "Who is this person staring back at me in the mirror?" That also had an impact on our marriage.

The first six to eight months of Bernie's retirement was a second honeymoon for us. We enjoyed doing what we wanted, when we wanted to do it. On my days off, we went to the beach, had lunch out, and spent time with friends who were also semiretired or retired. Then the honeymoon faded. Bernie and I experienced many ups and downs. Even though I am a psychotherapist and had counseled many couples about their relationships, including some in their retirement years, I felt I needed help. What could I do and where could I turn? As an action-oriented person, I decided to read all that I could on retirement marriages. I knew I wasn't the only one struggling with these problems.

When I looked at the material that had been published on aging, I discovered to my amazement that there was next to nothing about the retirement marriage. I decided to create a workshop for women who were anticipating their husbands' retirement or suffering through problems in their retirement marriages. The workshops were called "For Better or Worse . . . But Not for Lunch."

In the groups, we focused on specific issues and how to solve them—conflicts over space and time, housework, feelings of guilt and entrapment, and how much responsibility each spouse should take. We talked, cried, and laughed about mutual anxieties, hopes, fears, and expectations concerning the most important relationships in our lives. We faced a challenge expressed best by one woman in the group who said, "What can I do with him and myself? How can I sustain the marriage, his ego, and my strength? How can I be a person and still be part of a couple?"

The group experience helped all of us. I devised ways to negotiate new contracts between our spouses and ourselves. We drew floor plans to resolve territorial disputes within the house. We constructed time charts to explore how many hours we wanted to spend together or alone. We engaged in Relationship Review exercises—evaluations of what we wanted in our marriages and how to go about getting it.

Happily Married Retired Couples

Still, I wanted more information. I have a background in research; when I have a problem, my strategy is to investigate it. And so, I decided to study a group of couples in which the husband was retired and who identified themselves as happily wed. My goal was to understand what made these couples tick. Why were they so successful? What activities did they engage in? How did they treat each other? How did they deal with the inevitable conflicts arising from space, time, and intimacy in their marriages?

Dozens of middle- and upper-income couples over the age of 56 participated in my study. They were all unique, coming from varying ethnic, religious, and racial backgrounds. Married more than thirty years, the husbands had been retired for an average of five years. I wanted the adjustment memory to be fresh in their minds.

I interviewed each couple in their home for two to four hours. All were guaranteed anonymity; thus their names and identifying circumstances have been altered in this book. Specifically, I asked questions about how they handled the changes in their home, how they handled time together and time apart, how they resolved their inevitable conflicts, how they dealt with family and friends, how they went about making decisions, and how they resolved power issues like who makes the decisions.

These couples exemplified happy marriages. They enjoyed genuine sharing and togetherness. They had the capacity—in fact, they preferred—to spend time together but they did so without losing their identities. From this research, I constructed one of the guiding principles of this book—the Seven Marital Themes—the behaviors these couples engaged in for success.

The Empty Nesters

Seven years after Bernie's retirement, our daughter, who had already been living on her own for some years, got married. This presented yet another opportunity to address some important marital issues. In fact, I was so intrigued and had learned so much from the retirement couples that I conducted another series of interviews.

This time I spoke with midlife couples who had recently experienced the empty nest and were dealing with the transitions and dilemmas inherent in this life change. However, these couples were not necessarily happily married. They represented a wide spectrum of experiences. I wanted to understand the dynamics of their marriages—what worked and what didn't. I needed to understand so that I could help myself and others. I learned that the changes that occur during retirement often differ from the empty nest only in degree. During each stage, couples have the capacity to build upon their experiences from the previous transition. One stage prepares you for the next.

In the chapters that follow, I will have much to share about what I've learned from the couples I've studied and my own experiences.

What This Book Contains

There is help here for husbands and wives individually, with specific chapters for each. You cannot understand how you interact in a relationship until you understand how you, as an individual, are affected by these two major life transitions: retirement and the empty nest. However, the majority of the book is devoted to you as a couple; first and foremost, this is a book about enhancing your marriage. Even if just one of you reads it, however, shifts can occur. The laws of nature say that when one spouse changes, there is a change in the other—for every action there is a reaction.

I have included numerous exercises to do together that draw on the premise that good communication is one of the pillars of a fulfilling marriage. Use them as rehearsals for improved interaction and understanding—for change.

The notion of rehearsal is important. When you rehearse, you practice certain new behaviors. If they don't feel quite right, you change the behaviors until they fit. And doing your part over and over helps you to do it well. In this case, your part is the fulfilled empty-nest or retirement husband or wife. You don't have to rehearse in order to benefit from this book. But at least read these exercises. They usually highlight the issues you've just read about and may offer additional insights into your family's interactions. These provide the chance to change without risk.

You will also find many Questions for Growth and several Relationship Reviews to help you explore your own feelings and experiences in depth. You might enjoy and benefit from keeping a journal, either separately or together, where you can jot down your responses and think about them later.

All in all, you will learn how to initiate discussions with an eye toward solutions, how to make your home a haven during these changing times, and how to take care of yourselves and your marriage.

In Part One, we will explore what constitutes a happy marriage and how change and transition occur, especially when adapting to new roles and disengaging from old ones that no longer serve us. Parts Two and Three are devoted to midlife and the empty nest. We will elucidate how these phases in your life affect you individually and as a couple. We will discuss how to let go of your young adult children as well as how to enhance your marriage at this transitional time. In Parts Four and Five, we will cover the impact of retirement on you individually and as a couple, and I will share with you what my research has shown about what makes for a happy retirement marriage.

The focus here is to help you and your partner learn how to maximize these midlife years and beyond so that they can be the happiest of your lives.

I have devoted a major part of the last several years of my life to the improvement of my marriage, as Bernie and I have experienced his retirement and the empty nest. It has become my passion. I've read everything I could find on these subjects, conducted studies, interviewed couples, run groups, spoken to organizations large and small, written articles, and now this book. It has been an interesting journey.

There is much useful information, encouragement, and guidance in the following pages. Know that all of the suggestions in *Loving Midlife Marriage* have been tried out by yours truly, just as a cookbook author would test all of her recipes. They helped us—they can help you. We've been there, done that, and it works!

My wish is that your journey through this new phase of your lives will be a long and fruitful one, filled with compassion, good cheer, and love.

◆ ◆ ◆

Author's Note

Dr. Polston is available for speaking engagements, workshops, and corporate consulting.

She is also available for Retirement Relationship Coaching for individuals and couples.

You may contact her toll free at 1-877-LOVING4 (1-877-568-4644) or by e-mail at Drbettyp@aol.com.

PART ONE

Suddenly the Algebra Shifts

LIKE MANY PEOPLE, MY FAMILY and I have faced challenges during the midlife period. The emptying of the nest and retirement constitute two major transitions in most midlife marriages. You might think of them as parallel events: with the empty nest, you endure the loss of role as active mother and father; with retirement, you endure the loss of being workers in the world.

Time was—as recently as the turn of the century—when parents died an average of eighteen months after their children moved out. Midlife was short, and retirement almost nonexistent. Even in the 1930s, when Social Security was developed and put in place, the age of 65 was considered much older than the average life span.

But these days, with our extended longevity and the development of technology that makes it possible to bear children later in life, there is great variety in the age and circumstances of couples when their children leave and in how they manage their post-employment years.

Although in many instances the empty nest predates retirement, in some cases the reverse can be true, or both can occur at the same time. In my family, Bernie's early retirement preceded our daughter's marriage by seven years! And our son Josh, though out the door the day after his high school graduation, returned to the nest to live periodically for months at a time until he finally took up residence in a different city at the age of 28.

Whether they occur in sequence or simultaneously, the empty nest and retirement hold much in common. In both instances, the old order no longer applies. Issues in your marriage that seemed to have been settled years ago are up for grabs once again. Suddenly the algebra of needs and circumstances shifts. Both transitions have the potential for:

- The loss of important roles
- The retooling of your identities
- Increased time together
- An alteration in living space arrangements
- Renewed attention to activities (yours, mine, and ours)
- A new awareness of mortality
- Improved communication due to a lessening of stress (with jobs and/or children gone)
- Diminished conflict (your children's adolescence, in particular, is a difficult time for you as a couple) or increased conflict due to the absence of children as a buffer
- Greater dependency, especially on the part of men

People in retirement marriages face additional issues, including the reassignment of household chores, the effects of aging and illness, and more available time together.

The fact is, empty nest and retirement can throw into disarray even the strongest unions.

Besides, children and work are great distracters and buffers. Kids, for instance, can dilute intimacy with your spouse as you both focus on parenting duties; they can divert you from facing core dissatisfactions in the marriage. But with their departure after eighteen or more years of child-rearing (through college, their marriage, or simply moving out), you may suddenly find yourselves facing each other, a couple once more, but sorely out of practice in relating directly to each other. In some cases, sadly, the exit of the children dissolves the marital bond—they seem to be all that held together what was left of a fragile shell.

And some individuals use their careers as a refuge from stale, lifeless marriages. But even if a job does not stand in place of a good marriage, work fills many hours and can provide meaning, structure, and deep ego gratification. Indeed, with the children and work no longer a daily force to reckon with, all the energy you once directed toward these engrossing activities and all of the benefits you derived from them must now be redirected into individual and couple pursuits—and many challenges, if not out-and-out trouble, can loom as a result.

❖ ❖ ❖

How can you avoid this trouble? In Part One, we will explore the meaning and function of transition in your lives and we will propose a solution—what I call the Growth Circle—that will help you and your spouse in a spirit of goodwill and cooperation.

CHAPTER 1

Scenes from a
Midlife Marriage

A successful marriage is an edifice that must be rebuilt every day.
—André Maurois

I T WAS THE FIRST DAY OF FALL. Change felt imminent. Up in the hills above Malibu, the day seemed both hot and cool—the searing sun blazed in a bright blue sky, yet we were shaded beneath a grove of oaks whose twisted branches formed a protective canopy. Friends and family had gathered in this tranquil, bucolic place—the home of my dear friend—to celebrate our daughter's wedding. Everywhere there was evidence of fall—in the terra-cotta pots and the bridesmaids' earth-tone dresses and in the freshly planted flowerbeds and wooden planters filled with chrysanthemums all across the property. This was our vision coming to life in a place that we loved deeply. It was a serene haven for experiencing one of life's most important passages.

Our daughter Selena's wedding was a dream come true. I devoted five months to preparing it—it was a labor of love. As an all-accommodating "Super Mom," I needed every detail to be perfect. The newlyweds had an agenda, and I carried it out—campgrounds for friends; a beach nearby for parties, dinners and picnics; and of course, the main event.

And what an event it turned out to be. Selena wore a confection of seed pearls and silk moiré that hugged her body like spun sugar. Suddenly I was beholding a sensual woman rather than the girl I had always known. She danced with such depth of feeling, such passion. This was her glorious day to shine. I even sang a love song, "The More I See You," to the happy couple. It was one of the peak experiences of my life.

But the next morning when I awoke, I had the oddest feeling inside. I was empty, as if the light had gone out of me forever. I felt lost, and I wandered around the house aimlessly, asking myself, "Who am I? Who the hell am I?" Selena didn't need me anymore in the same way. It felt as if an internal organ had been cut out of me, out of who I was, and put somewhere else. I felt disconnected when what I wanted was connection. I felt awful.

Sure, I had been sad for a few weeks after my children had left for college, but nothing as profound as this. I felt a great loss, yet I had so much. Despite it all, I couldn't stop crying. For weeks, I couldn't stop crying.

My husband of thirty-something years, Bernie, reacted differently to the wedding. He wasn't as overwrought as I was. Rather, it was a paradox for him. He was glad Selena had gotten married. "I feel good having a married daughter, seeing that she's okay," he told me. "There's a certain pride in seeing her begin to form her own family. I'm happy for her." But at the same time he realized that "things would never be the same." For him it was the end of an era, but he seemed more concerned about the "new geometry," as he called it, of the family than he was about the changing relationship with his daughter.

Consequently, he was less than understanding with me. He complained that I was too self-absorbed; that I had less time to give him and our marriage. "First you were totally engrossed in the wedding preparations," he griped, "and now that it's over, instead of refocusing on us, you're unhappy and unavailable all over again."

He felt disappointed that this important event had not brought us any closer. He complained that we weren't having fun anymore, that my usually upbeat personality was missing.

I resented his expecting so much of me when I was feeling so lost. I resented his dependence on me. "Here I am so down," I retorted angrily, "and you're complaining about your social life? I didn't put those stresses on you when you were in a bad way. You need to be there for me."

We argued. Boy, did we argue.

Suddenly, our lives weren't working anymore. We needed to renegotiate our relationship. We needed to understand the effects on me, on him, and on us of this change in individual, parental, and marital roles. Now, it really was just the two of us, and we weren't quite sure how to proceed.

Our daughter's marriage was the second time during our midlife years that we had needed to reappraise and adjust our marriage. The first incident began innocently enough one evening seven years prior to the wedding. Bernie and I were sitting at the kitchen table finishing dinner as we had so many nights before. He had been picking at his food, however, without much appetite. He stirred his coffee and tapped his foot distractedly. The TV blared the evening news, and our dog Sami lay curled under the table.

Suddenly, Bernie looked up from his plate and turned his bright blue eyes toward me. With a determination that seemed tinged with sadness he said, "I've decided to semiretire from my practice. I'm leaving." He shook his head. "I'm out of there. I'll take a few of my biggest clients and work from home part-time."

"What?" I gasped. I could feel the heat rise in my neck and a tightness overtake my throat. My just-consumed dinner began to churn in my stomach. "You're quitting your practice?" I repeated in disbelief.

I knew Bernie had been unhappy. There had been some vague utterances before about leaving work. No matter what, Bernie is not one to do things rashly. Distressed as he was, I thought he'd go along anyway. A lot of men go through the motions even in the face of burnout. Besides, it's a living. I hadn't taken Bernie's complaints all that seriously until that night.

He looked at my stricken expression, and before I even had a chance to ask, he reassured me. "Financially, we'll be okay," he said. "Our lives will be okay. We'll have to tighten our purse strings a bit, but I'll be active. We'll be fine."

I didn't believe him. Not for a minute. Bernie didn't have one hobby. Nothing. Zip. His work totally and completely defined him. We used to jokingly call him "Bernie the Attorney." His selfhood was wrapped up in his career.

Moreover, Bernie and I are different in temperament. I am a take-charge, active sort of person; he's more laid-back. Our friends know us as a "She-Speeds-Him-Up" and "He-Slows-Her-Down" couple. I would get angry with him on weekends because I wanted us to do things together. I wanted him to take the initiative and plan activities, to have an upbeat attitude. I couldn't stand the long stints in front of the television, the newspapers strewn about the house.

And now I had visions of TV and naps . . . of books and newspapers . . . of his lying around the patio and falling asleep in the chair . . . stretching into infinity. I anticipated that his home office would be a mess, with contracts and letters all over the place. I didn't want him around all the time. I didn't want him underfoot. I had my routine. This was *my* house!

Lots of questions and anxieties buzzed around in my head, but mainly I was concerned about what would happen to him. To me. To our relationship. What worried me most was how Bernie's lack of outside interests would affect our marriage. Besides, he never was one to adjust easily to change—even if it was self-imposed. What would retirement be like for him, and how would this major transition in his life affect me and our marriage?

What Makes a Good Marriage?

Marriage is a precious commodity. Indeed, a good marriage is life-affirming. Research has shown that the happier your marriage, the happier and longer your life! Yet this most complex of human relationships is never static. Rather, it is a work in progress that requires constant tending in order to thrive. During midlife and beyond, you will encounter the greatest number of transitions ever—the children leaving home; your leaving work; your parents' illnesses and deaths; your own aging—and you may benefit greatly from reassessing and adjusting your marriage at these times.

But what exactly is a good marriage? Do you have one? And if not, can you create one at this late date?

Couples in a good marriage have a strong emotional bond that revolves around their shared feelings and involvements. Indeed, they often prefer to spend time together and take pleasure from joint activities, even as they maintain their individual identities. Certainly, the partners have conflicts—fighting that airs grievances can be healthy—but they handle them constructively and resolve them. They know well how to repair the rift. They work through their problems by adapting to changes in each other and in their circumstances. These changes, of course, can include the emptying of the nest and retirement.

Unhappy marriages, in contrast, are marked by continual belligerence and tension. These couples may mask their problems by presenting a façade of civility to the outside world, or their conflicts may spill out into the open as they publicly nag and belittle each other. Other less-than-stellar unions can begin with high expectations and good intentions, then gradually evolve into boredom and emptiness. The partners may share few interests or activities and may stay together because of family or religious pressure, or simply from inertia. And others are marriages of convenience in which partners have few expectations of each other—and derive few rewards. Each partner pursues independent, outside activities that keep the couple separate.

Questions for Growth

EVALUATING YOUR MARRIAGE

Before beginning this first exercise, a few instructions are in order. In a quiet moment, eliminating all distractions, and making good eye contact, tell your partner that you are reading this book and that you would like to discuss some of the issues I've raised. Make sure the phone or other distractions will not interrupt you and that you have each other's full attention. Creating this special time to talk sends the message that you give the relationship top priority, and that's a compliment.

And always keep in mind the words you use, your gestures, and how well you listen. At first, juggling what you say with how you say it may feel like patting your head and rubbing your stomach at the same time. Practice does not make perfect, but it does help you communicate more effectively and with more ease as time goes by. Now you're ready to try the first exercise.

Given the above descriptions of good and could-be-better marriages:

1. Where does your marriage stand? What is your spouse's opinion? Do you agree with each other?

> **2.** Discuss with your spouse where each of you sees areas for improvement.
>
> **3.** You might jot your ideas in a journal. Refer to your notes as you proceed to other exercises in this book. Keep in mind that this is just a beginning.

It's never too late to renew and revitalize; where there's life, there's hope. After all, with life spans stretching into the late seventies and eighties, even nineties and beyond, you can look forward to thirty or forty years together after the children leave—more time without them than with them! Even if you change your perspective or behavior ever so slightly, that may be enough to shift your marriage toward a more positive course. So no matter how you and your spouse perceive your marriage now, change for the better is always possible. Consider this merely a starting point.

Practice the Seven Marital Themes

From my research with couples in fulfilling marriages, I have discerned seven marital themes that contribute to the happiness of marriage. Let these serve as guiding principles as you navigate the transitions you will be making during the empty nest and beyond:

1. Accepting each other's individual differences
2. Nurturing each other
3. Reaching out to family and friends
4. Sharing values, goals, and marital responsibilities
5. Being flexible
6. Communicating your feelings and thoughts to your partner and listening to your partner's point of view
7. Managing conflicts

I will discuss these themes in greater depth throughout the book.

When put into practice, these Seven Marital Themes can help ensure that your marriage will be a haven of growth and development. This can be a fulfilling time in your lives. In fact, I often feel like shouting to midlifers who complain of getting old that they should wake up and look forward to the wisdom that comes with age!

Look Forward to the Wisdom
That Comes with Age

Most of us feel a good deal of ambivalence about midlife and aging. You hear over and over again from your friends and the media how aging is totally negative, associated with illness, the loss of attractiveness, and the advent of disability.

It's not necessarily so! So much is based on myths. In truth, middle age (which is now generally defined as the years from 35 to 70) can be life's peak experience. This is your prime. This is what you've been working toward. Research from the John D. and Catherine T. MacArthur Foundation Research Network on Successful Midlife Development makes clear that midlifers have the know-how to deal with life's changes more than at any other time in their lives. More than likely, you're at the top of your form in your ability to handle difficult issues with a sense of control and responsibility. You can look forward to a lot more than you thought you could.

Many retired people in this country have their finances well in place. And although many of us are still in midlife, we have been freed from the demands of the workaday world. We now have the time and the resources to spend with our spouses, to explore hitherto untapped interests, to indulge grandchildren, to travel, and enjoy our well-deserved leisure. This is a positive, growth-promoting time in our lives. Perhaps the retirement years (and not just midlife) are what we have worked toward all of our lives.

We have many things to look forward to at this time, and one of them is wisdom. After all, we have faced many challenges and witnessed many transitions, and we're still alive and kicking. We have matured and become wise from our experiences. Not only can we expect respect from others, but we can also respect ourselves.

The most valuable part of this wisdom, however, is not the kind that entails wagging a finger at an offspring and expounding, "Well, I've lived all these years and this is the way 'it should be done'" or "'this is what I've learned.'" The most valuable aspect of wisdom is that which we use internally for our own inner growth, our survival and consequently our peace of mind, and our ability to really embrace these years as individuals and as a couple.

	EXPLORING THE GOOD IN
Questions for Growth	**YOUR MARRIAGE**
	D iscuss together the positive aspects of your lives and your relationship right now.
1.	What had you hoped for when you first married?
2.	What have you actually achieved? If you've gained wisdom about your relationship, elaborate on this.
3.	Evaluate. Are you closer to the "it"—the essence—of your relationship?
4.	Contrast your positive feelings to the problems you might have unearthed in the "Evaluating Your Marriage" exercise.

Letting Go and Moving On

Eight months after Selena's wedding, we'd come through a difficult time, but our relationship was definitely better. I had had a lot of anxiety and, as a therapist, I knew this was to be expected. Intellectually, I understood that marrying off a child can bring on a crisis but this knowledge did not stop me from being upset. I was searching for a new reconnected self.

Since the empty nest seemed to affect me more than it did Bernie, I focused on understanding myself, my needs and motivations, and my early years with my family for insights regarding my reactions. Together, Bernie and I worked at letting go, moving on, and understanding the changing dynamics of the family. We both realized we needed to embrace new roles (besides Mom and Dad) with different activities and meaningful involvements. Indeed, the more roles we had, the better our adjustment.

Selena gave me a card at her wedding shower showing someone throwing many hats into the air. Inside, she wrote about how she sees me fulfilling so many roles—wearing many hats. I didn't realize how prophetic that card would be; it became a symbol of my coping skills and my ability to move on.

Now Bernie and I were both experiencing a wonderful time in our married lives. We talked constantly, reviewing our relationship, paying special attention to what we each wanted now. Soon, we decided that we were ready to take a honeymoon commemorating our second transition in midlife. And what more beautiful city could we choose than Venice?

We flew from Los Angeles to London, then boarded the Orient Express. Once in Venice, we stayed at beautiful seventeenth-century hotels and slept in big puffy beds. We wandered the streets and crossed the canals and got lost in the Old City. We drifted into marketplaces and bought fruit off the stands, which we shared as we strolled. We visited museums and, as Katharine Hepburn and Rossano Brazzi did in the classic film *Summertime*, we had a picnic near an ancient church on the picturesque island of Torcello.

One evening after our ramblings, Bernie rented a gondola and a singer to go with it. Our *cantatore* serenaded us with arias from *I Pagliacci*. The full moon illuminating the water was our only light. As the gondolier maneuvered us through those narrow canals, the water lapping at the sides of the boat, we snuggled closer. In a way it was symbolic—just the two of us hugging each other, going through dark, close passages, and emerging on the other side into the splendor of the Grand Canal.

The trip and the intervening months had given me a perspective from which to look back on the wedding and my intense reaction to it. It helped me to realize that the pain we had experienced was growth-producing. It had opened our lives as individuals and as a couple.

How else do we grow except by going through transitions? In order to move forward, we must let go, acknowledging that one phase of our lives is behind us.

CHAPTER 2

Some Things Change; Others Never Will

The need for change bulldozed a road down the center of my mind.

— Maya Angelou

Sharon: When Angela, our only child, was nine years old, we moved to Europe for one year. We went to Pienza, a little village in Tuscany. It was an important year for us in every way. At that time, we had been married for fifteen years. When you're married for a long time, you reach a point when you know everything so well. Everything is so predictable, and it's not just your mate, it's your life too. That's one reason I really wanted to go. If I don't change, I will die. Change, change. You begin to get so used to everything.

I told Jim the first couple of weeks, we may want to go home. And what a surprise! He was a tower of strength. He could calm me down, put things in perspective. He was my hero, even after fifteen years. It was the basis for many things. We had a most amazing year as a family, as individuals, and for our marriage. That year really made a difference in our marriage and in our lives. I was 42.

Jim: The year we spent in Italy was the happiest in our marriage. We had been apprehensive about it and spent the whole year overcoming our apprehensions. We did things that were unusual, different—things we never thought we'd experience.

We used a wood-burning stove for heat. At night, we read by candlelight. There were no telephones. We lived on a farm where we had access to food, but we had to forage for it. Sharon was washing clothes by hand and hanging them up on a line to dry. I was chopping wood.

These were almost adverse conditions for us as a family and also for Sharon and me as a couple. But not only did we fare well, we loved it. It was a whole new hemisphere of possibilities for when we are older. We found that we were much more adaptable to a radically different situation than we believed we could be.

Self-Knowledge Helps Us Negotiate Change

Sharon had stated that if she didn't change, she would die. But what does it mean to change? In my opinion, it means adapting to different circumstances—moving toward growth—according to our capabilities. It's the secret to our survival.

Sometimes individuals within marriages are out of sync and are changing in different directions or at different paces. With the departure of the children, for instance, a wife's long-delayed career may be taking off just as her husband feels ready to slow down and leave the rat race behind. And that can cause dissension. Indeed, a marriage consists of two changing individuals within a changing relationship living in a world that is constantly changing around them. We are each whirling in our own little orbits, which twirl around larger and larger trajectories. No wonder life sometimes seems dizzyingly confusing!

But for change to become growth—a movement toward a more positive adaptation—we need to have information about ourselves and our capabilities. This information helps us to feel more in control and to endure the difficulties and losses we will inevitably encounter. Self-knowledge is critical to help us negotiate change within ourselves and our marriages.

YOU HAVE CHANGED

Whether you're aware of it, you have changed the way you think about yourselves and your lives. Consider the idea of "happiness." Together discuss what happiness meant to each of you:

◆ In the second grade

◆ After high school

◆ Yesterday

Change comes into your life expectedly or unexpectedly. But one of the best ways to reduce the impact of change is to anticipate what's coming and plan for it.

Sometimes looking back can help you look toward the future. What major planned or unplanned changes have you experienced in your life? Use the following questions to stimulate discussion about how you have dealt with changes in the past.

Involuntary Changes
If you've lost your job in the past, how did you manage? What about other financial reversals? How did you cope when you were separated from loved ones due to an accident, financial problems, or some other crisis? Have you ever been forced to relocate to a new city? How did you deal with it? If a loved one died suddenly and unexpectedly, how did you find the strength to go on?

Voluntary Changes
How did you manage decisions about your life after you graduated from high school or college? How did you both deal with your first child? How did you adjust to career changes?

Clearly, you have displayed strength and courage throughout your lifetime. You have had rehearsals. Find a way to tap these resources now that you face new challenges.

Changing Roles in Midstream

Our sense of identity is closely linked to the different roles we play in our lives, as well as to others' perceptions of how we perform in them. Our roles create social status and a positive sense of self, and our life satisfaction may be dependent on our continued performance in them. We feel committed to our roles and consider them valuable. So change can be particularly challenging when it affects our roles as parent or worker. After all, these have formed a major component of our identities.

Traditionally, playing the role of mother means being important, involved, nurturing—necessary to the existence of another being. With fatherhood, we take on the mantle of provider and authority figure, and believe we have some control over our children's destiny. Being a worker means having power and status in the world; we are engaged in productive activity. The more invested we are in a particular role, the greater the loss when we must let it go. The questions we must ask ourselves are: "How can I give up something so important to my very being? When my role changes or diminishes, who am I? How am I defined? How and where am I connected? What is my sense of self?"

Sharon, for example, felt devastated when Angela left for college. "At first I thought I wouldn't make it," she told me. "I'm Angela's mom, and now I won't have anything to do for her. I thought to myself, how can I stand it without her around—for so many reasons, not least of which is the energy she brings into this house, with all her friends and activities. Those things make my life a lot fuller. It was scary to me, the solitude."

These changes can even call your marriage into question. As my interviewee Katy explained, "When the kids left, the dynamics changed. We had to decide if we wanted to live together as man and wife. We started focusing on what was good and on what was missing. How did we get along? What did each of us like? What did each of us want?"

Normal life events and changes may not be traumatic in themselves if we perceive that they are occurring gradually and "on time"—that is, when we expect them to. In contrast, life events that occur abruptly and "off schedule"—an early forced retirement, the untimely death of a spouse, a child's premature departure from the nest—can evoke stress and crisis. One of my interviewees, Marcia, suffered from the precipitous emptying of her nest:

> My younger daughter went to live with my ex-husband when she was thirteen. That was very painful for me. I didn't expect

to have my kids gone until they left for college. I felt like my heart was torn out—a part of me had been torn away. It was like losing a child. It wasn't the natural order of things. It happened fairly quickly and long before I ever expected it to. Instead of an empty nest, I had an empty heart.

Not all transitions need be as difficult as Marcia's. Most of us can weather the storm with minimal disruption and come out on the other side better than ever, especially when we are able to prepare ourselves for them by being flexible.

Is a midlife crisis inevitable? Although several of my interviewees seemed to suffer a midlife crisis, it is not a foregone conclusion that all individuals between the ages of 40 and 55 do so. According to many research surveys, the vast majority of people making the transition into midlife do so gently and gradually, with only 10 to 12 percent actually having a midlife crisis. Those who do have a true psychological upheaval (aside from disasters such as divorce, being fired, or serious illness) have had difficulties adjusting to change throughout their lives.

Most of us learn to rely on our brains and our acquired skills instead of our brawn or our beauty as we move forward in our lives. We recognize and accept our limitations and become more practical as we redirect our goals and choices. And women, in particular, recognize their new strengths at this time and often feel empowered by them.

Divorce is also not as common as we might believe during this period. Experts explain that most breakups occur during the first six to eight years of marriage, not at midlife. The likelihood of divorce declines after ten or fifteen years. Apparently, the frequency of midlife divorce is more myth than reality. Couples often stay together during this period, but their marriages may be conflicted or may lack vitality. It is also possible to have a very good time during midlife, as some of my interviewees can attest.

Anticipate and Adapt to Your New Role

Knowing or imagining what you will do as an empty-nest mother or father or a retired individual can also be a matter of rehearsal. Mental role playing can give you a taste of what's to come and help you to adjust.

Adapting to your new roles involves matching their demands with your capabilities. And, believe it or not, if you're a "worrier," your active imagination can stand you in good stead. It gives you the chance to try on new ways of being and doing. Try the following exercise:

Rehearsal	**MENTAL ROLE PLAYING**
	If you are not yet an empty nester or a retiree, imagine that you've already moved into your new role. Now ask yourself the following questions. You may want to write your answers in your journal.
1.	What activities am I engaging in? How do I feel doing them? Is there something more I would like to do?
2.	What people are involved in my life now? What part do they play?
3.	What role does my partner play? What are my expectations of him or her?
4.	What is our relationship like now? What are we doing to enjoy ourselves? What problems are we having in the marriage?
5.	What would my ideal day look like as an empty nester or retiree?
	Now share what you have imagined with your spouse. Explain the mental role-playing exercise you've just completed. Discuss whether your expectations of his or her participation are realistic.

Why make a mystery of what's to come? Through anticipation, you can begin to work toward this change and solve some problems in advance.

Dealing with Change

Change is inevitable, and yet it is in our nature to resist it and cling to what is familiar. In the case of the children's departure or retirement, many of us think it is the beginning of the last stage of our lives—and we don't want to face that.

Besides, when one person in a family wants to change, other members may put up roadblocks and resist. Families do not consist of individual units that just happen to be thrown together at random. Rather, like organizations, as family members we are part of a larger whole and are affected by anything that occurs within the system.

Similarly, when one family member grows and changes, it can intensify reactions in other members. One vibrating string resonates with the next. Your child's sexual maturation, for instance, can set off twinges of self-examination or discomfort in you. The same can be said of a husband's retirement. You may ask yourself, "With my husband around so much of the time, will I feel smothered?"

Loving Midlife Marriage is about the changes and transitions of mid-life and beyond—especially the transitions from being full-time parents into empty nesters and from being workers into retirees. Both of these stages in life involve going from a moment when you are in a "knowable place" to a moment when you are in an "unknowable place." During this time, it is as if you are traversing a bridge, moving from your old self and way of life toward a new one. The experience of crossing the bridge can fill you with anxiety, fear, loss, and confusion.

Several of my interviewees pointed out that after a period of insta-bility, life became smoother and sometimes improved as they crossed the bridge to their new realities. Consider empty nester Louisa's initial predicament:

> The impact of the empty nest didn't hit me until our young-est left. Suddenly I felt very lost. I missed the social time with her in the afternoons and evenings, especially since Cal often worked until 9 P.M. and even later. "Who will I cook for?" I lamented. We didn't seem as important. I myself didn't feel as important. No one needed me anymore.

After three months of confusion, Louisa found that she had made some big changes in her life and weathered the transition quite well:

> Although I had never been athletic before, for my forty-fifth birthday I joined a gym. It helped me to control my weight and gave me some social activity in the evenings when Cal came home late from work. I even began working out with a trainer twice a month. I started having dinners out with my single friends on weeknights. I increased my attendance at

professional meetings. Suddenly, my work took on new meaning and importance. Unhindered by my children's schedules and needs, I was able to put long hours into projects that might have seemed overwhelming before. I started teaching seminars at a local university. I took jobs that required me to travel on short notice and left for Washington, New York, and Atlanta for several days to several weeks, leaving Cal to fend for himself. Although we missed each other, he managed just fine and so did I.

Louisa moved from a state of desolation and uncertainty toward a new reality that suited her current situation. The transitions in our lives, as resistant as we may be to them and as chaotic and unnerving as they may feel, often follow this same pattern.

The Road to a New Reality

To make a transition, you have to think backwards. Instead of beginning, middle, and end, you start at the end of what you have known then move onto the bridge, a "nowhere place," and finally emerge at a starting point on the other side, a fresh start that had been unfathomable until now.

The End: Your Starting Place

It is natural for us to experience a sense of loss at the ending place. Indeed, like Louisa, it may feel as if something inside of us is dying. And perhaps it is. A piece of our old sense of self must wither so that we can step off the precipice, so that a new dimension can be born, take hold, and grow. It is difficult to separate ourselves from what seems so familiar, but that is the task of this phase.

Famed psychiatrist Erik Erikson tells the story of finding a sign over a bar in a western town that read: "I ain't what I ought to be, and I ain't what I'm going to be. But I ain't what I was."

Stories we have told ourselves and that had worked for us before ("I have the best kids," "I have the best boss") no longer operate. "That was then," we say to ourselves, "but this is now, and I can no longer live in the past." Indeed, the feelings of disenchantment and disorientation are signs that we are moving toward transition.

The Nowhere Place Can Be Frightening

It is difficult to let go of what we know and endure the "nowhere" of the in-between stage until we've latched onto a new reality. The experience of the Nowhere Place is a temporary state of fear, emptiness, and loss. We tend to pay the least attention to this stage of the transition process, but I believe that it is the most important. For even though it is the very thing we fear the most, it is the stage that will help us grow and move toward change.

You may find it helpful at this point to surrender to the Nowhere Place. Give in to the emptiness and stop struggling to escape. Go off alone to think or meditate. This can expand your reality and deepen your sense of purpose. Take a "Nowhere Place Respite"—a rest before the big changes to come. Or "just be"—stare at the clouds, watch children play at the park, let your mind go blank. Zoning out or becoming a couch potato is perfectly acceptable at this time.

Allow your emotions free rein. If you're feeling scared, be scared with the full knowledge that soon you will be fine; this is a transient state. And even if it seems as though nothing is happening, much important work is occurring internally.

Rehearsal | **YOUR NOWHERE PLACE**

With your spouse, brainstorm some activities that you can do right now or in the future to help you through the Nowhere Place.

1. Write down anything that comes to mind. (You might read funny books, take a trip, watch TV, work in the garden.)

2. Together, go over your list and label each of your ideas in order of difficulty (1 for the easiest to accomplish; 2 for something more challenging; 3 for the most difficult).

3. Try the easiest first. (You might save others for the future, since life is full of transitions. You'll have ample opportunities to use these again.)

A Fresh Start

Paradoxically, you come to the Fresh Start only at the end of the transition process. The realization that you are there can occur subtly; you have an idea, an impression, a dream that strikes a resonance within you. You can now begin to act in your new role instead of just getting ready, as you did in the Nowhere Place. You can envision yourself in this new place, you can take it step by step, and shift your focus from seeking a goal to the process of reaching that goal. For instance, after my midlife transitions, I began writing this book and developing a new adult-adult relationship with my daughter.

Can You Learn to Accept the Unchangeables?

Here is a conundrum—just as change is inevitable in our lives, there are certain things in ourselves, our partners, and our relationships that will never, ever change. These may be good qualities—the traits that drew us to our spouses in the first place. But they can also be unresolvable problems, those sticky issues that never go away that all couples face— the *unchangeables.*

Take my family. Bernie hates to shop. I have tried to convince him it's fun and exciting; I have argued that he's missing the adventure of making new finds and have even resorted to pleading—all to no avail. He won't do it! I am sure of that *now.* What have I done with this fact of life—this reality? I have accepted it and work with the fact that *it* will never change. In fact, *it* has almost become a joke between the two of us. I factor *it* in at home, and when we travel, we work *it* out. I look on his intractable feelings about shopping as an *it*—and therefore have gained some distance from the problem.

Every person you marry or could have married has a set of personality characteristics and preferences that he or she will not or cannot change. No matter how much this bothers you—it is a fact of life. I married Bernie. He hates to shop, he's stubborn, and he's always too early. If I had married Leo, I would be wedded to a bossy, stingy person. Stanley drank too much and dominated conversations.

In all marriages there are problems and issues that can be worked at and changed to some degree. We'll work on those in this book. But there are others that seem to be unsolvable. These lie in the realm of Acceptance—letting go of the struggle to change each other.

You must identify the things in your partner and your relationship that you can change, those you cannot, and as the serenity prayer says, pray for the wisdom to know the difference. Next, you need to accept the fact that the unchangeables simply will not change. Finally, it's helpful to adopt an attitude that says, "I want to work this out." That calls for a willingness to take responsibility for your own attitude readjustments.

If you can do these things, then you have taken the crucial steps toward dealing with the unchangeables. The following suggestions may also help.

Reframing Your Attitude

On a recent vacation to the desert, I looked out the window of our hotel room and remarked on the beautiful golden hue of the mountains in stark contrast to the blue, cloudless sky. "This is a special and unique beauty that you can only see in the desert," I commented to Bernie. But when I opened the window, the intensity of the colors diminished. I realized that the window had been tinted with yellow film to reduce heat from the midday sun. I had been looking through a different-colored glass, which altered my perception.

When you *reframe,* you look at a problem from a different perspective. The idea of reframing comes from the field of cognitive therapy. It is based on the premise that your thoughts influence your behavior. In this skill you intentionally deal with a negative perspective—an unchangeable quality in your spouse that annoys you ("He's so controlling!") but you put this image in a different frame ("Actually, he's determined and decisive and gets things done"). Reframing allows you to change your thoughts so that you can change your behavior, in this case, your tolerance of a spouse's formerly unacceptable quality.

Rehearsal	A NEW WAY OF LOOKING AT MY PARTNER
1.	Together list those unchangeable qualities in your spouse that bother you.
2.	Next to your complaint, make a reframing statement:
	He's loud at parties. *He's the life of the party and creates fun for everyone.*

She's too passive.   *She is calm and very accepting of me.*

3. Keep this skill of reframing in mind as you continue through the book.

"As If"

The field of attitude research has shown that when we engage in behavior even though we don't have the feelings connected to it (we play-act or pretend), eventually our attitudes and feelings start to change as a result. For instance, let's say you are angry with your spouse most of the time. Why not pretend that you feel loving toward him or her? If you act loving during short periods of time each day, you may see your feelings start to change as well. This is a definite step toward accepting those issues that plague your relationship and keep you stuck in negativity.

If you are full of negative feelings, begin slowly, build up, and be patient. It takes a while for the new "as if" behaviors to transfer to your attitudes and feelings. Being action-oriented can be good for your relationship as well; husbands tend to respond more positively to behaviors—"show me, don't tell me."

Even though we are dealing with unchangeables, there may be some instances where reframing and "as if" behaviors can alter your partner's response. But don't count on it. You're doing this to help you accept what you see as a fixed aspect of your relationship.

Rehearsal   **ACTING "AS IF"**

Knowing that changing your behavior has the potential to change your feelings and attitudes is very reassuring. The following exercise can help you focus on ways to bring about acceptance and tolerance on your part:

1. List negative feelings you have regarding your spouse.

2. Now, think of ways you can use "as if" behaviors to counter these negative feelings. For instance, you often

argue with your spouse on vacations because he's uninterested in seeing or doing the same things as you. You
suggest that he plan some of the activities on your next
vacation. Go along with the script and behave "as if"
you are enjoying yourself. You may be surprised to find
that acting as if you are having fun can change your
real feelings.

3. Now engage in similar kinds of behavior on a regular
basis for as long as it takes to see if there's improvement in your attitude. Use this skill in your daily interactions—it helps.

Discuss, Discuss, Discuss

Wives tend to respond more positively to discussion, so husbands—
discuss, discuss, discuss. This is the most important skill to employ
when dealing with the inevitable unchangeable issues or personality
traits in your marriage. A continuing discussion is the greatest tool for
handling those tenacious "won't go away" issues. Except now, if you
employ acceptance and a willingness to take responsibility for changing
your attitudes, you will discuss the "unchangeables" with some tolerance and maybe even an ounce of humor.

In fact, the unchangeable can become your issue—one you even
embrace as an old friend. Perhaps the two of you can distance yourselves from it by making it the enemy that interferes with the good feelings in your relationship. The more you can create this distance, the
easier it is to tolerate things you can't change.

"If I don't change I will die" is a dramatic way of saying what many
of us feel inside. There are so many times in our lives when we need to
take a risk and move on. Most likely, you have experienced change often
in the course of your marriage—when the children were born, for
instance, or when one of you got a big promotion or you moved into a
new home. The marriage must be renegotiated at these times of transition in order to remain vital and offer both of you areas for growth. In
the chapters to come, I will offer you many ways to do just that.

CHAPTER 3

The Growth Circle

Growth itself contains the germ of happiness.

— Pearl S. Buck

MANY OF US HAVE GROWN UP with the mistaken notion that human development ends some time during late adolescence or in one's early twenties. It seemed as if our personalities were set in concrete at that stage—and no further growth would occur. Of course, looking back on our lives, we know that this is just not so. Most of us continue to grow and change over the years as we gain insight and experience.

Sometimes change comes from within—an overwhelming urge to finally open your own business, a sudden recognition of your own mortality—and sometimes it comes from external circumstances—corporate downsizing or the departure of a child. No matter what the source, however, change is inevitable, and sometimes it can be dizzying, even frightening. But how can you manage that change so that it leads to personal growth? And how can you manage it so you grow within your primary relationship—your marriage?

The "I" and the "Thou"

Philosopher Martin Buber describes the "I-Thou" relationship in which each person is responsible for the growth and development of the other as well as the self. No person can be a healthy "I," he explains, without the support of a "Thou." (For the sake of clarity, I'll call them "I" and "You" from now on.) You can apply this principle to your midlife or retirement marriage. If you have a strong commitment to the marriage and your spouse, if there is equity in the relationship—fairness in the give and take—then it will feel natural for you to support each other through the sometimes difficult transitions to empty nest and retirement.

To make the most of these transitions, imagine that the changes in our lives occur within a Growth Circle. A Growth Circle is a positive, open system that promises goodwill, flexibility, and change for the better. It furthers the development of the individuals within it. (By contrast, a closed system, which is coercive both physically and psychologically, discourages change and depends on an authoritarian force that values power and performance over self-worth.) In a Growth Circle, change is not only welcomed, it is considered desirable.

One empty-nest couple in a good marriage exemplifies this sense of mutuality and growth. Louisa is a 49-year-old screenwriter married for twenty-seven years to an oncologist, Cal:

> Maybe twenty years ago, I had a dream that we both found ourselves in a cave. It was dark and dank in there. The only exit was an opening in the ceiling above our heads. Its walls were smooth and glassy, and it was impossible to gain a foothold to get out. To me, the cave represented our painful childhoods—we had both come from unhappy homes. Neither of us could get out alone. But Cal climbed up on my shoulders and pulled himself out, then turned around and pulled me after him. And that's the way it has been.
>
> I believe that we have each gone much further in our lives than we would have had we not gotten married. The synergy of the relationship has helped us both. One plus one definitely makes more than two, and maybe that's why we've always worked to preserve the relationship.

Cal, in his interview, concurred. In fact, he had difficulty talking about how midlife affected him individually.

> Lou and I have been married for so many years, there's a "we-ness" that's hard to separate from the "me-ness." That I

feel successful in my life is the result of the fact that we have a lot of cooperation and support. Even though we have separate careers, we have such a good collaborative relationship—one that's supportive and helpful—that it makes it easier for me to travel, do research, and pursue whatever professional goals I'm interested in pursuing and Lou is able to pursue hers.

This couple has enjoyed a reciprocity that is the hallmark of the Growth Circle. Keep in mind, however, that your "I" must be fulfilled in order for you to be able to contribute to the "You" and "Us" bank accounts. If you have enough inner reserves, you will always have something to give to your spouse.

Are Women the "Emotional Managers" in Marriage?

It may be up to the wife in your family to get the Growth Circle rolling. In fact, according to the latest research on happy marriages, when men are willing to listen to what their wives have to say, they are contributing to a healthier relationship.

From early adolescence, as a female, you have been socialized to be sensitive, to communicate feelings, and thereby resolve relationship issues. Most likely you have more experience with transitions, juggling multiple roles as daughter, single woman, wife, mother, volunteer, caregiver, friend, and career woman. In most instances you are biologically more adaptive. Anthropologists have found that women "go with the flow" more easily. And, many of you have experienced an empowering shift at midlife: you are more assertive, independent, self-assured, and adventurous.

Given these strengths, you may play the role of emotional manager in your marriage. You won't be surprised to learn that I often play this role in my marriage. I am continually opening up discussions and pointing out where changes could be made in our relationship, always encouraging Bernie to join in. At times his need to "fix" problems instead of just listening takes over. But generally he listens and then offers his take on the issue at hand. This did not happen magically to us. It has taken years.

The transitions of empty nest and retirement have given us the golden opportunity to take advantage of teachable moments—those moments at the beginning of new experiences when you are needing help and are more open to accepting it. Those transitions gave us the opportunity to take turns being either the kind teacher or the willing student. I often took the lead as the teacher, but not always.

Each of You Can Share the Roles of Kind Teacher and Willing Student

In our culture, men often have problems with expressing emotions. They may be afraid to appear vulnerable if they talk about feelings, which are frowned upon in the world of work where they operate so much of the time.

Yet as a husband, there is great value in your sharing your feelings about yourself with your wife. When you do so, you reveal to her your true self—a side that she might have been unaware of before. You also increase the level of intimacy between you, enhancing your marriage. But how can you accomplish this if you have had little practice or reinforcement in doing so? That's where your wife's skills as the "emotional manager" can be put to good use. Trust her and let her help you learn the emotional ropes,

Think of it this way. The Growth Circle consists of "I" and "You" interacting in a climate of reciprocity and acceptance. "I" act as the kind teacher to your willing student at those teachable moments when change comes into play. Teachable moments occur when "You" are experiencing a change and are at the point of needing help—and are more open to it. "I" as the kind teacher can help "You" go through this change, if you are the willing student. In fact, change sets the Growth Circle in motion and drives it. I helped Bernie during his retirement transition, and he helped me deal with the empty nest.

In some marriages there are emotionally in-touch husbands and emotionally reticent wives. When this is the situation, the husband can be the kind teacher and the wife the willing student.

As the Kind Teacher You Will:

1. **Take care of yourself.** Tend to the "I" as much as you can. You cannot teach from a dry well.

2. **Take it slow.** Ease into new behaviors. If your spouse does not understand at first, back off and try again. Wives, remember, you've had a lifetime off rehearsals; he may be new at this.

3. ***Use teachable moments to instruct your spouse about his or her emotions.*** That means you will:

    ◆ ***Be patient.*** Feelings can be quite fragile, especially if your husband is coping with retirement or your wife with the empty nest. Always keep that in mind.

    ◆ ***Listen attentively.*** Keep your spouse talking by saying "Tell me more," and give positive body language feedback by nodding when appropriate and making positive facial expressions (not frowning). Look at your spouse when he or she talks. Your posture, comments, and facial expression all communicate your interest in what he or she is saying.

    ◆ ***Ask, "What are you feeling now?" at opportune moments.***

    ◆ ***Offer your point of view when your spouse is stuck without putting words in his or her mouth.*** You might say, "It seems like . . . " and then check to see if you've understood.

    ◆ ***Really listen and accept.*** Keep your comments and questions to a minimum. Act as a sounding board. Your partner's emotions could be tentative and raw so if he or she wants to share them at all, show acceptance by simply listening,

    ◆ ***Show appreciation for your spouse's attempts at understanding.*** Express gratitude especially when he or she listens.

    ◆ ***Be tolerant.*** Allow some space to get the feel of things. Let your partner do things his or her way. Accept your differences,

    ◆ ***Be kind and affectionate.*** A hug, a kiss, a touch are reassuring.

    ◆ ***Keep your sense of humor alive and well.*** Routines, space, and time commitments will be evolving. Keeping your antenna poised for a good laugh at your adjustments, whether it's to the empty nest or retirement, can really help.

As the Willing Student You Will:

1. ***Be willing to learn the "new" language of emotions.*** Adopt a positive attitude toward learning. Listen to your body's reactions and give names to your feelings—sadness, loss, fear, happiness, anticipation, and so on.

2. ***Be aware of stonewalling—turning off your receptiveness to what your partner is trying to teach you.*** Yes, you may need to

pull back at some time during this learning process, but explain to your spouse that it is not his or her fault. Let your spouse know when you need space.

3. **Learn to tolerate ambiguity.** Allow yourself to feel more comfortable with being uncomfortable. The information you are learning is new. Know that it is all right; it is natural to have twinges of discomfort,

This book has many exercises (as rehearsals) for both of you to use together. But who is to initiate them? Here is another place where one of you (usually the wife) starts the ball rolling as the kind teacher, but only if you want to.

Struggling with Mixed Messages

If you're the emotional manager, how much responsibility do you want to take in your relationship?

Although contemporary society expects that women, first and foremost, be responsible for themselves, the "helping" duties society has traditionally imposed upon them (and they have traditionally taken upon themselves) are often in conflict with this imperative. The mixed messages we receive can be confusing and upsetting. The best strategy is to ask yourself some hard questions.

Questions for Growth	CLEARING UP MIXED MESSAGES
1.	Wives: What are the traditional messages for you regarding being the initiator of change in your relationship or helping your husband? What are the contemporary ones?
2.	How do you feel about being the one to open the discussion?
3.	Husbands: How do you feel about your wife initiating different matters in your relationship or helping you through some difficult times?
4.	Talk over your individual views.

Redefining Gender Roles

Nearly a century ago, the Swiss psychiatrist Carl Jung observed that at midlife we undergo dramatic changes in our perspective and character. He perceived life to be divided into halves, the second half beginning at about age 40.

During the first half of their lives, men are intent on developing the "masculine" characteristics that they need for mastery of the world: independence, assertiveness and even aggressiveness, logical focus, and an ability to ignore their emotions. The second half is devoted to discovering the inner, or real, self. To become a whole person, a man needs to integrate the neglected, more "feminine" parts of himself: introspection, tenderness, affiliation, and interdependence. He becomes more spiritual, more involved in mature, intimate relationships.

By contrast, women at midlife, with family obligations diminishing, may discover within themselves more "masculine" attributes. They may develop more independence, learn new skills, return to school or work, and become more creative, adventurous, and assertive. Once an individual integrates the feminine with the masculine, he or she will feel better equipped to face the challenges of aging. See Chapter 11 for a discussion of hormone changes at midlife.

Understanding this midlife crossover can enhance your adjustment to changes and transitions. It helps a wife, for instance, appreciate her husband's sudden need for support and affection as the children leave and he faces retirement. And it helps a husband accept his wife's newfound independence. Moreover, a husband's increased tenderness and emotionality can prompt him to help his wife through her sense of loss during the empty-nest transition. And by the same token, a wife's increased sense of mastery, confidence, and self-esteem provide her with more options. If she chooses, she can become the wise teacher, taking an active role in assisting her husband through his difficult transition. Such reciprocity is all part of the Growth Circle and is bound to improve your marriage.

One Starts Giving; the Other Begins Changing

As we will see, during the transition to the empty nest, a wife may need her husband's full support. And at retirement, the husband is facing many difficult stressors and often his wife must initiate the Growth

Circle to help him through. It will be to your mutual benefit to help each other since your marriage will flourish.

I have found, however, that wives need not always take the lead in the giving. One couple shared with me how gracious the husband had become since their retirement. Theirs is an excellent example of the Growth Circle at work.

Lola and Paul had always been involved in corporate careers even while they raised four children. Lola confided to me:

> It was hard. I kept getting promoted; I worked long hours, traveled for business, brought work home. It was almost impossible to focus on each other at night. There wasn't time to truly appreciate each other.
>
> But now, since we've retired, both of us have become more nurturing. It's the little things. Paul knows I have to feed the dog. It's my dog; I wanted her and he didn't. But even though she's mine, he feeds her and gives her water. He even cleans up after her. When he does things like that, it brings out tender, nurturing feelings in me. When I'm at the computer and he makes lunch for me and sets it down on the desk, I know he's thinking of me and I can't help but return those feelings. It's a two-way street. The good feelings just feed on themselves. Sometimes I'm overwhelmed with love and tenderness.

Admittedly, the Growth Circle is an ideal way of viewing your interaction as a couple. But by simply being aware of this ideal, this way of being, you can open the potential for change. When there is direct, clear, and caring communication; when change is welcomed and dealt with honestly; when you have the freedom to be and to do; and when you are flexible—all of this generates growth for both the individual and the couple, perpetuating the Growth Circle.

The Empty Nest and Your Midlife Years

T HE ABSENCE OF CHILDREN can be devastating to couples. A recent film brought this home to me. It revolves around two couples—a young, yuppie pair and a middle-aged, middle-class husband and wife. Both are yearning for children. The young woman aches for her cold and withholding husband to impregnate her in order to revive the marriage and fulfill her biological "destiny," while the older couple longs to be reunited with their only child—a daughter who eight years earlier had run away at the age of 16 and has not been heard from since. Both marriages languish and are devitalized by the absence of children. The older couple, blaming themselves for the untimely departure of their teenager, never have sex again. The wife lies in front of the television, day in and day out, watching old movies, while her younger counterpart leads a vacuous life, not knowing how to fill each day. Both couples wander about, aimless and bored until, through a series of chance encounters, each wife meets the other's husband. At this point, the young woman conceives a child with the older man and his wayward daughter returns. A happy ending? Maybe.

Studies show that children cause problems with couples, but they also add meaning to their parents' lives. Many of the people whom I interviewed spoke of how important their kids had been to them. For instance, when I asked Clara about their effect on her marriage, she looked at me as if to say, "Are you kidding?" "The impact of the children on our marriage has only been totally positive," she exclaimed with a shade of indignation that I should even ask such a question.

But as I'm sure you know, children can be a mixed blessing. Adolescents, in particular, can sap the vitality from a marriage, especially if there is tension in the home. Teenagers' emotional reactions and acting out can cause conflict between spouses who have different views on how to deal with the problems. Teen behavior can intensify our insecurities and anxiety as we question whether we did a good job raising them.

Isabel's son was troubled during his adolescence:

> We had a real trauma during our son's teenage years. If we were ever going to split up, it was going to be then. Our son was probably depressed, and he was very angry. He got kicked out of two junior highs and three high schools. He finally graduated from night school. We went to many family therapists to figure out what to do, but it was a horrendous four or five years. His teenage years put a big strain on us, and I think it pulled my husband and me apart. . . . Still I wouldn't change it, even for the five years that were bad. It was very important for me to have children.

Because our children are so important to us even if they're difficult, "losing" them to adulthood and independence can affect us deeply. The notion permeates our lives and signs of it are everywhere—on television, in the arts, even in politics.

- In a commercial for Tylenol, a bride walking down the aisle with her dad asks him how his headache is doing since he took the medication. "My headache's gone but," he replies, pointing to his heart, "it hurts a little in here."

- Barbra Streisand sings songs of expectations, dashed hopes, and protectiveness to her grown son on her album, *Higher Ground*.

- In Stephen Sondheim's play *Into the Woods*, the nasty witch longs for attachment, connection, and avoidance of the empty nest. "Don't leave me!" she cries to her daughter Rapunzel as she manipulatively instills guilt. "You know you want to live with your old mom."

- Architect Richard Meier, designer of the acclaimed $1 billion Getty Center in Los Angeles, treated his work of art as one would a child. "Now that his work is all but finished," comments writer Steven Proffitt in the *Los Angeles Times Magazine*, "he finds himself musing about feelings of pride tempered by a profound sense of loss— not unlike what a parent experiences when a grown child leaves home."

- Even First Families are not immune. President Clinton acquired a puppy, "Buddy," after his daughter, Chelsea, left for Stanford University.

In my interviews with empty-nest mothers and fathers, I encountered a wide range of reactions—both mothers and (contrary to popular belief) fathers spoke of being sad, depressed, grief-stricken, angry, ambivalent, worried, guilty, relieved, free, and even happy. Some expressed feelings of loss and abandonment, others became ill when their children left, and a few were surprised at the intensity of their response.

❖ ❖ ❖

In Part Two we will first look at the process of coming to terms with midlife and relinquishing your children to independent adulthood, and then we will examine how these issues affect your marriage. A balance must be struck in your midlife marriage in order to meet your needs as separate individuals and as a couple. We'll also introduce some strategies for letting go.

CHAPTER 4

Empty-Nest Mothers and Midlife Concerns

The only thing which seems to me to be eternal and natural in motherhood is ambivalence.

— Jane Lazarre

ALMOST TWO-THIRDS OF AN average woman's adult life will be spent either alone or with her husband. She will devote just 12 percent of her adulthood to being a full-time mother. But even if it's only 12 percent, look at how much of yourself you pour into that endeavor!

When Bonnie came to the door, I thought at first I was meeting her older daughter. At 52, she didn't look a day over 35, with her bright jogging clothes, young hairdo, and sparkling eyes. Bonnie revealed that hers had been a traditional marriage. Although she never worked outside the home, she had been attending school for the past twelve years, taking one or two courses a semester as she collected units toward a business degree. Her 22-year-old daughter had just been accepted to several law schools, and her 20-year-old son was in Paris finishing his junior year abroad.

When I asked Bonnie how she experienced midlife, she focused on how much she missed being a mother. "My license plate says 'GRT MOM,'" she told me with a giggle.

> When my last baby was born, my husband picked me up from the hospital with it. Everyone knows me by this plate! It's difficult not being an active mom anymore. It's not only filling the void of time. I came from a very crazy family, and I wanted the craziness to stop with my new family. I was always there for my kids without smothering them.
>
> But when my youngest left for Europe last July, I felt lost. I was like someone with a pain somewhere, and I couldn't find a place that was comfortable. I would run around all day, doing nothing, visiting people, going here, going there. I tried joining some organizations but I hated them, and I realized I had to do other work. I wasn't really depressed, but I had a sense of melancholy. I was aware that an era was over. But I put limits on my unhappiness. I gave myself a year. Now I'm feeling much better.

Her fluffy cocoa-colored puppy wandered in and gently nuzzled Bonnie's leg. She leaned over, picked him up, and held him in her lap. I asked her about her dog.

"I know. It's so sick. It's just . . . I'm embarrassed." She smiled and hid her face from me with her hand as she turned away. "It's just a tiny puppy," she continued with some chagrin. "It's something to love and to hold. It's nice to come home to a yipping thing. I'm ashamed to admit that a dog could make me happy, but I enjoy him."

Bonnie needed something to snuggle, to stroke, to feel connected with. This gave her comfort. Indeed, her puppy served as a transitional object, an emotional substitute for her children, something that she could cling to as she crossed the bridge from motherhood to the empty nest.

Traditionally, mothers have been so invested in the raising of the children that when the kids leave, many experience a loss of role as significant as a man's dispossession during retirement. The empty nest can, therefore, have a profound effect on mothers, ranging from a time-limited sense of loss and sadness to a full-blown depression.

Losing the Mothering Role

In many other cultures, women are expected to fill defined roles after they're finished with child-rearing and have higher status after menopause than before. But our society does little to provide women with meaningful family-based roles once their children are launched. Our emphasis on youth, and the feeling that mothers-in-law and grandmothers should stay out of the way of their children's lives, can be stressful to midlife women.

Women mourn their marginalization and the decline of their power and influence. We have no rites of passage to mark their entrance into this new phase of life. Their grief is disenfranchised; it's not socially sanctioned. "So what?" others may respond to their laments. "Your children are supposed to leave and get married. What's the big deal?"

Yet for many, it is a big deal. They grieve the loss of their role as if it were a death in the family. Among the women I interviewed, those who seemed the saddest and loneliest were invested in just a few roles, of which *mother* was the most prominent.

Questions for Growth

YOUR CHILDREN'S IMPACT ON YOUR MARRIAGE

This is a great topic for discussion. Getting these issues out in the open can prepare you for dealing with your children's absence. Each of you should take turns sharing your own perspective:

1. How have the children affected us positively?

2. How have the children affected us negatively?

3. Write your answer in your journal or store it in your memory. It will help to explain some of your reactions to the letting-go process.

Ambivalence

Letting go of the mothering role has much ambivalence attached to it. There is the relief at not having to wait up to see when (or if) the kids get home, the lessening of worry, the abatement of disagreements. But there is also the loss of feeling needed, the activities with our children that fill and structure our time, the nurturing that we have grown accustomed to, the fun we had watching them grow and develop. One mother expressed it well when she said, "I'm thrilled that they're on their own, but I want to tell my daughter, 'Come back again! Come home and be my little girl.'"

Some women focus on their relief at relinquishing the day-to-day parenting responsibilities and anxieties; others focus on the emptiness, the silence in the house, the sense that the family will never be the same; and some feel a little of both. No matter which side you come down on, however, one thing is certain: You feel something. You must! Too much has been invested for you to be indifferent.

Indeed, the mothers who have the most difficulty with the emptying nest may feel their children did not live up to their expectations. On some level, they feel guilty and responsible. They ask themselves, "What did I do wrong?" The situation need not be as dramatic as a child on drugs, on the streets, or in jail—it could just be a matter of the child's alienation from the parent.

In any case, there is a sense of loss, but as time moves on, this loss is tempered. Now the question becomes "How do I replace this loss?" Do you fill the breach with a puppy? With a career? With grandchildren? Keep in mind that both individuals in a marriage experience the empty nest, and that the marriage needs tending, as well.

The More Roles You Have, the Greater Your Sense of Control

For many, having a strong career identity can help mitigate the loss of a coveted role like motherhood. As Sheila explained:

> I was involved in my work and so many other things, I
> didn't miss the kids as much as I expected when they left.
> I find that when I'm working and involved in a project, no
> matter what's happening in my life outside, I'm completely
> engaged in what I'm doing. When things happened at home
> that were a problem, I'd go to work and be okay. It's a relief.

Still, career or no, how can you believe you will not experience a loss when your children leave? Louisa, for example, told me, "This was all a shock to me. I never expected to be so devastated. After all, unlike my mother, I had a career that was important to me beyond motherhood. I was busy with my work. It never occurred to me that I would suffer from the empty nest the way she had."

For eighteen years women are charged with the nurturing and safekeeping of their children. To believe that (in spite of the potential horrors of adolescence) a child's coming of age will bring on instant sighs of relief is ridiculous. Yes, women are more than mothers, but realistically, no other role takes up so much of their emotional and physical selves. Saying adieu to that role can be a major undertaking; after all, women thrive on connectedness.

Questions for Growth	CONNECTING IN NEW WAYS
1.	List all the roles you now play as an empty-nest mother.
2.	After each role, write whether you are feeling good or bad about the association.
3.	Now think about your connection needs. Do you need to ◆ feel a part of something? ◆ be with people who accept and like you? ◆ use your talents and have others show appreciation?
4.	Review your answers to question 3. Come up with at least two or three new activities you can engage in that would fulfill your current need for connection.

What Is Your Adjustment Profile?

From my interviews I have found that a midlife woman's adjustment to the empty nest is based on a number of factors, including:

◆ How far away her grown children live and how often she sees them—the farther away, the more difficult the adjustment.

◆ The quality of the relationship between her and the children. If the relationship is strong, there will be adjustments in the frequency and quality of contacts. If it is shaky, the relationship can be threatened.

◆ How successful she feels at having fulfilled her role as parent. Guilt can raise its head now.

◆ How many roles she currently identifies with. Remember, the more roles, the better.

◆ The quality of her marriage. If children were used as a buffer, she may have great concern about how to go about putting vitality back into a devitalized relationship.

◆ Her adaptability. How well she handled previous stresses and changes in her life. How able she is to roll with the punches.

◆ Early experiences in her family of origin. How she and her parents responded at the time of her departure can greatly influence her current response.

My interviews highlighted several categories of responses. Can you find your own profile?

The Eternal Mom

Life continues to be child-centered for the Eternal Mom. In fact, even after the children move out, they have frequent contact. These mothers may continue to focus on their children's lives as if they were still in the home—there is little individual growth. Like the mother in Philip Roth's novel *Portnoy's Complaint,* they live for and through their children.

Irene typifies an Eternal Mom. This strong, bright woman had funneled all of her creative energy into raising her three daughters. She couldn't stop crying during the first half-hour of our interview.

> The empty nest is the toughest thing I've ever had to do. I had a twenty-two-year investment in those girls; I was with them on a daily basis and all of a sudden, I wasn't anymore. I was fired. . . . Not being a mom anymore, not being responsible for anyone anymore, letting go and trying to be responsible for myself—it's hard on me. . . .
>
> When the kids left, their growing up and leaving broke my heart. It was so depressing for me. I was such an involved mom; I dedicated my whole life to their success. That's all I did. I worked toward their being successful children and scholars and getting them into the college that I knew would make them happy. It was a lifetime thing.

> I'm crying because the best part of my life is not here
> now. Being a mom was the best thing I ever did. I feel help-
> ing them grow up was my best success, and I miss them. I
> miss being a family every day. I didn't want to give that up.
> It's a real loss for me.

Indeed, Irene was so profoundly affected by the "loss" of her children that her body went into what she called a "hysterical menopause"
when the youngest one went off to college. Eternal Moms' marriages
often lack vitality since these women direct their energy toward thinking
and doing for their children rather than themselves and their spouses.

The Mourner

Mourners move on with life, but it's as if they're going through the
motions. They have infrequent contact with children who live out of
town. They may engage in activities but only halfheartedly. They have
many regrets about raising the children and wish they would move back
home again.

Catherine typifies this type of mother. She had been a nurse until
the birth of her daughter. She enjoyed the role of stay-at-home "car-
pool" mom. "It was the best thing I've ever done," she told me, echoing
Irene's feelings. But she misses contact with a child who holds her at
arm's length.

> I miss talking to my daughter. I want to see her more often.
> I'm a very busy woman, I really am. I volunteer at the hospital.
> I have a lot of friends and really enjoy working with children.
> But as busy as I am, it doesn't take my mind off Traci. I want
> her back here to take care of. I'm sad that my husband and I
> fought so much when she was younger. I wonder if that's why
> she doesn't want to be with us as much.

For many Mourners, the happiest time in the marriage was when the
children were young. Indeed, one mother with whom I spoke took in
other people's children to care for when hers left. "I'm really good at
this," she said proudly, "and the kids are better behaved with me than
they are with their parents." These women are more or less stuck in the
void of wanting to be mothers but not having their children to care for,
and their marriages often lack vitality.

The Realist

Realists have mixed feelings. They value the role of Mom, but realize their children must move on. Nevertheless, they still miss them. Sharon, the mother who took her family to Italy for a year, expresses these ambivalent feelings.

> Angela couldn't live in this house for another ten years. It's an impossibility. That's not just a thought, it's a fact. But I still wish I could be the mother of the most precious three-year-old. There's a part of me that still wishes I had my baby to take care of, but that's so far from reality. There's no way you can keep a kid. You just can't keep a kid.

Realists constantly work on reminding themselves to let go. They become active and may even change the circumstances of their lives. However, they are not necessarily focused on personal growth. Some attempt to search for new directions, and they also devote some energy to the marriage.

The Relieved Mom

These women are tired of taking care of adolescents; many have had conflicted relationships with them. Andrea, for example, had a difficult experience:

> There were a lot of problems with Sam at school. A lot of ditching class, some drugs and alcohol, stealing, lying. After psychological testing, he was diagnosed as ADD and anti-social. We dragged this child to therapy for a long time, but at some point in high school he said, "There's no way I'm going anymore." There was a tremendous amount of pushing and pulling between our younger child and us. Sam required so much attention—what he was doing, where he was doing it, why he was doing it. There was constant arguing among all of us.
>
> Sam had pushed and pushed us until we just couldn't take it anymore. One day we just had enough. We packed his things in a trash bag, put them out front, and locked the door. He took off, but he always called us to tell us where he was. That was a horrible way to empty the nest—painful and awful.

Relieved Moms look to their own growth now and feel as if this is their time to devote to themselves. One mother said to me. "Their leaving gave me a chance to focus on myself in a more whole way than at any other time in my life." In some cases, their marriages take second place to their individual growth.

The Grower

These women feel sadness at first, but they have worked at letting go and gaining new insights into their individual selves. Louisa is among those who adapted well:

> I anticipated that the transition to empty nest would be cushioned by my career, and I was profoundly surprised at how unhappy, lonely, and disoriented I felt after my youngest left. It took a while to adjust. Now, the nest doesn't feel empty anymore. On a day-to-day basis, I don't miss my kids like I used to. Mostly, I'm too busy with my work to dwell on it.

Many Growers are actively involved in searching for, or have found, new roles to occupy their interests. Louisa, for example, abandoned her nurturing role. "Now, when the kids come home for more than a week, I feel restless. Their presence impinges on my work and my privacy." Growers can have mixed feelings regarding attending to their marriages. These women see themselves as strong—survivors—and they can be career-driven.

The Thriver

Thrivers are happy with their lives. They feel it's acceptable for the children to have gone, that it's a natural transition. Their role changes are comfortable. Their strong marriages, work, and temperament seem to contribute to their comfort level.

Joyce seems to thrive as an empty-nest mother:

> It was great when the kids left. We loved it. It was such an adventure for them; it wasn't sad at all. The first time they went away to sleep-away camp, it was a little hard to say good-bye, for the first week only. Since then, it has been okay. They've always been very happy when they're away.

They have a lot of confidence in themselves. They were very independent from the time they were little. I think I fostered this in them.

I work in my husband's office. We've always been best friends. We've never had a problem communicating—we laugh a lot. We're true partners in every sense of the word, from raising our children to working together, to just having a friendship. My husband is a great communicator. We are in tune with each other; we can read each other pretty well. There is a huge bond of understanding. We're such close friends; we have respect and understanding for each other's feelings.

We turn conflicts into laughter—we have to. We don't take each other so seriously. My father died suddenly when I was eleven, and I learned not to take the little things so seriously.

Rehearsal	**LOOKING BACK TO MOVE FORWARD**

If you are an Eternal Mom or a Mourner, conflicts within your marriage may have been buffered by your children or made tolerable with the children around. There is danger now to your relationship with the children gone. In some instances, children serve as a diversion from dealing with your husband. Think back to your early years as a couple.

1. What activities did you and your husband enjoy doing together?

2. Pick one or two that still stoke the fires of interest.

3. Discuss this with your husband. He probably already knows how much you value your children, but if you've done the "Impact of Your Children on Your Marriage" exercise, he'll know for sure.

4. If he agrees, try some of the activities you once enjoyed.

Of course, at midlife the empty nest may be only one of your concerns.

The Invisible Woman

In *Fear of Fifty*, Erica Jong writes:

> So there I am . . . , facing my fiftieth birthday, and feeling hideously depressed. I am no longer the youngest person in the room, nor the cutest. I will never be Madonna or Tina Brown or Julia Roberts. Whoever the flavor of the month is by the time this book appears—I will never be her either. For years, those were my values—whether I admitted this to myself or not.

You have a striking way to mark your entry into midlife: menopause with all of its attendant physical and emotional markers lets you know that time is passing and that your roles (and certainly your capacity to bear children) are evolving. Yes, just like men, you will have more than merely the empty nest to face at this time in your life. But unlike your husband, you will be coming into a new sense of power and strength at this time. Even though you may no longer be the youngest in the room, midlife may be your time to fly.

"My friend and I were talking recently," Jane told me. "She had read something about when you become fifty, you become invisible. It struck me to the core. It sounds simple, but it explains a lot. I've always been flamboyant. I was a model, a dancer. I've always done things that called attention to me. It has something to do with sexuality, but really it's more about self-image. I still like that kind of attention, but I'm not getting it now. You are invisible."

In a youth-oriented culture, no longer being "the youngest person in the room" can be distressing. For women who have derived their good feelings about themselves and their power from their physical allure, aging and the "invisibility" that it can bring may be a terrible blow.

Nearly thirty years ago, Susan Sontag observed that "to be a woman is to be an actress," and her words still ring true. Our society's definition of femininity requires one to attend to makeup, costume, and a proper entrance. Women are constantly on stage, and their attractiveness is perpetually being evaluated.

To some, the ebb of youthfulness and the limited role of being beautiful or attractive can be devastating. This is especially so if the woman has been solely dependent on her appearance for self-esteem. But midlife is a mixed bag. Along with a diminished sense of attractiveness at this time in life comes a newfound strength.

Aging Parents

Statistics show that midlife adult children are the major caregivers for their aging parents—and usually it's the daughters.

"I feel we're the lost generation: We have kids who forget to call us and parents who can't remember us." This is a line from a musical comedy revue about menopause, *Is It Just Me or Is It Hot in Here?*, based on the life and observations of Los Angeles playwright Barbara Sher. It drew a big laugh from the audience the night I attended the play, and for good reason. We could all recognize our situation in these words.

Barbara's statement is funny, but sad as well. Midlifers have been called the "sandwich generation," and in truth, many of us are dealing with aging parents whose life spans and needs have increased exponentially. We can find ourselves caught between caring for our parents as well as helping launch our kids into independent lives. In fact, by some estimates, in this new "era of longevity," we may spend more years taking care of our elders than we have spent raising our youngsters.

Statistics show that midlife adult children are the major caregivers for frail elderly people in the United States. And recasting ourselves, not as our parents' children but rather as their caregivers, is a major life transition and a profound change in roles. As Connie, one of my interviewees, said:

> I always used to look to my parents for guidance, but I realize I have to take care of them now. They're making decisions about their lives that are not based on reality. I have to see them; I have to call them; I have to check up on them. They need to be cared for like they cared for me when I was younger. The empty nest had freed me, but I realize I'm getting more tied down now with my parents. I might resent the fact that I'm going to have to take care of them, but I know it has to be done.

You're Getting Stronger

Despite these difficulties, many women feel more powerful and even happier at this time in their lives. In fact, quite a few women over the age of fifty are thrilled with this stage. They are more satisfied with their careers and finances; they are less self-conscious about their appearance; and they feel good about their personal growth and development.

Alice saw herself as unfettered now that her children had departed and her elderly parents (for whom she had provided care) had died. "I feel a sense of renewal, freedom," she told me. "This is the first time in my whole life that I've had a chance to just *be*. I'm having a good time. Do I deserve this?" she asked with a wicked little laugh and a flick of the wrist. "You bet I do!"

Even my interviewees' husbands recognized the profound changes in their wives. Bud explained to me:

> Sarah has made a dramatic change from when we were first married. When I met her, she was painfully shy. In fact, she was so shy she wouldn't call a restaurant to make reservations because she didn't know the people on the other end of the phone. Since this change, she has become more sure of herself—a much stronger person. Through the years, Sarah has come to realize that she can do whatever she wants. She gained a tremendous amount of confidence. I like it. It think it's terrific, even though she's not so easygoing anymore.

Questions for Growth	**MY WIFE HAS CHANGED!**
	Husbands, have you noticed a difference in your wife? Tell her what you see.

Enjoying Postmenopausal Zest

What these and many other Growers, Thrivers, and Relieved Moms seem to be experiencing is *postmenopausal zest,* a term originally coined by anthropologist Margaret Mead to describe the vigor and renewed energy females enjoy as they reach midlife. Sheila was experiencing this wonderful phenomenon:

> I feel more secure with who I am now. I'm not trying to impress people anymore. I'm not trying to put on fancy dinner parties anymore. I'm really more relaxed. I wasn't quite sure what I was going to do, and then I found my

niche in advertising and marketing. I know I'll be doing more in the field. Now that I look back on my parenting years, I'm secure in that. I did all I could do and I think I did a good job.

Midlife women no longer have to worry about monthly mood swings or pregnancy. They no longer need to be seen as a sex object and can, as Carl Jung theorized, explore their more masculine attributes. Perhaps the change is also hormonal, as the balance between estrogen and testosterone shifts after menopause.

The change can even be found in a new enjoyment of sex. A recent survey of middle-aged women found that more than half claimed to have better sex lives now than they did at age 25. Karen, for instance, has found previously untapped sexual joy in a second marriage:

> My sex life is wonderful now. I have a new marriage, and it's better than I could have ever dreamed. I'm valuing my sexuality more than I ever have in my life. I have the freedom to explore in ways that I couldn't at other times when I had all sorts of moral and social constraints. And when the kids were growing up, there were so many physical demands, I was exhausted. Now, I don't have them—I have the freedom!

Nurturing Yourself

A number of women with whom I spoke shared their joy at finally relinquishing their caregiving roles. For instance, when I asked Alice about the happiest time in her marriage, "Now," she said, as a slow smile crept across her face. "Now, because I'm happy with me. I have a career, the kids are grown, and they're fine. I feel successful and relieved. My parents are deceased (I was an only child). I'm responsible only to my husband and me. No more caretaking! This is a period of renewal for me."

Louisa began taking care of herself for the first time in her life when the nest emptied:

> Since the kids are gone, I've redirected my nurturing energy toward my work, which is creative. I am also learning to be more nurturing toward myself. I had been so absorbed

with my children, that I often ignored my own needs.
Now I go for a manicure twice a month and see a personal
trainer. I've had more massages in the last five years than
ever before in my life. I have more money to buy myself
nice clothes and the car I really wanted. I could get used to
this!

Questions for Growth	PHOTO SESSION FOR WOMEN
	Get out your family photo album and find a favorite picture of yourself from between the ages of 21 and 35. While looking at this photo, ask yourself:
1.	What strengths do I have now that I didn't have when I was younger? How have I grown as a person?
2.	What wisdom have I gained over the years in regard to nurturing myself, self-acceptance, caregiving, dealing with different people in my life?
3.	Am I experiencing postmenopausal zest? If yes, how is this manifesting itself in my life?

Enjoying a Spiritual Midlife Passage

Psychologist Mary Gendler uses the term *spiritual menopause* to describe
the changes in self and focus that commonly occur in women at midlife.
Just as your body takes on new rhythms, so does the spirit. "Achieving
and doing are balanced more and more by appreciating and being," she
writes. "What to discard becomes as important a question as what to
pursue and keep."

And Rabbi Debra Orenstein also makes clear that along with this
notion come the themes we must all deal with: "mortality; fear of loss;
being part of a larger whole; the passage of time; the limits of our control over events, people, energy, and health; willingness to see our many
strengths and weaknesses; and the search for ultimate meaning and
inner peace"—these are all part of our spiritual quest at midlife.

I'm on this spiritual quest too. It takes the form of personally working at discarding outdated notions such as being the youngest, trimmest,
smartest, and best anything. With my own aging and the transition of

the empty nest and Bernie's retirement, I have gained a new sense of what really counts, what has meaning. For me, it has been a keen awareness of my connection—how I am connected to my family, to my work, and to my community. As I continue to make adjustments, I ask myself, "Are my thoughts and actions contributing to my inner peace, sense of fulfillment, and connectedness?" If my answer is yes, I know that my growing contentment will only enhance my midlife marriage—the spillover is inevitable.

CHAPTER 5

Empty-Nest Fathers and Midlife Concerns

Children want to feel instinctively that their father is behind them as solid as a mountain, but, like a mountain, is something to look up to.

— Dorothy Thompson

AT MIDLIFE, MANY MEN LOOK TO establish stronger connections with their offspring for the first time. But just as men become ready for closer relationships, their children are ready to move on, and suddenly, much to their frustration, they find that it's too late. It has even been suggested that fathers have a harder time with the empty nest than mothers. One reason for this may be that mothers have experienced the developmental journey with their children. Seeing them through infancy, their school years, and adolescence, they have gradually watched them separate and see it as part of a natural process. To a mostly absentee father who is now ready to deal with "the kids," their leaving can be perceived as a sudden break—an end to the family.

Many modern-day fathers have been deeply involved in the parenting role out of economic necessity, a profound enjoyment of the children, or a deeper need. The empty nest can be particularly difficult for these men.

Tears streamed down Dennis's cheeks as he shared with me how much he pined for his son. "I missed my son tremendously when he went away to school," he said. "I missed him powerfully. He was my soul mate. I get teary-eyed just thinking about the loss of him."

Dennis stopped for a moment to dab his eyes, and, by way of apology for his show of emotion, explained, "I lost my father when I was 10 years old. The relationship with my son was like a dream fulfillment; it was like filling up an empty space."

Along those lines, but with a different view, Michael Farrell talks about the "myth of patriarchy" in his book *Men at Midlife*. In this myth, the wife colludes with the children to protect and validate the image that the midlife man has of himself as the head of the family—the "beloved family patriarch." Perhaps some of the strain of midlife marriage has to do with upholding this myth. But by the time the children leave the nest, the myth can be discarded. Power and control issues between husband and wife can diminish as a consequence.

Losing the "Beloved Family Patriarch" Role

An empty-nest father might wonder "Who needs me?" And, if the myth of patriarchy was never upheld in the first place, a father can feel superfluous. This was true in Warren's case:

> Once I envisioned us like a solar system, with Eileen being the sun and our four daughters the planets, circling around her. I was a very large blue moon in the background. I tended to be the one who was left out when the five "girls" got together. This was certainly true during their teenage years. Eileen was so close to the girls, and everything revolved around her and them. I was separated from them. It can be very painful—you can feel lonely, not appreciated. Like nobody cared that much. It wasn't true, but that's how it felt.

A father's worst nightmare may be this fear of obsolescence. Such a terror was captured in a play titled *The Father*, written more than a century ago by the Swedish playwright August Strindberg. In this drama, a couple fights over who should control their only child's education.

Indeed, the marriage thrives in its own perverse way, when the battle rages over this control.

Using every tactic she can think of to win and slowly challenging her husband's sanity, Laura taunts him with the thought that their 17-year-old daughter may not be his offspring. She threatens to have her husband sent to an insane asylum so she can educate her child as she wishes. When he protests, she says with utter heartlessness, "You've fulfilled your unfortunate though necessary functions as a father and breadwinner. You are dismissed. I'm not as stupid as you treat me. Am I? I said, you're dismissed."

What could be more devastating than to feel you have outgrown your usefulness and are dismissed?

Many empty-nest fathers feel a profound loss at the departure of their children. Their role as father is very important to them, and the empty nest seems to leave behind an "empty man." This was not true of all the men I interviewed, but it was more prevalent than I had anticipated.

Men who are the most unhappy when their children leave:

- Find their marriage and friendships have become unfulfilling
- Recognize that the family needs less of their financial support
- Experience themselves as being more nurturing at a time when their children and wives don't need or value that quality in them

On the positive side, when all goes well with his kids, a father can feel validated in the successful completion of his parenting role. It is the culmination of his efforts. Midlife can also be a time when fathers find that their relative influence increases as their children mature, perhaps in part because their children now depend on them and value them as a resource.

Fathers are often wise in the ways of the world, and their grown offspring can be eager to seek out their counsel. My interviewee Cal had that experience:

> When the children left, my relationship with them changed. We became much more collegial. I was conscious of not wanting to tell them what to do. I wanted to be their advisor, the person they could confide in if they wanted to. And I wanted them to know that no matter what happened, we would be there—right or wrong—to help them through it.

Children may be closest to their mothers when they are young, but by adulthood a significant shift toward equality often occurs. This change may be most pronounced among fathers and sons.

What Is Your Adjustment Profile?

Your adaptation to the empty nest can vary depending on:

- Your relationship with your wife
- Your career or job situation
- Your perception of your own importance to other family members
- Your judgment of the job you did as a father
- Your feeling that this an end to the family
- Your belief that this is the beginning of a new life with your wife and a whole new journey for yourself at midlife

In talking with midlife fathers, I found that their responses to their children's departure could be grouped into several categories—each quite normal. Can you find your own profile?

The Eternal Dad

These men see their fathering role as primary—it's even more significant to them than their marriages. In fact, when I asked Harvey how his relationship with his wife compared to that with his children, he replied, "The children are more important. They're more important than us—absolutely—they're more needy." And when I asked how he felt when his last child left for college, he said, "I missed her; I missed her; I missed her. When someone is in your life all those years, and suddenly you don't have that anymore, you can't help but miss it."

These dads feel great pride in their children's accomplishments and view the nurturing and care of their children as paramount. Because they enjoyed raising their children, they have frequent contact with them. If they live long distances away, they make plans to see them often. Some feel overly responsible and engage in self-blame if their children are having problems. One father wept as he recalled a painful situation with his grown son. "I didn't agree all the time with what they were doing with their lives, and perhaps I should have exerted more guidance at the time," he said ruefully.

The Mourner

These men miss their children deeply. They generally have less contact with their children than Eternal Dads and mourn for "what could have been." Phil told me:

> When our youngest son left, that was very hard. I missed him a lot. He went to school in Vermont. He brought a lot of brightness into the house. He was fun and naturally out-going—there was a happiness, a glow about him, and his glow left and went to New England. I was somewhat depressed about his going away. It took me a month or two to get over it. It was worse in the beginning. My wife encour-aged him to go so far away, and I was upset with her for that. She's less sentimental in that way. She puts up a better front. She didn't become as sad as I did! I guess I was just more melancholy.

Mourners can see their offspring as central to the vitality of their marriages. Like Dennis, who lost his father at the age of ten, they may think of their children as soul mates or confidants, and sometimes their offspring can substitute for a good marital relationship. For these men, the happiest years of the marriage occurred when the children were small. Their departure can cause them to change their lives—go back to school, switch careers. Like Brent, often they miss their children more than their wives do.

The Relieved Worker

After their children leave, Relieved Workers fill their time with their careers. They claim that they don't miss their children and are often pleased to finally have their wives all to themselves. As one man put it, "This is the happiest time in our married lives. We love our time together now. We have a lot of freedom."

These men may also feel relief because their children's adolescent years might have brought chaos to the family. Another dad shared, "The kids were very stressful to have around. Now it's very relaxing. . . . I'm happy that the kids are out doing their thing, and now it's just Fran and me together. I like that better." Relieved Workers are usually comfortable in their marriages.

The Pragmatist

Pragmatists take pride in knowing that their children are launched. They feel successful in the job they did. They also feel good about their careers and find them enjoyable. Their goal was to get the children grown and independent. They feel the children's leaving reflects the natural order of things. As one dad told me:

> The moving away—I consider that to be a normal, even a sought-after event in their lives. But I do expect some filial affection—a feeling that the word *Dad* is positive. I don't expect them to be beholden to me or to feel guilty about me. But I haven't let go. I'm connected by invisible threads—the threads are stretched longer now. It's not a web or an umbilical cord. It started out as a thick rope and has gotten thinner and thinner, but it's still a form of connection. I don't have to let go of the filament and I don't want it to snap or sever.

Rehearsal	**LOOKING BACK TO MOVE FORWARD**
	If you are a Mourner or an Eternal Dad, your relationship with your wife may have been buffered by having the children around. There is danger now to your relationship, with the children gone. Children sometimes serve as a substitute for dealing with your wife. To reconnect, try to remember the early years of your marriage.
1.	What activities did you and your wife enjoy doing together?
2.	Pick one or two that still stoke the fires of interest.
3.	Discuss these activities with your wife. She probably already knows how much you value your children, but if you've done the "Impact of Your Children on Your Marriage" exercise in Chapter 4, she'll know for sure.
4.	If she agrees, go back to some of the activities you once enjoyed.

Just as with your wife, the empty nest may be only one of your concerns at this transitional time in your life.

The Aging Process

"Is there something you can do about [aging]?" asks humorist Dave Barry in his book *Dave Barry Turns Forty*. "You're darned right there is! You can fight back. Mister Old Age is not going to get you, by golly. All you need is a little determination—a willingness to get out of the reclining chair, climb into that sweatsuit, lace on those running shoes, stride out that front door, and hurl yourself in front of the municipal bus."

Just as their children are leaving the nest, the signs of aging hit many men with pangs of fear. But, in truth, the thinning hair, the changing physical abilities, the decline in sexuality are not a disease. They are simply part of the normal aging process, and as such, need to be addressed.

Men at midlife seem to become preoccupied with their health. Constantly monitoring their bodies, they worry about loss of physical prowess and, understandably, about heart attacks and prostate problems. They get the first inklings of what their "shell" is doing to them, and it's usually a jarring reminder that they're not 19 or 20 anymore.

Fifty-nine-year-old Frank, for instance, told me, "I've always looked younger. Until a year ago, that is. It's a sign my body is starting to decay. I'd always felt like Dorian Gray before. For the first time, I'm feeling and looking my age."

When I asked Frank about the copper bracelet he wore on his wrist, he remarked candidly, "It reminds me on a daily basis that my body is disintegrating!"

But sometimes physical ills do confront us. Indeed, medical problems can be a wake-up call, a reminder that life is finite, that there is no time like the present. Hal, 48, told me how a massive heart attack had irrevocably altered his life ten years earlier:

> I was in the hospital for four weeks. I was lucky that the ambulance came so quickly and the hospital was close to my house.
>
> The heart attack changed many things in my life. I had been a career naval officer, but after my attack, I retired. I had wanted to be an entrepreneur all my life, to create something for myself, but my wife was always too scared. I had had a very bitter relationship with her. But when you're in bed in the hospital—you see only daylight and darkness through the window day after day—it gives you perspective.

So I decided in order to be happy, it was better for me to divorce my wife and start all over again. I retired my commission and moved across the country. I began my own business. I married a wonderful woman who supports me in my dreams for the future.

Hal used to put everything and everyone else around him first—he didn't pay attention to himself or his own needs. After the heart attack, he made the decision that he would be at the center of his life. He felt he had to do that in order to live.

Questions for Growth	PAY ATTENTION!
	Now is the time to attend to your body, especially if, like Frank, you fear you're "disintegrating."
1.	Take the time for a personal health checkup. Take stock of the following areas related to your health:
	◆ Physical: diet, weight, cholesterol levels, exercise, detrimental behaviors such as smoking or substance abuse, existing illnesses
	◆ Emotional: stress levels and the issues that are creating tension in your life, the presence of friends and others who are supportive of you, feelings of fulfillment from your work, the status of your marriage
2.	Share your concerns with your wife. Together discuss how she can help you and how you can help yourself. This is a time when you can put the Growth Circle into practice.

Dealing with Aging

Our changing bodies and illness can certainly evoke a sense of our own mortality. But the death of a parent can underscore it. Many men with whom I spoke brought this up as an issue. Ron told me:

My father died just a few months after Eric moved away so there have been many changes. It's like my dad was always

there in my mind, but no longer. It feels like a series of con-
centric ripples, like when you throw a pebble in a stream.
The first ripple is the shock that he died. Then, there is a
shift in the way I see my own mortality, like, am I next?

Ron's feelings are common among midlife men. Mortality is no
longer just an abstraction. It is real and anxiety provoking. It can cause
you to begin thinking about how you want to live the rest of your life.

Another of my interviewees, Brent, is a police lieutenant who comes
in contact with death on a weekly basis, but he seems to have made
peace with it:

I had a midlife crisis about twelve years ago, when I hit 40,
and it was tough. I see death more than most people. You
start to worry more. But it doesn't bother me as much now.
Then, I was just into my job and the family, but now I do a
lot of writing. I look at my mortality more philosophically
now. I read and write about religion and this helps me to
relax and feel more in control.

Questions for Growth

FACING YOUR MORTALITY

Midlife isn't the first time you've thought about your
own mortality, but it may be the first time you've
begun to take it more seriously because of your
parents' illnesses or deaths or your changing health
patterns. Death is an eventuality for all of us—there is
no argument with that. It can be useful to think about it
in a more structured way.

1. How have your experiences with the deaths of family,
   friends, or heroes affected you?

2. What attitudes about death did you absorb from your
   parents?

3. How do you view death? As the extinction of life with
   no meaning attached? A way to a better life? A relief?

4. Is death a dreaded enemy or a welcome friend? Explain.

5.	What kind of death would you like to have?
6.	What part does religion play in this?
7.	Review your answers. Now that you know your thoughts and feelings, what can you do? Talk to others. Coming to terms with death can be one of the most positive steps you can take in midlife.

Changes in Sexual Responsiveness

The astonishing popularity of a new anti-impotence drug, Viagra, highlights men's vulnerability to the loss of sexual function. The enormous demand for this medication is bringing impotence—a previously hidden subject and one that men preferred to avoid—to light. A man's self-esteem can be linked to his performance in bed. More than likely, declining sexuality is not a disease, but rather a part of the normal aging process. You should expect certain changes in your sexual response.

For instance, it is typical for erections to take longer to occur, to require more physical stimulation, and to be less firm than they were previously. The urge to ejaculate and the force of ejaculation may also diminish. These signs do not necessarily constitute impotence—which can be related to illnesses such as heart disease or diabetes, blood pressure medication, antidepressants, prostate surgery, substance use or abuse, or psychological factors such as anxiety or depression—but they do indicate changes in responsiveness that may be disconcerting.

You'll find suggestions on how to reawaken your sexual selves in Chapter 11.

Is Work Losing Its Luster?

Whereas some men at midlife can feel that they're at the peak of their productiveness, others like Dennis begin to experience disenchantment with their life's labors. They may believe that they have reached a plateau from which they can ascend no further, they may have been skipped over for promotion or downsized, circumstances of the workplace may have deteriorated, or they may simply become bored or worn out from their efforts. Dennis had this reaction:

I've been a real estate broker for thirty years. Half the time I enjoy it, and half the time I don't. But I do need to work. I don't like the fact that my work is difficult, though. It's pretty demanding, and as I get older, those things get harder. It's stressful timewise. You have to work longer hours and faster to make a deal, and sometimes I just don't feel like doing it anymore. Sometimes I'm just going through the motions.

Questions for Growth

REAWAKENING YOUR INTEREST IN WORK

Work may be central to your life, but if it no longer holds meaning, you may become disenchanted. The following questions will put you on the road to reawakening your interest in your present work or direct you to some other kind of work that you might want to do.

Change
Always respect the fact that you are a changing person within a changing relationship in a changing world. That's a starting point—one that will give you reassurance that you're not the only one.

1. How have you changed since you began your career?
2. What do you value now?
3. Is there a mismatch or disconnect?

Talents and Abilities
Identifying your "calling" means recognizing your skills and abilities and using them in productive work. This gives you a strong sense of meaning and connects you to your work.

1. List your interests, values, and personality characteristics.
2. Do you prefer working with people, data, or things?
3. Are your talents and abilities being utilized at your present job? If not, where could they be applied?

> **Balance**
> We all play many roles as worker, husband, son, father.
> The challenge is to find a balance.
>
> 1. How can you create a balance between your work and outside interests?
>
> 2. How can you balance your time?
>
> 3. How can you create a balance between your work and your marriage?

Middle-Aged Men Crave Connection

Carl Jung predicted that at midlife, men would turn from aggression toward affiliation, and I found this to be true with my husband. I remember when Bernie attended the tenth reunion of his law school class, which was held in the elegant banquet hall of a fancy hotel. After a sumptuous meal, each member of the class rose to speak about "what I've done since I got my degree." Most of them celebrated their professional accomplishments. There was a sense in the room of "Look at how well I'm doing!"—a sort of competitiveness.

At the twenty-fifth reunion, however, the tenor at the banquet changed. Most of the attendees, now in their fifties, shared stories about their families. In fact, the attorney who garnered the most applause spoke mainly about his nine children and all the pets that lived in his house. The emphasis had shifted from competition and pride in one's achievements to connecting with other people and pride in one's family.

I found a similar outlook and behavior among the midlife men I interviewed. In fact, I was surprised at how many of them wept as they revealed how much they missed their children and how much they longed for stronger connections to their wives.

John spoke of the primacy of his relationship with his son and daughter who live far away. "Most people use their vacation to rest and recuperate," he told me, "but we use it to spend time with our kids. That's something we really enjoy. I call the kids every evening after I come home from work. Occasionally, I'll even call from work. My son and I are good friends, but there is a different kind of warmth with my daughter. She's more available and emotional. I can talk to her more easily about feelings."

◆ ◆ ◆

If ever there was any thought that men breeze through their mid-lives as avoiders and deniers, my interviewees give the lie to that belief. Brent, the police officer who dealt with his mortality; John, the emotionally involved father; and Frank, who experienced his bodily changes as "Dorian Gray–like," attest to the many issues midlife men face.

Acknowledging and then understanding that you are neither "sick" nor alone in what you're experiencing can help you cope with feelings at midlife that may seem overwhelming.

Questions for Growth	**PHOTO SESSION FOR MEN**
	Get out your family photo album and find a favorite picture of yourself from between the ages of 21 and 35. Considering each of the above midlife topics (health, mortality, sexuality, work, emotionality), ask yourself:

◆ What strengths do I have in the above areas now that I didn't have when I was younger?

◆ How have I grown as a person?

◆ What wisdom have I gained over the years?

Taken together, these empty-nest and midlife issues indicate that you are experiencing many transition points at this time in your life. It should help you to know that you are not alone.

CHAPTER 6

Letting Go and Finding Your PPQ

I know from personal experience that the intense work of parent-ing does not end after a few exhausting months of round-the-clock feeding and diapering. I know it involves far more than teaching children to go potty, feed themselves, read, write, and respect other human beings, control hostility and anger, overcome sadness and disappointment, forge close relationships with others, and maybe someday find a mate and have children of their own. . . . It involves the extraordinary capacity to cope with one's own frustra-tion—and sometimes even one's own rage—to balance one's own needs with the often unpredictable needs of another, to tolerate terrible anxiety and even dread about their safety and well-being, to give and give and give when there is no "please" and "thank you" and finally, in such a bittersweet finale . . . to let go!

—Suzanne Gordon, the *Los Angeles Times*

WHAT A POIGNANT AND CRAZY-MAKING activity parenting can be! It is a role fraught with incongruities and contradictions, with passions beyond our wildest imagination. For eighteen years, we have been watching and teaching and nurturing our children as they grow and develop, and now we're asked simply to let them go. It almost seems unnatural, and yet we are told that to be healthy, to allow ourselves and our children to flourish, this is what we must do.

Granted, letting go is easier for some than for others, as the different kinds of empty-nest parents attest. Many factors can be involved:

- Your early experiences in your family of origin; how attached you still are (or were) to your parents—the model they created for you
- Your marriage
- Your support system in addition to your family and the number of other roles you fill
- Your and your children's temperaments
- The number of children in the family (it may be more difficult to let go of an only child)
- Your relationship with the child who is leaving
- Your child's success and your beliefs about his or her ability to function well in the world; your feelings of guilt or responsibility for your child's failings
- Your child's and your previous ability to cope with life-cycle changes
- The ways in which you occupy your time; the value you place on independence

In truth, we never, ever stop being parents, even if our children live far from us and conduct their lives independently. But at midlife, big questions loom, nevertheless.

Questions for Growth

TIPS FOR BECOMING HEALTHIER PARENTS

Now is a good time to ask yourselves the following questions:

1. How do we become parents who continue growing and who foster growth in our offspring now that they're gone?

> 2. How do we transfer the responsibility for their lives from our broad shoulders to theirs, and do we want to?
>
> 3. How do we accept the reality of their lifestyle and of who they really are?
>
> 4. How do we cultivate mutual respect?
>
> 5. How can we deal with separateness and yet create balance in the relationship?

I believe the answer is in learning to accommodate and adapt to change. In this chapter, we will be looking at some strategies that may help you do so.

Let Go of Your Offspring

Some families push their children out of the nest, either because they believe they need to be independent or because the child creates so much distress in the family that keeping the bonds strong seems destructive to all. On the other hand, mothers and fathers who are Mourners or Eternal Parents can have much difficulty letting go of their parenting role because they so enjoyed or needed it.

And for some, the opposite can also be true. The more disappointed you feel about how your children's lives have turned out, the more tenaciously you hang on, as if to try continually to better the situation. In some cases, the children also serve as a shield. Letting go can be frightening if your marriage is fraught with conflict and the kids are the only glue that holds you together. Indeed, some couples pay undue attention to their adult children's problems to avoid their own marital issues. They fear that focusing on the marriage will force them to acknowledge how truly unhappy it is.

But no matter what the situation in your family, you still need to learn to deal with your children leaving and eventually to let go of them. As one interviewee told me, "I realize my children are no longer a permanent part of my life. They are guests in my life." This is true for all of us.

When you let go of your offspring, you open up more space in your life to take care of yourself and your marriage.

The Role of Expectations

Consider how to let go and create a positive relationship with your young adult children. If "goodbye child, hello friend" doesn't work for you, perhaps "goodbye child, hello adult" may work better. But however you envision the relational shift, it's important to bear in mind that this is all a process. Letting go and creating a positive relationship doesn't occur overnight—and it would be unrealistic for you to expect that it would.

A good place to start cultivating your adult-to-adult relationship is to analyze your expectations for your children. This may not be as easy as it sounds, since your own emotions and your expectations for yourself may get in the way. After all, from the moment your child takes his first breath, you are making plans for his life. You might have looked to your offspring to fulfill your own disappointments or to make up for mistakes you had made. That's a heavy-duty set of expectations. It could cause you to engage in "shoulds," which might run something like this: "He or she should have studied harder, gone to college, or not taken up with that girl/boy who had such a troubled family life."

Or, you as the parents could have joined in the "self-blame game," in which case, the "shoulds" would be as follows: "I/we should have paid more attention to him/her, been more strict in setting and keeping to our rules," and on and on.

Questions for Growth

WHAT DID I/WE EXPECT FROM THE CHILDREN?

With your spouse, list your expectations of your children. Now ask yourselves:

1. Did your children meet most, some, or none of these expectations?

2. What about those unmet expectations?

3. Are you able to come to terms with them?

4. Can you acknowledge that, yes, your expectations were unmet to some degree, but that's the past and now you need to move on?

If so, you are ready for an adult-to-adult relationship.

Your children know full well that you have expectations for them. It might be useful for you—and it would certainly increase your understanding—if you thought back to when you were growing up and leaving home. Remember what your parents' expectations were of you. Did you meet them? If yes, how did you feel? If no, how did you feel?

You can create a feeling of understanding by recognizing that you have been in the same position yourself. This softens your view and allows you to take a step back—judgmentally, that is—to appreciate that expectations are a two-way street. Your children have them of you too, and if you don't already know it, you have disappointed them to some degree also. So a major first step in the letting-go process is realizing and then accepting the fact that none of us can totally fulfill each other's fantasy ideals. That's true with your children, your parents, and your spouse!

Change Your Grown Children? Forget It!

A next step in creating a positive relationship with your adult child is to let go of trying to change him or her. Deep down, do you hear some little voice repeating, "It's your fault; you should be ashamed; make some changes in him"? If you listen to this inner voice, you might resort to manipulative behavior. Relinquish the following unproductive efforts to change your children; they only create resentment. Author Eleanor Lenz offers the following list of manipulations to which I've added examples.

- **Bribery:** "I'll buy you some new clothes if you come home for a while . . . "

- **Appeal to Guilt:** "When you don't call, I get upset and then my headaches start up . . . "

- **Threat:** "If you don't come with us to Aunt Sally's for Thanksgiving, I'll . . ."

- **Shaming:** "What a ridiculous idea . . ."

- **Power Play:** "As long as you continue to live this way, I won't lend you any money . . ."

- **Appeal from Authority:** "I've already been through that and from experience I can tell you . . ."

- **Unfavorable Comparison:** "Jan's son visits her every day . . ."

- **Dire Prediction:** "Running around with people like that . . . you'll be in trouble in no time . . ."

These are clearly hurtful. Remember, the unchangeables apply to your children as well as to your spouse. And face it—your children are no longer under your control. (Ask yourself if, at this late date, you *really* want the control anyway?) In fact, sometimes the more we try to control them, the more they act out.

Attachments—Past and Present

Our personalities, backgrounds, and coping skills help to determine how we respond to the empty nest. Our attachments to others (especially our mothers) are an important part of our early experience and deeply influence our well-being and our adult relationships. We all need to feel loved and to love others—it's instinctive. Indeed, most of our intense emotions arise as we form, maintain, and renew these profound relationships.

By the same token, the attenuation or rupture of these bonds can be frightening—even terrifying. A child who finds himself without a parent could be in mortal danger. We carry memories of our early attachments into our adult relationships. Sometimes they affect how we relate to our spouses and our children.

My interviewee Karen told me about the difficulty she had in leaving her family of origin when she got married and moved to another city. Her mother had lost her own mother at a young age and revisited that trauma when Karen decided it was time to create her own life. "When I left, my mother became physically ill—she had to be hospitalized. That was pretty dramatic. She went into the hospital with 'malaise'—they never really diagnosed what was wrong with her. She couldn't handle the separation. It was a very painful, intense, horrible experience for her and for me, even though she still had my twin brothers living at home to take care of."

Questions for Growth	**REVIEW ANCIENT HISTORY**
	Recall how your family of origin dealt with your leaving:
1.	Did your parents hang on tightly?
2.	Were they grief-stricken?

3.   Were you "kicked out"?

4.   Was there a lot of conflict?

5.   Were you reluctant to leave?

6.   Did you feel supported in your journey toward adult-
      hood?

This awareness can help you understand how you have
been handling your child's departure. It can also help
you decide how you want to move on.

Karen's past pushed her toward making some decisions about how
she would separate from her own kids. "I didn't want to have the same
reaction my mother had, so I protected myself from it. I was deliberate
about it. I wanted to have multiple focuses in my life and not be so
intense about my children or burden them with my neediness. I didn't
want my children to be so responsible for my happiness."

Think Positively and Proudly

You have launched a relatively well-functioning, soon-to-be adult into
the world. You gave him or her the best you had to offer at the time. Forgive yourself your errors. You might not have been perfect, but most
likely, you were a "good enough" parent.

Many parents were able to express their pride in their children during our interviews. Diane told me,

> I really like my children as people. They have excellent
> values and caring souls. I feel proud of them as they define
> their lives and become more and more independent. Our
> son is about to go into business for himself. He is anxious,
> but we feel confident he will succeed. He has been building
> up to this for a couple of years. Our daughter just became a
> social worker. She has a difficult job, but she is hanging in
> there and hopes to do good. As a parent, you put a lot into
> them and then set them free in the world. It's exciting to see
> what develops.

It's also useful to remember that young adults may pull away with great vehemence at first, as they try to establish their own identities out in the world. But often, if the basic relationship with their parents is solid, they eventually come around. As Sheila, whose daughter was "headstrong and difficult" during adolescence, explained,

> I think my relationship with our daughter is better than ever. She sees, now that she's away, that we were really good parents. Her boyfriend comes from a dysfunctional family so she can see that she really has something good in us, as parents. She's been calling us more. She used not to call. It's amazing that we really like each other because it used to be a one-way street. Now she's coming around, and it's great.

Find a Way to Connect

If your children live out of town, create a comfortable way to see each other and communicate. In addition to frequent phone calls and visits scheduled no more than six weeks apart, Louisa and Cal also plan family vacations with their daughters and their live-in partners. "We've met them in Yosemite and Kauai," Louisa explained. "There's no reason not to expand the boundaries of 'family' to include the girls' significant others. And since we all have such happy memories of family vacations there together, the kids were eager to accompany us and introduce their boyfriends to places they had enjoyed as young children."

Questions for Growth	CONNECTING THREADS
	Most of us want connections with our grown children, whether by a filament or a thick rope. With your spouse discuss:
1.	Who you'll connect with
2.	How
3.	How often
4.	Where

Respect Their Boundaries

Your children deserve your respect. Remember, what goes around comes around, and that's particularly true when it comes to respecting your children's boundaries and sense of self. Rather than telling your children what to do, offer emotional support with an attentive ear and words of encouragement. Treat them as you would your friends. Let them know that you have confidence in their ability to run their own lives. You might say, "I know this is a tough time for you, but I'm sure you'll find a way to figure things out." Listen more and tell less. Become conscious of loosening your grip on the "ties that bind."

Be careful in how you offer an opinion. Introduce it by saying, "This is just my opinion. You may or may not agree with me." Wait to be asked, and when you give advice, give it one time only. Remember, being right is not as important as starting a new adult-to-adult relationship.

New Roles

Letting go of being a full-time parent and becoming, once more, the person you were before this role became so prominent in your lives is a gift that you can give yourselves. It's an opportunity to take up again where you left off eighteen or twenty years ago. There is great value in participating in varied roles—you are the healthier for it. Now, when parenthood is no longer your major role, it's time to cultivate new ones.

Questions for Growth	**BACK TO THE FUTURE**
1.	What did you enjoy doing as a teenager or young adult?
2.	What got your blood flowing?
3.	How can you incorporate these past dreams and interests into your present life?
	The options are endless.

Moving On—Together

Focusing on your children may be a way for you individually or as a couple to avoid moving on in your own lives. As one Eternal Dad told me:

> We all went through a developmental period when the kids
> left. Now we're focused on ourselves more, learning how to
> take care of ourselves. That's an area where the relationship
> was lacking. We put so much energy into taking care of the
> kids, we neglected our relationship. We find ourselves differ-
> ent from a lot of couples, and I'm not sure it's a good thing.
> They took more time for themselves when they had young
> kids. They went out more to the movies—things like that.
> We missed that, but now we're forced, by default, to develop
> our relationship and focus on our needs.

For years, this husband and wife had colluded in neglecting their
relationship. Clearly, the children had become a buffer in a dull and
conflict-ridden marriage. This couple had directed all of their loving
energy toward their offspring and when they left, they realized the marriage could use some help. This husband and wife are more mature
now, and the outlook for positive change is good.

Your Parental Power Quotient

It's gone now—that coveted commodity—parental power. Or if it's not
gone, it's greatly diminished. Your parental power quotient, or PPQ, is
your ability to say something and have your words be taken seriously
and acted upon, maybe even with a modicum of respect. The fact of the
matter is, when your children are grown, you no longer have as much
power with them. This can represent a real loss, and many of us go
through fruitless gyrations to recapture it. This can be negative for your
relationship with your kids. You can invent it in other spheres, however.
That's growth. You do have choices. In fact, you are now free to recapture the power you have over your own time and interests. You don't
have to take your kids' needs into account anymore!

Rehearsal	**LOOKING THROUGH NEW WINDOWS**

Y ou might try the following reframing exercise, especially if you feel stuck in the letting-go process:

Imagine you live in an old Victorian home with
many large windows, each affording you a

different view. Imagine that you have a favorite window from which you often gaze. In your mind's eye, sit in front of it now. As you look out the window, see your relationship with your child. Notice all the details—I'm sure you're armed with much information. Now pick up your chair and move it to another window. As you gaze out, envision a different way to interact with your child. Notice the details. What are you doing? What is your child doing? Now move to a third window and gain yet another perspective on your relationship.

This exercise illustrates how many possibilities we have in terms of relating to our adult children. It can help you reframe your relationship to your children, and that in turn can facilitate your putting into action many of the suggestions I've made for letting go. Use them as a jumping-off point for self-exploration.

"We're Baaaack!": When Your Kids Return

You've finally begun to let go when suddenly the kids come back, and for all kinds of reasons: financial reverses, divorce, schooling, job loss, or other changes. No matter what the cause, you have to adjust all over again. Perhaps worse than the cluttered or crowded nest is the unexpected return of a grown child to the home. Joyce had such a boomerang daughter, and it was tough at first:

> Janet didn't like the school she had enrolled in. She couldn't get all of her classes; she hated the party atmosphere. She was a workaholic and was commuting a lot so we said, "Just come home. This is silly."
>
> She's been home for seven months now. It was difficult at the beginning, observing the rules of the house—pick up your clothes, don't leave dishes in the sink—the usual. She's a woman now. It was different having a big person around. I was used to having my house clean, not doing laundry, but now there are people in the house—it's a full house again.

Over time, it has gotten easier—tolerable. We enjoy it at times. We don't see her a whole lot because she's either at school or at work. The hardest thing about having her home is watching her struggle with coming to grips with what she wants to do with her life.

As Joyce makes clear, there is the potential for myriad problems when grown children move back home. Many individuals I interviewed spoke of how difficult it was to deal with their children's comings and goings. Once your offspring have left the nest, their return can jar your expectations, your internal calendar, your own adjustment, your marriage. Problems can arise from the most mundane things like space and time issues: the use of bathrooms or the phone, mealtime planning, the lack of privacy, your sexuality (and theirs!).

The change can bring on regression—you all revert to your old ways of dealing with one another—and that's not good for you or your adult children. Guilty, angry, bewildered, you may want to avoid the intrusion ("Whose house is this anyway?" you may ask) or you may lapse into a "good mom" role in which you do all the cooking, washing, and waiting on, or an old "pop" role in which you suddenly feel the need to discipline and control. Worse yet, you may infantilize your child, treating him like a teenager again instead of an adult. Resentments and clashes are bound to occur when you regress. The entire family suffers, and so does your marriage.

You and your spouse must discuss the parameters if a grown child is moving back in, even temporarily. Privacy is a major concern. Which areas of your home will be designated off-limits? Respect is key here. There must be some discussion about how each of you wants to be treated.

You might draw up a set of guidelines for living in the house. Brainstorm with your spouse and write down anything that comes to mind. Then hold a family meeting regarding:

- Chores—designate who is responsible for what.

- Space—clarify who uses which room, when, and how.

- Meals—decide who buys the food, who cooks it, whether you eat together or separately, and who cleans up.

- Money—resolve who pays for what. Do you charge your child for rent and expenses? This can be a real boondoggle if not cleared up early.

◆ Length of stay—expectations need to be clarified. What do you do if the child exceeds an agreed-upon duration?

Make every effort to maintain your own independence as well as your grown child's. Keep the lines of communication open. Heart-to-heart talks are crucial before irritating situations get out of hand. It might help to think of your boomerang child as a houseguest. How would you treat him or her under those circumstances? How should he or she treat you?

With flexibility, tolerance, and respect, you, your spouse, and your adult child can negotiate an arrangement that will balance your need for independence with your child's need for support.

Rituals to Mark the Empty-Nest Passage

There are few, if any, rituals marking our passages through the midlife period, and especially the empty nest. Yet we feel the absence of these ceremonies. Many of the couples with whom I spoke lamented that there was no formalized way to chronicle this important change in their lives. And without it, the transition feels less meaningful, even invisible.

Rituals create predictability and the feeling of safety at moments when we're going through a transition and feeling frightened and insecure. They make us stop and think about what is happening at a particular stage in our lives—we pay attention. Sometimes rituals help us reassess our direction, sometimes they give meaning to our pain. They dignify and elevate our experience of everyday life. We need rituals for the changes we are undergoing at this time when our children are leaving us, but society provides us few if any guidelines.

Interestingly, two of the women with whom I spoke created their own spontaneous rituals to mark the departure of their children. In both cases, these self-generated activities helped the women come to terms with their loss and move on.

Louisa told me:

> The first three months after our youngest left, I was in disarray. I felt confused, unsettled. Cal saw the kids' departure as an opportunity to increase his commitment at work. He was offered a position that required a good deal more travel than we were used to, and he felt that since the kids were no longer home, he was free to pick up and go. "What about me?" I had cried at the thought of being abandoned even

further. "Am I chopped liver? The kids are gone and now you will be too. How will I handle so much aloneness? Don't you care about me?"

To which he replied, "Get a life!"

We fought a lot during those three months, but he did take the job over my objections. (Of course, if I were offered a job that required me to travel more, I would have resented his objections to it too.)

I was drifting around in a muddle. It was even hard for me to sit at my desk. To help me find my center again, I decided to take an art class, just for fun. It was called "Developing Your Creativity," and I thought the concepts might cross over into my work as a screenwriter. One of the last assignments was to draw a self-portrait in pastels. As I was working on mine, the instructor came up behind me and asked, "What's wrong? Your portrait seems so sad." I took a fresh look at my work and realized that it was, indeed, a very melancholy portrayal.

"I guess I really miss my kids," I told her. That picture put my feelings in focus, and the tears began to flow.

The following week we were to create a collage. I decided to try something different. I made color photocopies of my daughters' high school graduation photos. Then, I cut them into pieces—the eyes, the noses, the mouths, the cheeks, the chins, the hair. I then cut the self-portrait I had drawn into the same pieces. On a fresh piece of paper, I glued our features together in the same general areas—our eyes, our noses, and so on—in roughly the same spots as they should go. I connected the features with jagged, irregular lines.

What emerged was a jumble of chaos. The kids were part of me, but not me any longer. We were together but separate. My self had felt shattered by their absence—despite the frequent contact—and I saw where my internal work needed to take place. The old identity I had had throughout adulthood had broken apart, and I needed to create a new one. As I explained this to the class during the critique period, I became weepy. But the exercise was extremely helpful in concretizing exactly what was going on inside of me. Once I had this insight, I was able to move forward.

Sharon told me:

> Recently I was alone for six days. Jim was out of town. It was
> close to Angela's eighteenth birthday, and I was going to
> make a tape for her of me singing all of her favorite songs as
> a gift. That was my first idea, but I got so bored with myself
> that I lost the motivation.
>
> Then I noticed the boxes of audiotapes I had saved. They
> ranged from when Angela was an infant to her twelfth birth-
> day. I listened to them for hours and hours. I relived my
> motherhood with those tapes by myself for six days. I was up
> until 4 A.M. some nights, listening to them—I couldn't stop.
> I even edited them into one tape.
>
> It was so delightful. I was so pleased with all of my
> memories of motherhood, this kid, our lives. I cried and was
> sad, but it was like a purging. I relived it all.
>
> "Now she's gone and a new person," I told myself. "We
> have to change; she does too." I sent the tape to Angela and
> kept a copy for me.

Create Your Own Ritual

Louisa and Sharon created rituals for themselves, not even realizing
beforehand that that was what they were doing. Once they had completed the task of the ritual, however, they became aware of how the act
had given them a sense of comfort so that they could "move on" in their
lives. They had acknowledged the past, dealt with their feelings of loss
and sadness, and in so doing freed themselves from constantly having
to revisit their pain. You could almost hear, at the completion of
Louisa's collage, the slap of her dusting her hands clean of the full-time
motherhood experience and then opening them wide in a gesture of
"Next!"

Several of my midlife interviewees mentioned that had there been a
ritual for their children's leaving, they would not have felt so alone. Our
culture does not sanction or support a couple's grieving for a lost parenting role or their children leaving. By performing rituals, we provide
ourselves with an anchor, a sense of predictability and safety in times of
change, loss, and transition. They give form and structure to painful
emotions.

How would you create your own ritual to deal with the empty nest? I can't suggest the exact form it might take for you or your spouse. I have no way of knowing what has deep meaning in your lives. But I would like to propose a structure into which you could fill the elements that are the most meaningful. You can do this alone or both of you can participate as a way to mark this turning point in your marriage.

In surveying many religious and nonreligious rituals, I have found that they seem to have three elements in common:

1. ***Creating an atmosphere.*** Think about the setting in which you will perform your ritual. Will it be indoors or out? What will the light be like? Many rituals use candles since they seem to impart a soothing, nonintrusive, mood-setting ambiance. Indeed, rituals often begin with the kindling of tapers, an act that can create a zone of safety and may open the internal space for your next step in the process.

2. ***Performing healing acts.*** With the atmosphere chosen, think about:

   - What it is that you experienced over the years with your children, their meaning in your life/lives.

   - What has changed since they've grown.

   - What you want to accomplish now. What do you want for your life/lives as individuals and as a couple? What do you want for your relationship with your grown children?

As Louisa and Sharon demonstrated, there are creative or artistic ways of performing healing acts. But many others exist. You can:

- Assemble objects that represent the highlights of the years spent with your children while they were growing: photographs, toys, clothing, videos, certificates. The list is endless.

- Together plant a new tree at each child's departure and watch the trees (and your children) grow.

- Invite friends and loved ones to your home to talk about the years spent together with your children as they were growing up.

- Individually write about your memories and your current desires and read this aloud to each other.

◆ Meditate individually or as a couple. For instance, you might create and repeat to yourself your own mantra of healing phrases such as: *I've had many wonderful years with you, Tracy. I will miss the _____ and the _____. Things have changed now in these ways:_____. And now, I want to _____.* This may help you to think about what has been and what will be.

◆ Get in touch with your "higher self." One of the gifts of aging is wisdom. There is wisdom in all of us that comes into play at times like these. Here is a golden opportunity to put your higher self/inner wisdom to work on your own behalf.

All of these activities are meant to help you through the experience so that you don't have to keep revisiting the loss and pain.

3. ***Release, give thanks, and let go.*** This third step provides energy to let go and move on. It allows you to acknowledge all that has gone before, to appreciate what you have had with your children, and to look forward to what you want for yourself as well as your relationship with your grown offspring. The expression "letting go with love" is apt here, for the more positive this third step, the better the outcome for all of you.

The way in which you perform this third step is also quite personal.

◆ You might say something to the effect of "I'm letting go."

◆ You might write about releasing the ties.

◆ You might think about it, sing about it, dance about it.

◆ You might blow out the candles or watch them as they burn down.

Create a ritual that is custom-made to your own talents and experiences. I've suggested a structure. Now it's up to you to fill in the blanks as your feelings and needs dictate.

PART THREE

Enjoying Your Midlife Marriage

We've never had a "golden" time in our marriage. From the very beginning, we would scrap like siblings. In years past, I just felt more comfortable when he left the house. Then, there were no criticisms, no demands. I was always tense when he was around—my stomach was in knots.

I've been a very traditional wife, always trying to meet his needs. Our kids allowed me to focus outside myself. When my husband was in law school, he had almost no interaction with them. I practically raised them by myself. I was a total mom, and the kids were a buffer between my husband and myself. The dog also helped. But then the kids left home, the dog died, and now there's just the two of us.

L ORRAINE'S MARRIAGE IS A good example of how couples can use their children as shields. But now that the buffers are gone and Lorraine is choosing to stay married, how will she continue on in her midlife years and beyond as an individual and as part of a couple?

In Part Three, we will explore various ways to add to your enjoyment (both individually and as a couple) of "life after the kids are gone." For, just like Lorraine and her husband, you may wonder, "Where do we go from here?"

This question is inevitable. Situations around you are changing. You are changing. That's a fact of life. Consequently, your marriage is changing as well. But in what direction is it moving?

- Is it lacking vitality?
- Do you find it comfortable but duller without the challenges and excitement that kids can bring?
- Are you arguing more?
- Do you feel that after all of the years and energy you devoted to your kids, the two of you have lost track of each other and now you have little in common?

If your answer is yes to any of these questions, you can replace sadness with hope. For, in truth, you have the opportunity to develop skills that you will use for the rest of your lives. Understanding that marriage is not static gives you room to work out your problems.

Marriage carries with it a sense of unfinished business. So let's get down to the business of tending your empty-nest relationship. Whether it's reevaluating, redefining, restructuring, renegotiating, or recontracting—whatever you call it—it all boils down to your reinventing your marriage.

CHAPTER 7

Replenishing Your "I" Account

First learn to love yourself and then you can love me.
— Saint Bernard of Clairvaux

S ELF-ACCEPTANCE, SELF-ASSERTIVENESS, and self-nurturing can fill your emotional coffers. Let's look at these more closely.

Accept Yourself

In a scene in *After the Fall*, Arthur Miller's dramatization of his marriage to Marilyn Monroe, the lead character imagines a grotesque creature on his lap. He comes to realize that this ugly beast represents some unacceptable parts of himself—parts he has split off and rejected but that ultimately he needs to accept and integrate before he can become a whole person.

Self-acceptance is reassuring and certainly powerful. It helps you "feel your center"—the part of you that represents your strongest, best-functioning self. When you accept yourself—your whole self, "the good" with "the bad"—you are more apt to be in touch with your needs. You can recognize when you are giving too much or too little to your marriage. You sense when the situation is becoming unbalanced.

Part of self-acceptance is your understanding that genetics has much to do with your temperament—how you respond to your environment. Recently scientists have found that, despite our beliefs to the contrary, our genetic inheritance may greatly influence how we behave. For instance, Jerome Kagan, the developmental psychologist at Harvard University, recently wrote, "I have been dragged kicking and screaming by my data to acknowledge that temperament is more powerful than I thought and wish to believe."

All of us have inborn traits that influence who we are in the world. Moreover, we have bona fide temperamental variations from one another. Some of us are born to be more outgoing, while others are more reserved; some are more active, while others are quieter; some embrace change, while others shrink from it. No temperament is better or worse than another—they just are. As Chilean biologist Humberto Maturana makes clear, "organisms never 'make mistakes'; they simply respond to events in terms of their current structure."

Starting from a position of being "okay" with your temperament, whatever that may be (rather than believing that something is wrong with you), gives you permission to be fully yourself. And self-acceptance leads to partner-acceptance. It's a step toward dealing with the un-changeables.

Use Positive Self-Talk

We talk to ourselves all day, internally criticizing our mistakes, real or imagined, and lauding our successes. We can use self-talk to tear ourselves down ("How could I have been so stupid?!") or build ourselves up ("Boy, do I look handsome today!"). We can also use self-talk to accept ourselves.

The self-talk of acceptance might follow a pattern such as: *I accept who I am.* You might wish to repeat this sentence as a sort of mantra when you shower in the morning, drive to work, or take an evening walk. The reiteration of such a positive statement—even if you are saying it *as if* you believe it at first—will soon make its content part of your emotional repertoire. Remember the "as if" solution—changes in attitude often follow changes in your behavior.

The following exercise can help you along the road to self-acceptance.

Rehearsal | **SPRING CLEANING**

1. On a piece of paper, list all the things you like about yourself and your life: temperament, personality traits, talents, achievements, what you do for others, and so on.

2. Next, list all the things you dislike about yourself and your life: temperament, personality traits, things you have neglected to do for yourself or others, weaknesses, fears, parts you are ashamed of. Get it all out.

3. Now review your lists. Say each item out loud and after each make the statement, "I accept who I am."

4. Pay attention to which emotions surface, especially after you go over your inventory of dislikes.

5. You have already looked at letting go of your children. Now try to let go of your disappointments in yourself. Ease up on the self-blame and accept yourself for who you fully are.

   When you go through this process of spring cleaning, you provide yourself with a platform for moving on. This can be a freeing activity.

Self-Assertion and Setting Limits

Lydia told me:

> For the past eight years, I have been taking care of my parents, who were both very ill, and now they are deceased. I also worked full-time, raised the kids, and handled most of the household chores. Now, Ken is tired of working; he wants to retire early. But one of us has to work to make ends meet, and I don't want to be the one. After my parents died, I was sure, for the first time in my life, that if it were at all possible, I would pay attention to my own needs. I earned it.
>
> The surprising thing is that Ken isn't thrilled, but he accepts and respects the position I've taken. And our marriage is all the better for it.

Lydia drew a line in the sand. She needed a break after the many years she had put into caring for her family and her ailing parents and she said so, in no uncertain terms. The limits and boundaries she established enhanced her sense of self, while they contributed to her marital well-being.

The crossover at midlife often finds women like Lydia enjoying more assertiveness than they had experienced earlier in their marriages. But becoming suddenly assertive when that has not been your style can be disconcerting to those around you (and even to yourself). During this transition, it helps to remember that we are always reinventing the work in progress—ourselves and our marriage.

As an assertive individual, you are entitled to certain rights and privileges. Acceptance plays a role here too.

Your Rights and Privileges as an Assertive Individual

- You always have the right to change your mind.
- You always have the right to make mistakes without excuses.
- You always have the right to be the judge of your emotions, thoughts, and behavior.
- You always have the right to dismiss others' opinions of you.
- You always have the right to refuse to take responsibility for others and to find solutions to their problems.
- You always have the right to ask for what you want.
- You always have the right to just say no or just say yes.

Keeping these rights and privileges in mind, use some of the pointers below to help you define the boundaries of what you are or are not willing to do in your marriage.

Defining Your Boundaries

1. **Engage in a self-search.** Define just what it is that you want to change in terms of setting limits. Lydia, for instance, decided that she needed respite from work and that she was unwilling to support her husband in taking an early retirement.

2. **Consider how willing you are to negotiate.** You may be averse to giving ground on this issue. You clearly want your needs met, but at the same time you want to protect your marriage. Think about how to communicate your needs to your spouse. You may

put your concerns in writing or call for a "couple meeting" to discuss them. Lydia sat down with her husband to talk after they had spent a relaxing day on the golf course. They were both calm and could hear each other out.

3. ***Be aware of what you say and how you say it.*** Keep your statements short and to the point and avoid any attacking expressions such as "You never . . ." or "What's wrong with you?" These will only make your partner defensive. Instead use "I" statements such as "I want to get closer to you," or "I need . . ."

4. ***Use the roses-and-bricks approach.*** As trite as it may sound, the roses-and-bricks approach can work. Lydia told her husband, "You've been working really hard and I understand why you want to retire, but the last few years have been a nightmare for me. I'm just exhausted and I need time to recuperate." In this way, she validated her spouse's feelings (roses), while still asserting her needs (bricks).

5. ***Be prepared for your spouse's reaction.*** He or she may become angry, sad, resigned, defensive, or silent. Standing firm demonstrates your decisiveness about your limits and needs. Still, you can express your understanding as Lydia did above or you can agree to revisit this issue at some designated time in the future. "Let's talk about this again six months from now," Lydia had told Ken. "Maybe then, I'll feel ready to get back to my job."

You can apply these five steps to any major or minor issue for which you feel you must set limits.

While women are learning to be more assertive, their husbands may be trying to reach out to get what they need. Their midlife changes often dictate a softening of their outer-directed male traits—a need for more affirmation and involvement with others, for example. Assertiveness in line with meeting these new needs is now in order. Your new boundaries can be porous or fluid, capable of being opened or closed, as need be.

Peter, for instance, was missing his children, especially his involvement with his son, which had filled so much of his time. With the kids gone, he needed more time with his wife. He approached Lisa for some special activities they could do as a couple.

In breaking down boundaries, you can use the same assertiveness techniques outlined above.

This Is Your Time: Nurture Yourself

Women have a long history of denying their own needs. With the children growing and many of us working, who has the time to indulge? But now that the children are gone, you have no excuses. This is your time to pay attention to your needs. When you take care of yourself, you are no longer so needful of others to provide you with a sense of fulfillment, happiness, or well-being.

Men have not been paragons of self-care either. They often engage in practices that undermine their health. For instance, they visit the doctor less frequently and have fewer checkups than women. They don't sleep as much or eat as healthfully. They are less physically active than women. Consequently, Jed Diamond claims that more men than women are overweight. They are more apt to abuse alcohol or other substances. They engage in riskier behavior and tend to be more violent. They have fewer social supports than women.

So how can you take better care of yourselves? You may find the following guidelines helpful:

Taking Care of Yourselves

1. ***Take the time.*** Time is one of the most important elements in your life. Indeed, making time for self-nourishment is essential to your mental and physical health. It's important to factor in time to take care of yourself daily or several times a week. Use your assertiveness skills to carve out time for self-nurturing. If you don't do it, who will?

2. ***Learn to relax.*** Tensions are everywhere in your busy life; that's all part of being a midlifer. But there are many things you can do to relax: meditate, jog, listen to music, read, sew, garden, paint, build furniture, just sit and stare, hide under the covers.

3. ***Be sure to play.*** Explore the world around you as a child might, with all the wonder and freshness of youth. You might enjoy tennis, golf, electric trains, swimming, or bike-riding. Sex can be a form of play. Or just get silly—collect jokes, watch funny videos, paint your dog's toenails!

4. ***Enjoy sensual pleasures.*** Although many of us disregard it in our lives, touch may be our most important sense. Did you know that there are thirteen hundred nerve endings in every

square inch of your fingers? Pay attention to your sense of touch. Blindfold yourself and touch various plants or fruit. Explore your body and your partner's during sexual activity. Enjoy a warm, luxurious bath. Try showering in darkness—it helps you to focus on the sensual pleasure of your body.

Your sense of smell provides another source of pleasure. Become aware of the scents around you: clean sheets, a perfumed bath, cookies in the oven, or fresh-cut flowers. Your sense of hearing is another resource. Listen to the birds' songs or the trickle of water in a fountain. Allow music to inspire you.

Your Dreams and Goals

Having a mission or purpose for your life (and following it) is one of the greatest nurturing gifts you can give yourself. Consider your favorite hobby. There is a good reason why you enjoy this activity. If you think about it, you might discover something about what makes you unique and forms your character. Getting in touch with this uniqueness can help you articulate your dreams and goals.

Rehearsal

DEFINE YOUR DREAMS AND GOALS

Ask yourself the following question to get in touch with your dreams and goals: *If I could do whatever I wanted without worrying about money, time, my husband's/ wife's approval, what would that be?* You'll probably come up with more than one dream. Write down your answer. Take time to look at it each day. Add to it when additional ideas strike you. This is your "big dream." After studying it for some time, perhaps you will begin to act on it.

Without letting go of the "big dream," begin to envision smaller desires (such as eating at a certain restaurant, taking a karate class, and so on).

Make a list of at least fifteen of these that you would enjoy doing over the next several months.

◆ Keep this list where you can see it several times a day. (The refrigerator is the hub of our house; every wise saying, joke, recipe, diet, and list is magnetized there.)

◆ Make a contract with yourself to put two or three of these desires into action.

Pursuing your "big dream" will have added meaning in your retirement years. Much of what will help you during the empty-nest phase of your life will certainly apply as you continue to age.

CHAPTER 8

Your "You" Account: Taking Care of Each Other

When the satisfaction or security of another person becomes as significant to one as is one's own satisfaction or security, then the state of love exists. So far as I know, under no other circumstances is a state of love present, regardless of the popular usage of the word.
—Harry Stack Sullivan, *Conceptions of Modern Psychiatry*

INTERESTINGLY, IN MY INTERVIEWS, more husbands spoke of the esteem they feel for their wives than the reverse. This may have to do with the reversal of roles at midlife. Men are looking around, noting attributes, interested in their more tender and loving side. Women are more assertive, maybe even less tolerant, and they are expecting more of themselves and their spouses.

As these men focused on the "You" in their marriages, they admired the new growth and strengths their wives were exhibiting. One husband spoke of his appreciation for the changes his wife had gone through:

> She had a life struggle of finding herself, and it just came to the surface in the last few years. She has recognized that her

entire life has been devoted to others—she felt responsible for maintaining relationships across the board, not only with her family but with my family—and people have taken advantage of her. She has come to realize that over the past few years, and now, she has backed off. She's not taking on the responsibility like she used to.

In fact, there has been a call for change on my part. I never did anything with our relationship—most women take charge of that department. With our situation it was maybe 99 percent to 1 percent. We're working at being maybe 90 percent to 10 percent or 80 percent to 20 percent. I want to be realistic. Fifty-fifty is far in the future. I need to recognize more of her needs now, especially since she has learned to sit back and let me take more responsibility for the marriage.

I think ultimately the net effect of this change in her will be a positive one for both of us because it will allow us to interact more and have a more intimate relationship.

Emotional Intelligence and the Growth Circle

An emotionally intelligent spouse will accept the notion of the Growth Circle in action. Those who are emotionally intelligent:

- Know themselves well (their strengths as well as their weaknesses)
- Understand how to handle upsetting emotions and impulses
- Are motivated and hopeful and have the energy to follow through on goals
- Are empathic and are able to read others' emotions from facial expressions and body language
- Have good social skills and don't bully others

Indeed, according to psychologist Daniel Goleman, research has shown that such emotional intelligence predicts about 80 percent of a person's overall success in life. And an individual's success bodes well for the couple's success.

Easier said than done? Perhaps. This is especially true if your partner feels threatened or is unwilling to go along. In that case, you must take responsibility for yourself first. Someone has to start the Circle rolling.

Helping Your Husband
Express His Feelings

In the spirit of the Growth Circle and remembering your roles as kind teacher and willing student, you can help each other through difficult situations. In fact, women, as the emotional managers in the family, can teach their husbands to express their feelings. Here is how this worked with one couple.

Joe loved classical music and Sandy could take it or leave it. During intermission at a performance of the orchestra, Sandy met a friend she had not seen for a long time. When the break was over, she told Joe, "I'll join you soon." Joe waited and waited. A half-hour into Beethoven, Sandy quietly slipped into her place next to her husband.

Joe felt annoyed and hurt. "Why aren't you there with me to enjoy the things I do?" he whispered angrily. "You know I've been looking forward to this concert for so long."

Sandy didn't know what to say except, "Sorry. I guess I got carried away talking to Cindy."

Joe, however, wouldn't let go of this incident, even though Sandy asked him to. This slight served as a metaphor for what was occurring in their relationship. Joe was unhappy at work and wanted to get closer to his wife, but he was unsure how to share his true feelings. How could he tell Sandy without feeling so vulnerable?

Fortunately, Sandy was understanding. She had been wondering for a long time how she could encourage Joe to open up and talk about what was really bothering him. The following are some simple steps that Sandy (or any wife) could use to help her husband express his emotions, to be a kind teacher to her husband's willing student.

Helping Your Husband to Open Up

1. **Don't force the issue.** Many husbands need to express their unhappiness, but like Joe, they don't know how to go about it. He, for instance, needed to tell his wife that he wasn't getting the love and attention that he longed for from her. Yet he feared disclosing this and losing face. While aware of his fear of disclosure, Sandy could use Joe's dissatisfaction as a discussion opener. She might say, "I can see that you're unhappy about this incident. What's on your mind?" Then, without offering advice or defending her actions, she could let him take the lead. Admitting

he had a problem was threatening enough for Joe without her pouncing on him about it.

2. *Self-disclose.* It can be helpful to model the behavior you're after. Because women have so much more permission in our society to let it all hang out, expressing emotion comes naturally to most. Indeed, they can model this behavior for their husbands. Sandy might say, for instance, "Joe, when I came back to sit down, you gave me a look that made me feel as if I'd disappointed you. That made me feel sad."

3. *Make it easy for him to talk.* Asking questions is a simple way to help someone talk. When Sandy shared her feelings, she might have followed up with: "It made me sad to think that I disappointed you. Did I?" She could also use phrases such as "tell me more" or "I didn't realize that." These are nonthreatening invitations to keep talking.

4. *Be aware of your body language and facial expressions.* It's important to communicate to your partner that you are nonjudgmental and that you are listening with empathy and understanding. This will help your spouse feel safer. Lean forward, make eye contact, and uncross your arms. These gestures convey openness and interest.

5. *Be brief and to the point.* In the world of business, men talk about the "bottom line." Your spouse will be more open to listening and sharing if you don't overload him with details.

6. *Be patient.* If you see your spouse become quiet and nonresponsive, it's best to withdraw yourself. Most likely, he's not reacting to you. He just needs his space. Be patient. He is learning new ways to communicate his feelings. It's a process that takes time.

When your husband feels more comfortable sharing his feelings, he will be a more willing participant in the give and take of the Growth Circle.

When Both of You Work

There are so many stresses at midlife. And to all this we must add one more: the dual-career couple. Wives enjoying their newfound strengths may relish their careers now more than ever. Some midlife husbands may still be fully engaged in their careers, but others might feel bored or disillusioned with their life's work. They may compensate by looking to their wives for affirmation and fulfillment.

Jealousy can easily rear its head if a woman forges ahead in her career during midlife while her partner is stuck in the doldrums. Moreover, in his need for greater attention from his wife, a husband may feel, "I'm number three on her list, after work and the kids." No midlife husband covets the role of second or third fiddle.

Besides, the workplace is a demanding entity. The furthering of marital happiness is not its bottom line. Most of the recent family-friendly changes that have been made in the workplace such as flex-time or in-house daycare centers are meant to help parents deal with their children and are not directed at enhancing one's marriage.

The Myth of Shared Household Responsibilities

Let's not forget the ever-present issue of housework. In most cases, working wives continue to handle most of the household responsibilities. Women with full-time employment outside the home work an average of fifteen hours longer each week than do their spouses. That time adds up to an extra month of twenty-four-hour days a year, and over a dozen years that adds up to an extra year of days. Unfortunately, the concept of shared household responsibility is often still a myth.

Resentment can build when a wife feels she is unfairly saddled with all (or most) of the household chores, and that in turn, creates tension and power struggles. As one wife told me, "I'm worn out and don't want to make dinner when I come home. He doesn't lift a finger to help. Or when he does, he leaves the kitchen such a mess, it just makes twice as much work for me. I'd rather do it myself."

Unfortunately, many wives have bought into the "superwoman" myth as they try to flawlessly juggle career, family, household, children, and husband. Such unrealistic expectations might have arisen from how women define success—high achievement at home and on the job—while for men, only the career is important. Women may believe that they have to handle everything well; they give themselves little slack.

But perfectionism conflicts with a happy marriage. Midlife stress can turn into midlife crisis because of your perception that you can't control everything to your satisfaction. It is a reminder of your limitedness, your mortality.

If you're a superwoman and are ready to give up some control and perfectionism for the sake of marital harmony, try this exercise with your husband.

Rehearsal	**OUR HOME–SHARING THE LOAD**
	Wives, are you guilty of being "superwoman"? Husbands, are you supporting this role in your wife to the detriment of your relationship? To enhance your mutual "You" account and promote fairness, try to create a new reality of shared housework.
	Husbands, imagine you are sitting in a comfortable chair in your living room, relaxing, maybe sipping a glass of wine or a cup of coffee while a maid is bustling around the house, attending to all the chores.
1.	Share with your wife your fantasy of the different things the maid is doing.
2.	Which of these chores would you be willing to take on for the next week?
3.	Do this one chore for a week.
4.	The following week, drop this chore but take responsibility for another one.
5.	Repeat the next week and so on for four weeks.
6.	At the end of the month, take on two chores and continue as above. You are taking small steps toward big changes.

Restoring a fine balance in giving and getting will help relieve some of the stress in a two-career midlife marriage. Flexibility, communication, and negotiation are essential.

CHAPTER 9

The Seven Marital Themes and the Empty-Nest Marriage: Tending to the "Us"

To be loved for what one is, is the greatest exception. The great majority love in another only what they lend him, their own selves, their version of him.

—Johann Wolfgang Goethe, *Wisdom and Experience*

THE QUOTE THAT OPENS THIS CHAPTER refers to acceptance—one of the Seven Marital Themes that emerged from my research into what comprises a happy marriage. These themes include:

- Accepting each other's individual differences
- Nurturing each other
- Reaching out to family and friends

- ◆ Sharing values, goals, and marital responsibilities
- ◆ Being flexible
- ◆ Communicating your feelings and thoughts to your partner and listening to your partner's point of view
- ◆ Managing conflicts

These Seven Marital Themes (taken in conjunction with the other suggestions I have made throughout the book) incorporate many of the attitudes and behaviors you can use to revitalize your empty-nest marriage. Indeed, they build upon one another to support your reinvigorated relationship.

Accept Each Other's Individual Differences

Accepting your partner as he or she truly is can be a tall order. As Goethe points out, it is far more common for us to love in our mates the reflection of ourselves than who they really are. But to try to change your spouse to more closely match your "ideal" can lead to frustration and conflict.

When you accept your partner, you relinquish the struggle to "fix" him or her. And ironically, the more you let go in this battle of wills, the more likely you are to achieve what you want. Think of the Chinese finger-cuffs we used to play with as children. The harder each child tries to pull his finger free from the flexible straw tube, the tighter it holds. The reverse, of course, is also true. Gracefully accept what you can't change.

When you stop labeling something you don't like a problem and start labeling it a fact of life, you will realize that it's not your differences but your resistance to differences that causes you pain. It is inevitable that you will disappoint each other. But the difference between couples who thrive and those who don't is that the former accept and adapt to their spouses as they are. They take the good with the bad—but they focus on the good and on what they love in their mate!

You can learn to tolerate certain anxieties, fears, and even behaviors that overwhelm you by slowly and systematically introducing yourself to them in a step-by-step fashion. Professional therapists do this all the time with people who fear flying, heights, and so on; it is called *systematic desensitization*. For instance, let's say that you are afraid of heights. Anything above the eighth floor of a building terrifies you. First, understanding the problem—talking about it—helps you to get a handle on it. Next, the therapist might lead you to the eighth floor of a building, and again you would explore your feelings. When you are ready, the therapist might then encourage you to ascend to the ninth floor and then the tenth and so on, thinking and talking all the while about your feelings and understanding them. When you reach the top floor of a twenty-story building, you look out the window and congratulate your-self for understanding, taking control, and tolerating your feelings.

You can also apply this principle to building up a tolerance to behaviors in your spouse that make you uncomfortable.

Rehearsal	### SYSTEMATIC ACCEPTANCE

In systematic acceptance, you and your partner take graduated steps to reduce the "hot spots" that can plague your relationship. A good dose of compassion is in order here. Realize that when your partner does something that seems unpleasant to you, he or she may be trying to feel better—to survive. The behavior isn't necessarily meant to annoy you.

Systematic acceptance is more effective if you practice it individually on your own time. Before you begin, relax and take some deep breaths. You are going to do some imaging and self-questioning.

1. ***Think of one "hot spot."*** Imagine something that bothers you about your partner's behavior, something that is unlikely to change.

2. ***Ask yourself the following desensitizing questions:***

   ◆ How is this behavior helping my spouse feel better?

   ◆ How is this meeting his or her basic needs?

   ◆ What can I do to help? (Give reassurance and avoid criticism.)

   ◆ How can I reduce my annoyance with this behavior in the future?

> 3. **Let go.** In a don't-bother-with-the-little-things mode, let go of those issues in your marriage that are extraneous to your marital survival. On the other hand, trust, loyalty, and respect are bottom-line and always essential for a marriage.
>
> 4. **Repeat as needed.** This exercise can help you address the "I," the "You," and the "Us" of your marriage. Your spouse isn't a bad person—just different from you. Through systematic acceptance, you can begin to let go of your anger.

Let Go

The theme of accepting is also tied to "letting go." Earlier, I spoke of letting go in relation to your children. But letting go is a part of the Growth Circle as well. To help your empty-nest marriage, it is essential to let go:

- ◆ of the need to mold your partner to your "ideal"
- ◆ of the idea that the differences between you are intolerable
- ◆ of your need to be or have the "perfect" husband/wife
- ◆ of the need to control your spouse

My clients Millie and Joe had struggled during their twenty-nine years of marriage with the issue of control and letting go:

> When our first child was born, our biggest problems began. It was really hard on Joe when he wasn't the center of attention anymore. I guess he had to adjust to the fact that the baby needed more of my time than he did.
>
> We fought a lot then. In fact, most of the arguments we've had throughout our marriage were over how to raise the kids. My father was really strong and self-assured. He provided well financially. Joe is definitely not like him; he's more scattered, going from job to job. He has always just barely made a living, and I guess that part of him disappoints me.
>
> My mother was always there for us. Dinner was ready at six. She came to all of our school functions. She was patient

and understanding—nothing like me. And to keep the peace, my mother usually just gave in to my dad.

Because of Joe's going from job to job, I've had to work throughout our marriage. I also had most of the responsibility for taking care of the house. To tell you the truth, my disappointments in Joe have made me resentful, and I felt entitled to have the greatest say in how we raise the children.

Joe had his own version of the conflicts in the marriage:

Millie is a take-charge person. I admire that in her, but it created a lot of problems especially when it came to raising the kids. I was an only child and the center of attention. I didn't have a lot of experience in a large family like Millie, but I know that you can't spoil a child with too much love and affection. I always felt she was more of a "manager" than a warm and caring mother. We argued a lot about my paying too much attention to the kids and her paying too little.

Things did change, though. After our youngest moved out, we were faced with each other. We couldn't argue about discipline or curfews anymore. After twenty-seven years, we didn't know what would happen next.

Millie and Joe's struggle exemplifies how a couple can use children to buffer the real issues between them: Joe's need to have his wife be more nurturing and attentive toward him; Millie's need to turn her husband into the self-assured, financially successful ideal. Indeed, Millie's attempts to control Joe set off a power struggle between them that was reflected in their dealings with their children.

But then things changed. Millie's dad died, and in therapy she came to realize that her parents' marriage was far from perfect. Her father, though charismatic, had also been dictatorial, and her mother seemed weak in her role as second fiddle. "I don't want that for me," Millie said after reaching this insight.

Over time, the conflicts in Millie and Joe's marriage began to ease. "With the kids out of the house," Millie told me, "I realized how much we had neglected each other. Over the last few weeks, I've done some serious thinking, and I know I want things to be better." And they did become better. Millie was less insistent that decisions go her way all the time. "This has really changed with age, experience, and wisdom," she told me. "I've let go with the children, my husband, and myself."

Rehearsal	CLEARING THE AIR
	The following activity will help you and your partner work toward acceptance.
1.	Sit at a table with a small bowl or bag in front of each of you.
2.	On three slips of paper, write down three problems each of you is having with the other. Phrase the issue as follows: "It's a problem for me when you . . ."
3.	Fold up the papers and put them in your partner's bowl.
4.	Your partner reaches into his or her bowl and reads one problem aloud.
5.	Let your partner explain in one minute why he or she acts, feels, or thinks this way.
6.	He or she should then ask you, "Now that you know why I do this, can you accept it?"
7.	Give one of three responses: "Yes," "Yes, if . . . ," or "No, because . . ."
8.	Save all your "No's" for further negotiation.
9.	Now it's your turn to read one of your partner's grievances.
10.	Did you make some inroads? Were some behaviors accepted?

Respect Your Partner's Needs

Respecting your partner—his or her need for privacy, for experimentation time, for personal space—is another aspect of acceptance. Respecting the changes in his or her life helps put the Growth Circle into operation. Respect also works within you. Knowing that you have a right to ask for what you need, to say no, to make mistakes, and still to feel good about yourself are all a part of assertiveness and self-acceptance.

Nurture Each Other

At midlife, your spouse may feel on top of the world while you are down in the dumps. Or, the reverse can be true. Whatever the circumstances, we all need support, validation, and caring. A kind word, look, or act; tenderness when one of you is ill; a steadying hand when a parent dies—who better to support you, hold you, and listen to you than your spouse?

In the stressful busyness of midlife, it may seem difficult to find the time for nurturing your partner, but taking a few minutes a day can do wonders for both of you.

Imagine the following scene: "Honey, I'm home," Ed calls out as he drops his briefcase by the front door. There's no response. Liz is upstairs on the phone with a girlfriend and ignores Ed's arrival. He's frazzled from the long drive home; she's equally stressed from a hard day at work that ended with a trip to the supermarket and a stint in front of the stove. She wants to relax talking with her friend. He feels ignored; she feels underappreciated for all she does and so does he. When she comes downstairs, tempers flare. Anger, hurt, and frustration color the rest of the evening's interactions.

Ed and Liz need to establish a reentry ritual. It might be as simple as a brief kiss and hug or as involved as sitting down for a few minutes to outline how each of their days went.

Rehearsal | **DESIGN YOUR OWN REENTRY RITUAL**

Like Ed and Liz, think about what you can do to reconnect for a minute or two after a long day. How could you show each other caring and appreciation? Design a reentry ritual that works for you and remember to discuss reentry behaviors that backfire: continuing to talk on the phone when your partner comes home or going straight for the mail and phone and bypassing your spouse are ways of disconnecting.

Rehearsal

LOVE AT FIRST, SECOND, AND THIRD SIGHT—A RECOLLECTION

Expressions of appreciation go a long way toward enlivening a stale union. This exercise is effective in helping you stop taking each other for granted.

1. List the qualities that attracted you to each other in the first place and the loving experiences you had early in the relationship.

2. Share these with each other with each allowing the other to speak without interruption.

Reach Out to Family and Friends

Years ago, extended families, the school community, the church, and the neighbors all worked together to form a protective shield for your marriage. Now, with the extended family scattered, school no longer relevant, and friends and neighbors moving on, your external supports may be weaker than they once were.

To this diminished societal support add the fact that most likely you and your spouse have always had some areas of incompatibility. In fact, this is a mathematical certainty. A recent study, for instance, found that the average person dates only five other people more than casually before marriage. This means that most of us may not have had the opportunity to find a partner who is compatible with us in many aspects of the relationship. When you add to this the stresses of midlife and the empty nest, you can see how you might have trouble meeting each other's needs at this time.

The children may have acted as buffers in your relationship. But, paradoxically, with them gone it may be a mistake for the two of you to close ranks and exclude all others from your circle. Indeed, this can stunt your growth as individuals and as a couple.

To feel fully a part of life, it's important to reach beyond your "coupledom" to include others in your lives. New community involvements will enrich your life with fun, new experiences, even a smidgen of adventure. What better way to nurture yourselves? Besides, you set in motion a pattern that will serve you well during retirement. Laughter and having fun with others was high on the list of reasons why the retired couples in my study said their marriages were so fulfilling.

Indeed, such community contacts can be good for your physical well-being! In its extensive research on midlife issues and aging, the Mac-Arthur Foundation found that a "high level of social support results in lower blood levels of stress-induced hormones that can promote disease."

Rehearsal | **ENRICHING THE TWO OF US BY REACHING OUT**

A three-legged table stands firmer than a two-legged one—adding outside relationships enhances your marriage. Connection, support, fun, and laughter are all good for your health as well as the health of your marriage.

1. Together, on a sheet of paper, list in a column all the community, friends, and family involvements that you have. Be specific and name each one.

2. Now rearrange these names under two columns: Positive (fun, supportive, uplifting) or Negative (boring, creates bad feelings, saps energy).

3. Now add a wish list of involvements that you would like but don't have.

4. Discuss how you can make your wish list come true.

5. Make a commitment to include at least two positive involvements in your couple life each week. You may not be able to eliminate all the negatives, but you can accentuate the positives.

Social, family, and community contacts are not only good for your health and mental functioning, they're also good for your marriage. Reaching out to include others in your lives can help ease the expectation that you should provide entirely for your partner's emotional needs. It may also help counteract the loss you feel with the departure of your children. Reaching out can bring new and exciting roles into your lives.

Share Values, Aims, Goals, and Marital Responsibilities

"Mort and I are a couple," Julia explained to me. "We think and act like a couple; we share a lot of the same interests and do things together. It has always been that way, and now that the kids are gone, it's just more so." Julia and Mort are fortunate. They're best friends. They share many of the same values and identify themselves as a unit.

In my study of long-term happily married couples, I found there was an 88 percent agreement on major issues in the marriage such as lifestyle, activities, and family. These couples agreed on areas that were fundamentally important to them, such as values and goals, but they also left room for tolerating differences.

So much togetherness need not be stifling. Even though a healthy relationship is based on a sense of "we-ness," the fostering of one's individuality is equally important. If either partner needs some time alone, he or she can establish a boundary. But if more closeness is desired, the boundaries open and intimacy flourishes. Fulfilled couples create a rhythm in their marriages that allows for ebb and flow across these temporary boundaries.

"What can I do to lighten your load?" This is a powerful question that is sure to evoke a sign of appreciation in your spouse—a smile, a gleam in the eye, a deep sigh, a hug and kiss, a tear. What better way to contribute to the happiness of your midlife marriage?

The multitude of pressures you face at midlife can be daunting. Sharing the many obligations of married life at this time and offering a helping hand when needed are positive steps you can take to further the fulfillment of your marriage. When you nourish yourself and maintain goodwill toward your partner (including being more accepting of him or her), you will want to demonstrate that goodwill by being helpful.

Rehearsal	**WHAT CAN I DO TO LIGHTEN YOUR LOAD?**
	What a beautiful and appreciated question for husband or wife—a question that surely furthers sharing and marital well-being.
1.	Make a list of five to ten burdensome activities, such as making dinner every night, feeding the dog, washing the car, visiting Uncle Myron at the retirement home by

yourself. Exchange lists. Ask yourself, "What would I be willing to do?"

2. Pick at least three activities that you feel ready to help your partner with.

3. Take turns telling each other which loads you would consider sharing, each telling the other what, when, and how you choose to do it. Doing it your way eliminates unrealistic expectations and demands.

4. Each do one activity for the other for two weeks.

5. After two weeks are up, take turns asking: "Did my performing this task please you? How?"

6. The following week, pick another task or repeat the same one. Nothing succeeds like success.

Intimacy is at its height when you and your partner let each other know your most private thoughts and feelings. Such emotional sharing demonstrates your deep trust. But not every conversation has to be profoundly meaningful. Even ordinary discussions of everyday issues like household tasks add to your sense of working together—working on your partnership.

Be Flexible

My research has shown me that the more you are equipped to "go with the flow" of events as they unfold, the greater are your chances for a fulfilled marriage. When you are flexible in your outlook and actions, you are better able to withstand any changes that come along in your marriage, including aging, ill health, job loss, depression, financial setbacks, and even the death of loved ones.

No doubt you've had a good deal of practice being flexible and adaptable until this point. Consider what it took to bring up your children. Like Millie and Joe, it's unlikely that you and your spouse always agreed on how to parent. Instead, as the kids grew, you probably became aware of how challenging they were to raise. Most likely, you consulted friends, your parents, and Dr. Spock, or perhaps you looked toward the heavens and asked, "What should I do now?" Yes, child-rearing requires an enormous amount of flexibility, but so does the creation and mainte-nance of a happy midlife marriage.

And many times, when we're inflexible, we cling to ideas or behav-iors that no longer work for us. This could mean that we are concealing some hidden fears or self-doubts. I found this to be true when I coun-seled Maria and Sam, who were struggling in a conflict-filled marriage. Often their arguments arose from Maria's need to rigidly stick to "rules" she had constructed for both of them. For instance, dinner was always served at 6:30 P.M. sharp, every dish was washed the minute it was dir-tied, and nothing in the house was out of place.

These rules infuriated Sam, and to show his distaste, he did what-ever he could to upset the applecart. Often he'd arrive home late for dinner (with myriad excuses, but late nonetheless); he'd drop his clothes on the bedroom floor like a teenager; he'd leave glasses and dishes about in the den. These passive behaviors were designed to pro-voke Maria, who experienced them as a personal affront. Indeed, these were passive-aggressive behaviors.

As their therapist, my first task was to help uncover the reasons for Maria's rigidity. Many of our strongest emotional reactions are deter-mined by our "self-talk"—the stream of thoughts that course through our minds night and day. Sometimes this monologue gives us incorrect or inadequate information, so it's important to evaluate its accuracy. I used the following self-questioning technique with Maria to help uncover the hidden fears and self-doubts that contributed to her inflexibility. You can try this "Why Technique" on your own. Here is how I used it with Maria:

> *Expectation.* I have to be neat and organized in running my home.
>
> Q: Why?
>
> A: Because it gives me a sense of comfort knowing things are in their place.
>
> Q: Why?
>
> A: I've been like this since I was a little girl. People would comment on how neat my room was. I did it myself.
>
> Q: Why?
>
> A: My mother was always working. She had to. My father left us. The house was always a mess. I thought maybe he left because she was a bad housewife.

Aha! Perhaps Maria's hidden fear was that her husband would leave her, just as her father had, if their home were messy. Once she uncovered this fear, she could ask herself another series of questions to evaluate the accuracy of her self-talk.

> *Q:* What evidence do you have that Sam would leave if the house were untidy?
>
> *A:* I don't know.
>
> *Q:* Does an immaculate house guarantee that he'll stay?
>
> *A:* No.
>
> *Q:* When you work so hard at keeping the house clean, what happens to your relationship?
>
> *A:* Actually, we fight.
>
> *Q:* Are you willing to look for another way to handle this situation?
>
> *A:* Maybe.

Once Maria had the awareness, I encouraged the couple to negotiate some new behaviors. Dinnertime was now set for somewhere between 6:30 and 7 P.M. And the dishes could pile up in the den as long as Sam put them in the dishwasher at the end of the evening. As a result of Maria's new understanding of her behavior, she began to loosen the reins, and as a consequence, Sam relinquished some of his negative behaviors.

Rehearsal | **BEING MORE FLEXIBLE**

As you work on becoming more flexible, be sure to be patient with yourself. This process takes time. Add a touch of compromise, be aware of power issues and think about being more accepting. It also helps to view your partner with an attitude of goodwill.

1. Become aware of what you want to become more flexible about.

2. If you're feeling rigid about your behaviors, try the "Why Technique." Can you identify some long-hidden fears that contribute to your inflexibility?

3.	Rehearse new responses (both physical and emotional) to old situations. Act "as if" you feel comfortable when trying a new behavior.
4.	Reframe your perceptions.
5.	Think about how you complement each other, even if you're "incompatible." The old saying "opposites attract" holds true at the beginning of a relationship when your new love is fascinating in his or her uniqueness. But this can break down over the years. Bringing a new appreciation for your differences at this stage of your marriage helps to jump-start your flexibility.
6.	Eulogies are often laudatory, poignant, funny, loving remembrances of the departed. Pretend that you're giving one at your partner's funeral—a morbid thought, but one that might be helpful. What would you say? Try to recall these positive thoughts when you're feeling unyielding. Draw on your natural store of empathy.

Communicate and Listen

Communication is the lifeblood of any relationship. In fact, whether or not you are talking, you are still communicating. The words you share or withhold; the way you listen; your gaze, gestures, body language, and facial expressions; and how you touch (including sexual touching) all convey your thoughts and feelings. Communication is so important, and how you carry it off can enhance or undermine your relationships.

Men and women have differing expectations for verbal communication. Women feel that things are better when they talk out a situation, whereas men feel that something is wrong if they have to talk it out. It is wise, therefore, to iron out your expectations before beginning a discussion with your partner.

Communicate Love

How better to enhance your midlife marriage than to communicate love! How do we accomplish this? There are many simple ways. Private, shared jokes create an intimate connection. One study found that 70 percent of a couple's marital satisfaction might stem from the ability to make each other laugh. Eye contact is vital in conveying your feelings. Poets have called the eyes the windows to the soul, and rightly so. Even activities as simple as dancing or rocking in unison on a porch swing can relax you and help you get in sync with each other.

Snuggling in a nonsexual way also conveys affection. When you curl up together and simply hold each other, you are fulfilling a primal need among all humans to cuddle and touch. You might enjoy some music as you lie together, relaxing in each other's arms.

Pay attention to how you use the words "I love you." People often use those three little words as a plea or demand for a similar response. Indeed, you can use "I love you" to interrupt an uncomfortable silence or a difficult conversation, to warn your spouse, to apologize, to ask for attention, to excuse your behavior, to make sexual overtures, or to attack (as in, "I love you! How could you hurt me like that?"). Say, "I love you" when you really mean it and watch the benefits flow.

Listening Is a Vital Communication Skill

This is especially true when you're listening to each other's feelings. In fact, when you are listened to, you will feel cared for, understood, respected, and loved. We all yearn for these attributes. They further your connectedness and coupledom and decrease the spaces between you.

You validate your partner's feelings when you let him or her know that you have heard and understood his or her emotions. You do so by listening and then paraphrasing and reflecting back what he or she has said. ("You're saying you feel anxious about the possibility of losing your job.") Your body language—good eye contact, a smile, unfolded arms—also help you to reach this goal.

The essence of good listening is empathy. To be an attentive, empathic listener, put aside your self-preoccupations and enter your spouse's world. Your empathy also helps to validate your partner's feelings.

Rehearsal | **TELL ME A STORY**

Telling stories to each other enhances your relationship: It promotes active listening, self-disclosure, self-discovery, acceptance, and sharing. This is especially helpful when one or both of you have problems revealing your most intimate thoughts. Just listen and avoid interpreting negatively.

Create a story:

◆ About your switching roles with your children.

◆ About the two of you as kids having an adventure together.

◆ About you and your spouse living happily ever after. How did you each contribute to the happy ending?

◆ About switching bodies. What would it feel like to be in your partner's body for a day or a week?

◆ About a courtroom scene where you are defending all the good you have brought into your relationship.

Or create your own scenario.

Manage Conflicts

"I was always someone who needed to talk everything out, and Andy would internalize it," Sonia told me heatedly. "He grew up in an 'Ozzie and Harriet' home—you know, the perfect mother and father who never fought. When I would start to blow, he would say, 'I need to leave the room. I don't want to say anything I will regret later.' Well, that just unnerves me. If I'm angry about something, I need to talk about it now." She lowered her voice. "We don't fight, we have *differences*," she said with disgust. "If I say anything, he gets very quiet and that's it. Conversation stops. We never get loud and angry. I probably keep a lot of my anger inside."

Yes, Sonia does rein in her anger, but it filters out in many other ways, and Andy is aware of them. "She is very tense and has been for quite some time," he tells me. "On weekends, she can't sit still. She has to be out of the house, and she's on the go all the time."

Sonia and Andy are caught in a futile dance of avoidance—they dodge the inevitable, for conflict is a certainty in every marriage. Odds are good that you married someone quite unlike you. This is as basic as our genders! Male and female brain physiology differs, and we are socialized to behave differently. You and your spouse come from unique family backgrounds. In addition, your temperaments vary: you're practical, your partner is frivolous; you're emotionally open, your partner is more contained; you like to experiment, your partner is cautious. Being different, you will each have your own perspective on the various issues that replay themselves in your lives such as the children, money, sex, and work.

Conflict Has a Bad Rep

Conflict has been misunderstood. In truth, it's not our differences or the conflicts that can arise from these differences that cause the problem. Rather it's the way we handle those differences that creates distress in our lives.

Conflict is a natural extension of our differences. A healthy marriage provides a safe zone for the expression of these inevitable flash points and grows from your ability to work toward the resolution of conflicts with humor, empathy, and reasonable negotiation. When you and your spouse air your differences, it helps each of you become more loving. You will probably never resolve all of them, but it's important for the health of your marriage that you keep working at it.

Don't Stonewall

Sonia and Andy's struggle is a good example of the bad reputation that conflict has acquired. Andy, believing that conflict is bad (and to be avoided), closes down and withdraws when Sonia is angry. Andy's reaction is common among men, especially when their wives become emotional, but it may not be entirely due to his parents' modeling, as Sonia believes. Indeed, men experience a more intensely unpleasant physiological reaction during marital conflicts than their wives do. Their hearts beat faster, they perspire more, they're more agitated. They become flooded.

In response to this physical reaction, men "stonewall" to remove themselves from the source of their discomfort. Stonewalling can involve a lack of facial expression, little eye contact, a stiffened neck, and reduced listener responses. And once they have tuned out physically, can emotional disconnection be far behind? If a man experiences himself as flooded by his wife's feelings, he may avoid any potential conflicts with her, which means he may avoid contact altogether.

A woman doesn't take well to stonewalling. Research has found that the level of stress hormones in women rose and stayed elevated for hours after a marital conflict. These hormones are known to weaken the immune system. Indeed, the greater a husband's withdrawal, the more upset his wife will be and the higher her stress hormone levels. Be aware, however, that this situation is sometimes reversed, but in most cases it's the husband who feels flooded and then stonewalls.

Like Sonia, a wife feeling stressed by her husband's stonewalling may respond by pursuing him ever more strenuously, which can cause him to retreat further. Or she can withdraw too and simply say, "We don't fight." But inside, they do. The anger and frustration don't go away. Rather, they seethe beneath the surface, deadening interactions. Intimacy withers. At some point the partners ask themselves, "Why bother?" and withdraw from each other. Sonia, for instance, found ways to spend weekends away from Andy. Eventually, the couple begins living parallel but separate lives, and the marriage loses its vitality.

What's the solution to this dilemma? It may be unrealistic to expect to resolve every conflict that you encounter in your marriage, but you can learn to manage it by applying the principles of acceptance, compassion, sharing, flexibility, and communication. The following can also be helpful:

Rehearsal	**CREATING BOUNDARIES FOR DISCUSSING CONFLICT**
	Conflict is inevitable, so some tips prior to the next "big event" could be helpful in dealing with it.
1.	If possible, go for a time-out. Take a break and cool off. Pick a good time to discuss your issue when both of you are away from the intensity of it.
2.	Deal with one issue at a time.
3.	State your side clearly and beware of negatives such as criticism, name-calling, sarcasm, or other below-the-belt tactics. All of these are sure to evoke a stonewalling (or an enraged) reaction.
4.	Be self-aware. Are you being defensive? Note your physiological responses when faced with your spouse's anger. You can choose to respond differently. Take responsibility for your part.

5. Yes, it's natural to be emotional, but try to engage your intellect. Analyze the problem. Think of it as an "it" that you both need to solve together. You are not adversaries. Attack the problem, not your spouse.

6. Remain calm. Learn self-control by taking deep breaths, being aware of tense muscles and words that push your spouse's buttons. Because of men's physiological response to conflict, it would be helpful for wives to present their issues without attack. This can avoid stonewalling on the husband's part.

7. To de-escalate intense anger, prepare a written or verbal time-out contract—a signal that means stop immediately, leave, return at an agreed-upon time, and see whether your partner is ready to discuss the issue.

8. Choose your fights wisely. My happily retired couples often used the expression "Don't pick with the chickens," meaning don't bicker over every little thing.

9. Humor helps. The comic Victor Borge says, "Humor is the shortest distance between two people." How true. Much marital satisfaction can be traced back to your ability to make each other laugh—even during an argument. People often use the expression "you break me up" to describe someone who tickles their funny bone. Yes, humor does break up your line of reasoning, and in the case of conflict, it provides a much-needed deflection from intensity.

10. Discuss possible solutions.

11. Make an appointment to revisit issues if you haven't resolved them.

12. Show appreciation when your partner understands your side.

If your goal is to "one-up" your spouse—that is, win at all costs, or seek revenge—none of these recommendations will work. In this case, it's important to review the themes of acceptance and sharing.

Negotiate and Compromise

Negotiating and compromising are part of being married. The overriding value of negotiation and compromise is each partner's willingness to use these skills to deal with the many changes that we all face in marriage. This willingness helps to avoid, or at least reduce, some of the inevitable conflicts that arise.

Compromise is inextricably interwoven with flexibility. For instance, if you have difficulty adapting, you may find it hard to compromise, especially if you perceive it as "giving in" or "losing the battle." Suddenly, you find yourselves in a power struggle.

John and Nancy argued over paying off their son Tony's student loans for him, as he was struggling financially in his new job. Nancy wanted to pay them off in full; John felt that Tony should assume total responsibility, as John had after college. In a quieter moment, they discussed the problem. Nancy expressed her reasons for her position while John listened, and then they traded roles. They brainstormed solutions and rated each from 1 to 10 (10 being best). Finally, they agreed to make the payments on Tony's loans for the next six months, until he could get on his feet. They agreed to revisit their decision in ten months.

Rehearsal	NEGOTIATION SKILLS
	Using the Boundaries for Discussing Conflict, do the following:
1.	State the problem.
2.	Get an honest dialogue going. Each give reasons for your position as John and Nancy did and listen to your partner—good listening promotes understanding.
3.	Brainstorm solutions. Rate each from 1 to 10 (10 being best).
4.	Agree on a resolution you can both live with—the one closest to a 10.
5.	Keep alternative solutions in mind and agree to revisit the issue at a specified time.

CHAPTER 10

Use Relationship Reviews to Enhance Communication

There is no pleasure to me without communication; there is not so much as a sprightly thought comes into my mind but I grieve that I have no one to tell it to.

—Montaigne

ATTENTIVE LISTENING; KNOWING HOW to use words that convey appreciation, avoid blame and sarcasm, and validate your partner's feelings and good body language (eye contact and an open, welcoming posture) are all aspects of effective communication. You can use all of these skills and behaviors effectively when conducting a

Relationship Review, one of the most important ways to help your marriage get and stay on track in your movement toward growth and change.

Relationship Reviews involve you and your spouse discussing various aspects of your marriage every few months. They may take several forms. Taking an inventory of where you've been and what you've done, you may evaluate your shared history. Or, analyzing your present situation, you may determine what you want now. To help you plan effectively for what's to come, you can also anticipate future changes during such a review. This self-examination and sharing with your spouse will help you to set the groundwork for your post-empty-nest relationship.

I have found Relationship Reviews to be most helpful in filling your "I" and your "You" accounts. You are expressing your wants and needs while attending to your spouse's as well, and this plays into the success of your marriage. In fact, when successful marriages are studied, those that do best are the ones that are periodically evaluated and renegotiated. Be sure to follow the guidelines I suggest in Chapter 1 for setting the stage.

Keep in mind that since all marriages are works in progress, the Relationship Review is an ongoing process. Conduct one frequently.

Your Couple Coping Capacity

The keys to getting along can be found in your past successes and strengths. Yet I have found that couples often fail to take the time to understand, evaluate, and acknowledge their ability to cope with adversity. Few appreciate how much they have been through together by the time they reach midlife. Among the most critical measures of successful marriage are your problem-solving skills.

Your Couple Coping Capacity (CCC) refers to how you have faced and dealt with the myriad issues confronting you through the years. Bear in mind that these are your unique patterns of coping—the tools you've used to confront the various stresses and changes that have affected your marriage. No general rules apply to all couples. Your CCC can include how you adjusted to your marriage, dealt with the fact that your spouse is imperfect, blended with each other's family of origin, incorporated the birth of children into the marriage, accommodated career disappointments, including the loss of a job, and contended with health issues.

TAKE STOCK OF YOUR
COUPLE COPING CAPACITY

Review your common history, especially the major turning points and challenges. Your couple history will offer clues to how you will face the challenges of today. Ask yourselves:

1. What are some of the difficulties we as a couple have faced during our marriage?

2. How did we deal with them?

3. What were our problem-solving skills?

4. Was I (were we) satisfied with the outcome?

5. What would I/we have changed, now that we look back?

Then create a Marital Lifeline showing the stressful events in your marriage, how you reacted to them, and how you resolved them. The value of this exercise is in enhancing communication with your spouse and reinforcing your ability to draw inspiration from past strengths as you build toward the future. Use Gerry and Marta's CCC and Marital Lifeline to guide your own explorations.

Gerry and Marta's CCC Lifeline

My clients Gerry and Marta have been married for twenty-seven years. Now, with their three children out of the nest, they no longer have the kids to distract them. Marta works at home, writing and illustrating children's books. Gerry is busier than ever as an executive in an accounting firm. It's a she-goes-her-way, he-goes-his kind of marriage—the "we-ness" is gone from the relationship. As Marta explained, "Even with all the freedom I have, I still feel lonely. Sometimes I think back to the early years before the kids were born, and I long for the closeness we used to have. Where has it gone?"

It was time for this couple to reexamine how they had coped with problems in their marriage in the past. After reviewing their long history together, Gerry and Marta constructed a timeline that recapped the most stressful events in their marriage, how they reacted to these events, and how they resolved them. (During the intervening years, their lives proceeded relatively smoothly.)

They had met in college and married in 1971. They were both active in the antiwar movement and were as idealistic as they come. Plus, they loved each other; they could do no wrong. But then:

Year 1: Marta was feeling discouraged and resentful because she worked and tended the house with little help from Gerry. They fought. Then Gerry brought roses and they made love.

Year 3: Their first child was born. Gerry felt jealous of the attention the baby was getting. Marta was exhausted. Gerry avoided Marta, staying at work late. After some time, Marta hired a baby-sitter and planned a romantic evening out so they could talk.

Year 8: Gerry lost his job. They now had two children and a mortgage. Gerry was at loose ends and became depressed. Together they brainstormed alternative solutions, and he agreed to ask a cousin for work.

Year 13: With three kids at home, Marta felt overwhelmed but bored. Now Marta was at loose ends and became depressed. Gerry suggested she seek counseling. She did, and it helped.

Year 15: Marta was stronger and more focused. She attended art classes and held a part-time job. Gerry felt slighted and began a brief affair, which Marta discovered. After Gerry shared his unhappiness with a friend at work, the friend suggested Gerry and Marta try marriage counseling. They did, and it helped.

Year 20: Gerry had a serious car accident that required surgery and three months of recuperation. Gerry needed help. Marta quit her part-time job to take care of him. The whole family pitched in to help, and Gerry felt very loved.

Year 25: Their youngest child was in trouble with drugs and truancy. Gerry's new position required a lot of travel and Marta bore the brunt of caring for their troubled teen. They argued over who should take responsibility for their child. A school counselor suggested Marta join a support group. She did, and it helped.

In reviewing this couple's CCC Marital Lifeline, we see that they used a number of strategies to help them through difficult periods in their lives. In some instances they talked, in others they sought outside help; in some Marta initiated the resolution of the situation, in others Gerry did, and in some they did the work together. This couple has weathered many storms, and despite the troubles, their marriage is still intact, though in need of an infusion of a new burst of energy. Studies show that the longer a marriage endures, the more opportunities there are for revitalization.

Rehearsal | **WHAT IS YOUR CCC? CREATING A LIFELINE**

Like Gerry and Marta, the two of you can create your own CCC Relationship Review and Lifeline. From your perspective, write individually about the stressful times and the solutions you found. Then get together with your partner to discuss your Lifelines and create one that represents the difficult periods in your marriage. You may find it interesting to note how many coping skills you already possess. As you discuss your Marital Lifeline, keep in mind that you will listen attentively to your partner, that you will refrain from judgmental remarks, and that you will endeavor to share your honest feelings and show respect for what your partner has to say.

Define What You Want for Your Marriage

Another type of Relationship Review focuses on your current situation rather than on the past. It will help you assess where you stand today and assist you in planning for the future. You can repeat the Now and Future Relationship Review on the following page as often as you feel comfortable—every couple of months or so. You might want to record your individual and joint responses in a journal. Sometimes it is helpful to look back on these thoughts as you formulate your next steps.

Relation-ship Review	**WHAT IS YOUR VISION FOR YOUR MARRIAGE NOW AND IN THE FUTURE?**
	Together discuss your answers to the following questions:
1.	What values are important to you and your marriage individually and as a couple? (Openness, communication, togetherness, separateness, respect for each other, more understanding and tolerance of yourself and your spouse, more support from your spouse for activities you want to pursue, and so on.)
2.	What changes have you seen in yourself? In your spouse? How have these changes affected the marriage?
3.	What, specifically, are your goals for yourself? What are they for your marriage?
4.	Has the departure of the children left a gap in your lives? What impact does this have on you individually and as a couple?
5.	What changes do you foresee in the future? (Your career demands more of your time, for instance, taking you away from the relationship.) What do you want to change, individually and as a couple? (You want more time together.)
6.	How can you accommodate wants that conflict with reality? How can you deal with changes you neither anticipate nor desire?
7.	If your parents are still alive, what is (or will be) your relationship with them? How often do you see them? Who will care for them if or when they need it? What do you want individually and as a couple?
8.	What is (or will be) your relationship to your grown children? If they live out of town, how often will you talk or visit? How do you foresee this relationship developing?

9. When conflict arises (and it will), how will you handle it? Reviewing your CCCs from the past will give you clues, but what additional coping skills might you need in the future? What ideas do you have individually and as a couple regarding dealing with expected conflicts?

10. Have either of you felt misunderstood lately? Have you felt intruded upon when you wanted private time? Have you felt your partner has not listened to you? Have you felt irritated with your spouse but been unable to share your feelings? How do you want to communicate your thoughts and feelings to each other? What methods would be comfortable to you individually and as a couple?

11. What activities do you want to engage in individually and as a couple? What kind of work do you want to do? How do you anticipate relaxing? Playing? Nurturing yourselves and each other? How do you plan to make time for the relationship?

Taking your marital pulse every few months is helpful for you and your relationship. On a regular basis, Bernie and I sit down for an evaluation of how each of us is feeling about ourselves and our marriage. These talks cover all areas of our lives: our friendships, relationships with our children, activities, sex life, health, and more. To us, it's an essential part of existing in a fulfilling way in our marriage. These Relationship Reviews are as vital to our positive emotional coexistence as breathing.

CHAPTER 11

Sex and the Midlife Couple

*As in all other experiences, we always have the sexual experience
we deserve, depending on our loving kindness towards ourselves
and others.*

—Thaddeus Golas, *The Lazy Man's Guide to Enlightenment*

SEX IS WONDERFUL. I have more freedom than ever. No demands
from the kids!" This wife says it all—more time for privacy,
more time to enjoy each other.

"Sex has always been good from the time that we first met. We're just
more tired than we used to be." Even in a thriving marriage, the
many pressures of midlife can intrude on a couple's ability to fully
enjoy their sexual relationship.

"I'm not into sex. I was never very much interested. If my husband
wanted something, I did it to please him. He doesn't know. He
thinks I like it. My mother wasn't interested either, but my father
was a lusty man. I've often wondered if it's genetic." Catherine's
marriage is strongly devitalized. The fact that she never enjoyed sex
reflects the anger and alienation she has experienced throughout
married life. The power struggles, the arguments, the shutting down
have erected a wall between her and her husband when they get into

bed with each other. And aside from her marriage, Catherine has never allowed herself to get in touch with her more passionate self. This is a problem of self-nurturing.

"I worry that I'm not satisfying Tina. It used to be that even before her clothes were off, I had an instant reaction, I would be ready for sex. But now it doesn't happen so fast. We both lie naked in bed and there's nothing. It's dark in the room so I can't see her face, but I imagine her twisting her mouth as if to say, 'What gives?'" Robert is experiencing normal physical aging. The natural lowering of his testosterone levels affects how quickly his penis will respond to visual stimulation. But along with the physical reaction comes an emotional one—fear. He worries about his diminished responsiveness, and he worries that his wife, with her newfound strengths, will find him less desirable.

All of these statements reflect the variety of reactions that individuals and couples experience when facing their changing sexual selves at midlife.

Sexual Rejuvenation

A fulfilling sex life provides the basis for good physical and emotional health for you individually and as a couple, and it increases your sense of personal and marital well-being.

Your sexuality can help restore your self-esteem and assertiveness; it can help mitigate chronic pain; as a form of play, it can rekindle your sense of humor, which is so necessary in dealing with everyday stresses. It also does wonders for improving your communication. Just the skin-to-skin contact (even without penetration) speaks volumes about closeness. Touch is reassuring, reinvigorating, and growth-producing for the relationship.

With all of the changes and losses that occur at midlife, you and your partner may turn to each other now more than ever. A sexual rapprochement at this time can be a healing act—an act of renewal, replenishment, and rejuvenation.

Sexual desire is essential to our ability to enjoy sex. The sensual, the erotic, and the romantic all contribute to our feelings of desire. But these elements are not interchangeable. *Sensuality* refers to your five senses. Different sensual experiences such as listening to music, taking a bubble bath, wearing silky lingerie, or walking in the woods after a light spring shower can all enhance our sexuality.

The *erotic* has much to do with stimulating you in a distinctly sexual way. It could involve smelling your partner's perfume, giving and receiving a massage, reading erotic literature (either by yourself or aloud to your spouse), or watching an X-rated movie.

The *romantic* involves your emotions and sensuality without physicality. Romantic acts include giving flowers or gifts to your partner, calling him or her on the phone to express your caring, or preparing a special candlelit meal just for the two of you.

Your personality type, your sexual history, and your attitudes all contribute to your desire. As my interviewees' stories reflect, however, desire can be disrupted at this time in your life—not all is well in some midlife bedrooms. Some of the difficulty, as in Catherine's situation, may be related to the buildup of resentment over the years. But for others, midlife sexual difficulties can stem from normal physical and emotional changes that diminish desire.

The Sexual Equation at Midlife

"You win some, you lose some," as the saying goes. This of course, can apply to many aspects of our lives, but it is certainly true when we talk about our sexual selves at midlife. The equation goes like this:

You Lose Some

Men can have performance issues at this time. Decreases in testosterone levels can lead to:

- Less intense orgasms
- Delayed or less firm erections; longer wait between erections
- Decreased sexual desire

All of these changes can be worrisome to a man, and sometimes anxiety over diminishing virility can further erode his ability to perform.

Women's sexual issues during midlife often correspond to the physical changes that accompany menopause. Decreases in estrogen levels can lead to:

- Less vaginal lubrication, causing pain during intercourse
- Loss of vaginal elasticity and thinning of the vaginal walls, which

can also cause pain during intercourse, and can increase suscep-
tibility to infection

◆   Diminishing sexual desire over time (in some cases this may be
due to painful intercourse; it may also be due to diminishing
levels of testosterone)

These changes can increase the chances that a woman will respond,
"Not tonight dear," when her husband is feeling amorous.

You Win Some

If your present level of enjoyment does not meet your previous stand-
ards, that's called *change*. If you are flexible, you can reframe these physical and emotional shifts. Use your wisdom and experience to redirect
your perceptions and actions in order to realize a heightened enjoyment
of sexuality. There are many ways to compensate and adjust:

For men:

◆   Now that you are more into your nurturing and affiliative self,
think of sex as an around-the-clock experience. It doesn't have
to mean penetration, but can involve all kinds of play, touching,
and tenderness.

◆   If achieving an orgasm takes you longer, why not enjoy the process more? Use the additional time to savor the sensory pleasure
that you might have passed over previously in your haste to
reach your goal.

◆   You're in a position to please your partner more. Many women
enjoy a lot of sexual foreplay, touching, and caressing. If you
take your time, you can heighten your wife's desire and her
responsiveness—and that can mean more exciting sex for you.

◆   Now that you're older and wiser, you can better understand
your partner's responses. Women, for instance, love to be com-
plimented. Tell your wife what you find interesting and attractive about her. You might say, "Your skin is so soft," or "I love
your hands," as you caress her. A word of praise goes a long way
toward helping the two of you have a great experience.

Broad lifestyle changes such as exercise, quitting smoking, or using
less alcohol can also help. Exercise, more than anything else, reawakens
your body's capabilities and instills new confidence in your body image.
It also helps to get the blood flowing. (Many cases of impotence are due

to vascular problems.) Moreover, men who exercise on a regular basis are more willing to experiment in bed. Their erections are more reliable and they also enjoy more satisfying orgasms.

Humor is a great aphrodisiac too. It distracts and relaxes you. It confirms your creativity and connectedness. And it is forgiving. Laughing together in bed to your gyrations can expand your enjoyment and help you to ease up on your expectations.

You also need to like and accept yourself in order to enjoy yourself sexually. Positive self-talk can become a self-fulfilling prophecy.

If you are experiencing long-term erectile dysfunction (failure to achieve or sustain an erection), then it's important to pay a visit to your urologist. He or she can evaluate your overall health as it relates to sexuality (heart and blood pressure medications, antidepressants, diabetes, and dropping hormone levels, among other factors, can all diminish your responsiveness) and make recommendations.

For women:

Many of my female interviewees described the benefits that midlife brings to their sexuality:

◆ You have a newfound desire for self-fulfillment, and that can include fulfillment in your sex life.

◆ Your new assertiveness may embolden you to take charge and ask for what you want sexually. This can excite your husband. Many husbands tell me of their pleasure in having their wives initiate sex—it reaffirms their desirability.

◆ Mothers often sleep with one ear attuned to their children. With the youngsters gone, privacy, spontaneity, and freedom reign once more. You can run around the house naked if you feel like it, and you no longer have to worry about a child hearing or interrupting.

◆ Menopause brings a welcome end to contraceptive/pregnancy worries, not to mention monthly bouts with backaches, cramps, premenstrual syndrome, and related discomforts.

If you find your desire has diminished, there is much you can do as well. The lifestyle recommendations I made for men are also appropriate for women. Exercise and proper diet both enhance sexuality. Typically, women have difficulty accepting their bodies at midlife, but exercise and a low-fat diet can improve your self-esteem and body image. And these good feelings can flow into your sex life. Positive self-talk is key.

If you are having problems with desire for sex, vaginal dryness, or other issues associated with menopause, a visit to your gynecologist is in order. He or she may prescribe hormone replacement or recommend lubricating gels.

Emotional factors and stress can also diminish your desire. Investigate these with your partner (be sure to use good communication skills) or, if need be, with a licensed therapist. Also bear in mind that your partner's erectile dysfunction can have many causes (including physical ones) and most likely does not reflect his level of desire for you. You have the potential to further your relationship with patience, humor, and understanding. Your husband needs this now more than ever.

With wisdom, kindness, a sense of adventure, and compassion, both of you can make the sexual equation at midlife add up to win-win.

Our Sex Hormones

From conception onward, our sex hormones—estrogen and testosterone—have regulated the development of our female and male bodies and our reproductive capacity. As we age, these hormone levels naturally drop. Women undergo a rapid decline in estrogen at menopause, while men experience a continual (but not precipitous) decrease in testosterone. As Jed Diamond put it in *Male Menopause*, "Women fall off a cliff, and men sort of roll down the hill." Interestingly, both genders need both hormones, but men have more testosterone than women and women have more estrogen than men.

Testosterone

Testosterone has gotten good and bad press. It has been blamed for many socially aggressive acts from rape to corporate raiding to declarations of war. But it can also be called the hormone of youth, making men strong, protecting their hearts, and fueling their sex drive and the physical attributes that propel it. Lower testosterone levels can also alter a man's mood and may cause depression. Testosterone is a leading hormone in metabolism for males and females.

Women also need testosterone—especially after menopause. In females, testosterone has been called the "hormone of desire," since their sexual responsiveness is dictated by how much of it is in their bodies. Indeed, this "male" hormone is essential for a woman's healthy sexual functioning.

Estrogen and Progesterone

Estrogen gives girls their womanly bodies. It helps to preserve the elasticity of their organs, and also protects their hearts, bones, and muscle mass. Especially at midlife, women become gradually aware of its decline. However, while estrogen gives women their femaleness, it does little to promote desire. That's the job of testosterone, which stimulates the desire factor.

Perhaps the postmenopausal zest we discussed earlier can be traced, at least in part, to the hormonal shifts that take place at this time. At menopause, when both estrogen and progesterone exist at lower levels in the body, the effects of "unopposed" testosterone can be felt more distinctly. Women become more assertive in the world, and they enjoy themselves more lustily in the bedroom.

Men also need estrogen. It can have much to do with a man's need for love and intimacy along with his sexuality.

Much has been written about estrogen replacement for menopausal women, and there is a great deal of controversy surrounding this issue because of the increased risk in some women for breast or uterine cancer. Hormone replacement may be inappropriate for women who have a history of stroke, a family history of breast cancer, or liver disease. These issues should be discussed carefully with your physician. Interestingly, however, testosterone replacement is also a consideration for men whose moods are affected by a deficiency in this hormone. Again, thoughtful discussions with your physician are in order here.

The Desire Discrepancy

Do you find yourself using the following tactics at bedtime when your partner is interested in having sex and you're not?

◆ *Getting busy.* Do you suddenly identify myriad tasks that need doing without delay, even though your spouse is turning in for the night? Do you find it impossible to tear yourself away from The Late Show? Must you catch up on work-related correspondence at 11 p.m.? Many spouses use these and other strategies to avoid going to bed at the same time.

◆ *Making excuses.* "I don't feel well." The headache, backache, stomachache . . . a multitude of physical ills can be brought to bear. As we age, all of us experience some aches and pains, but it's the ways in which you use those daily discomforts to avoid getting close that can be so detrimental to your marriage.

- ◆ **Complaining.** "I can't come to bed with you," Muriel exclaimed. "I've got too much work to do and you never help me, so the whole burden is on me. I can't leave the laundry for the morning. I've got an 8 a.m. meeting and I won't have time." Muriel complains that she's overworked and underappreciated. Her husband, feeling put down, quickly turns off.

- ◆ **Conveniently forgetting.** Sometimes spouses behave passive-aggressively. After having jointly made an "appointment" for sex, one partner seems to have lost all recollection of it.

These are all signs of a desire discrepancy—the state in which one spouse is more interested in sex than the other. That's what happened with Barbara and Matt. "Sex has always been good in our relationship—not as frequent as Matt would like it—but frankly more than I want it," Barbara told me. "My sex drive isn't as strong as his."

It is natural for couples to be sexually incompatible to some degree. No two people have identical needs all the time, and it's unrealistic to expect otherwise. But, as we have seen, midlife issues may heighten an already disparate rhythm.

Many factors may influence the desire discrepancy. We cannot overlook the role that diminishing hormones play. Moreover, interpersonal issues such as anger, power struggles, passive-aggressiveness, resentments, or depression can also thwart desire. In general, sexual desire tends to decrease over time for nearly all couples. Unfortunately, sometimes it decreases unevenly. An "out of sync" midlife couple might respond as follows:

Wife: "I want more sex, more often."

Husband: "I want more tenderness, more caring. I'm scared that my body is not responding like it used to."

Another common misconception is that one of you is destined to have the higher level of desire while the other must have the lower. Imagine, instead, that you are both involved in other relationships in which the roles are reversed. Suddenly, the more amorous of you feels like a stick-in-the-mud, and the more reluctant one seems lusty. Desire levels are relative to your current partner.

So before you play the "blame game," realize that in your particular relationship, the fact that you are out of step with each other is normal. No matter how many exercises you do, how many hormones you ingest, how much you polish your relationship skills, there will always be a desire discrepancy—it's a fact of life.

I recommend that the spouse whose desire is less intense control the frequency of intercourse. This may seem unfair, but there is a reason for it. Over time, if you have sex less often, the disinclined spouse will feel less pressure to perform, and this can relieve anxiety. He or she may also need time to build up a yearning for more. If one is feeling sexually satiated, there's little interest in additional contact. In fact, sometimes it's useful to refrain from sex altogether for a period of time when there is a disparity in desire. During the hiatus, focus on affection and tenderness. This will set up conditions to reawaken the willingness for sex.

You might try these other strategies to get the two of you on the same wavelength:

- Meditate together.
- Dance with each other either at home or at a club.
- Go swimming together.
- Sing or harmonize together.
- Go to bed and awaken together.

But what if you really don't want to engage in sexual relations at one time or another? How do you say no without feeling guilty and your spouse feeling rejected? The naysayer should always give a reason for declining the invitation while suggesting another time that would be better. Or he or she could promise to initiate sex the next time.

In another approach, the person with less desire could ask his or her spouse why he or she wants sex so often. The interesting part of this question lies in the possibility that you might find nonsexual means to satisfy the lustier partner's needs. For instance, Sophie asked Jay, "Why do you want sex four to six times a week?"

"I need the physical release," he responded. "And I feel very close to you during sex." But Jay could satisfy his need for release by jogging, and he could get close to Sophie in other ways, like cuddling and intimate conversation. Intercourse is not the only option.

This reminds me of a story my husband, Bernie, used to tell me. When he was living with his grandmother, she would make him a bologna sandwich every day to take to school. Day in and day out. Bernie hated bologna. Finally one day he asked her, "Grandma, why can't you make me something else for a change?"

"You don't like bologna?" she marveled. "Why didn't you tell me?"

This point brings us right back to the bedroom. Perhaps some men don't realize that they can ask for more closeness, a sense of being needed, or intimate conversation. You may believe that the only road to intimacy is through the bedroom door. Ask for what you want. It's a powerful aphrodisiac. Try these on for size:

- ◆ "Could you sit here with me and just hug me?"
- ◆ "I need you to listen to a problem I've been having."
- ◆ "Would you massage my shoulders?"

If you're experiencing a desire discrepancy and you're the one who is asked to put your ardor on hold, ask yourself what you are getting from intercourse that you could get some other way.

Deepening Your Intimacy

A wonderful aspect of the mature marriage is the opportunity you both have to deepen your intimacy. I hope that trust has been built over the years so you can let some of your vulnerabilities show. Since healthy communication is so essential to a well-functioning marriage, utilizing it if you are somewhat out of sync can be immensely helpful.

In your Marital Lifeline perhaps you reexamined the strengths and coping mechanisms you had used in previous years to deal with problems. Most likely, your marriage has lasted this long because you have been able to work things out to some degree. Now it's time to conduct a review of your sexual history and explore what you would like today. Speaking honestly and openly about your likes and dislikes with your spouse during this Sexual Relationship Review will help you make changes.

Relation- ship Review	**THE SEXUAL REVIEW**
1.	In the first years of your marriage, what did you like about your sex life? What did you dislike?
2.	When children came along, how did it affect your sexual relationship?

3.	What is your sex life like now? How do you feel about it?
4.	Have you changed physically or emotionally? How has that affected your sexuality?
5.	Deal with negative thoughts (such as 'All he wants is sex; he doesn't really care about me,' or "She doesn't think I'm performing well enough") by checking them out with your partner. Ask if your thoughts are correct. If you reach an impasse, you might try the "Why Technique" suggested in Chapter 9.
6.	Share with your partner what would make you feel safe and comfortable now: the setting, the mood, the frequency, the specifics of touch, and preferred methods of stimulation. Reveal to your partner your honest feelings about your sexual lives together: what you like and dislike; what you want to keep and what you want to change.
7.	Plan baby steps for grown-up rewards. What small actions can you take together to build toward your goals? (You will find the suggestions and exercises that follow helpful in this regard.)

Try a Little Tenderness

Perhaps in your Sexual Relationship Review you have found that the desire factor in your long-term marriage needs perking up. Familiarity can breed boredom and devitalization. Remember Erica Jong's lament, "I'm hideously depressed. I am no longer the youngest in the room nor the cutest"? If ever you needed reassurance that you are still desirable, it is now at midlife. A loving touch, word, or gesture—any sign that your spouse still finds you physically attractive—is most reassuring. Indeed, many studies confirm the importance of touch to your physical and emotional well-being—even to prolonging your lives. In this case, however, I am suggesting that affection can be the precursor to loving sex in an otherwise devitalized relationship.

Interestingly, jumping into bed and "getting to it" may not be the answer. In fact, your spouse's character and personality override the sex factor in marriage; that is, spouses who are gentle, kind, and caring, and who make their partners feel important contribute more positively to the marital relationship than those who are not. No surprises there. Thus the first steps on the road to better midlife sexual relations lead in the direction of affection and tenderness, not eroticism.

Rehearsal	**PRACTICE WAYS TO SHOW AFFECTION**
1.	***What's working now?*** Begin by recognizing what you are already doing well. Jot down every sign of affection in a notebook. At the end of the week, assess how affectionate you have been. Perhaps you've been more withholding than you realize. This is the base from which you will be operating.
2.	***Give each other clues.*** What more would you like from your mate in the way of affection? What does he or she want from you? You might each finish the sentence "I feel your affection when you _____." Fill in the blank as many times as necessary. (Some common responses: "kiss me," "pat me gently when I pass by," "take my hand when we're walking," "snuggle when we get into bed.")
3.	***Observe the "Five or More" rule.*** Use the results of the previous suggestions to guide you in being affectionate with your partner. Implement at least five of his or her suggestions a day.
4.	***Give compliments.*** Expressions of appreciation go a long way in establishing affection and tenderness. Try "That was a great meal" or "You look handsome/beautiful today."
5.	***Set the scene.*** Start the day with a show of affection. Kiss and nuzzle upon awakening. Smile over breakfast. Lavish compliments. This establishes the tone for the rest of the day.
6.	***Be playful.*** Think of ways to put a sense of surprise

back into the relationship. Call or send a loving fax or e-mail during the day. Kiss your partner when he or she least expects it. Plan a mystery getaway—that means not telling your spouse where you're taking him or her. If your mate needs to travel without you, plant a love note in the luggage. Opening a suitcase and finding "I love you" is a positive stroke for any relationship.

7. **Help your partner.** "What can I do for you today that will help you?" is a powerful show of affection.

8. **Engage in verbal intimacy.** A good marriage is built on safety and trust. The opportunity to be open and consequently vulnerable, knowing your partner honors your best interests, is more than reassuring. Take a chance. Revealing your feelings is one of the most intimate acts anyone can perform. Women revel in such sharing, and men can discover, to their surprise, that it does not threaten their manliness. (Step 6 in the Sexual Relationship Review can encourage this process.)

You Can't Change the Past but You Can Ruin the Present by Worrying about the Future!

Normally, June had no problems becoming aroused or having intercourse, but lately she has been so tired and harassed at work that her level of desire has become quite low. After dinner, she could think of nothing better than to kick off her shoes and lie on the couch. But when her husband Tony settled in next to her one night, she froze. "Oh no," she thought. "He wants to have sex, and I'm just too exhausted. If I kiss him or smile or show any reaction to his touching me, he'll want to go all the way. I know him. I'd better turn away. I don't want to lead him on." June's behavior left Tony feeling confused and rejected.

Adam had another problem. For the first time ever, he lost his erection after foreplay with his wife. This caused him so much consternation that he began to think, "What if I try this again and can't keep it up? Maybe I'd better lay off the sex for a while."

Both June and Adam are engaged in negative self-talk and future thinking. Both need to learn how to remain in the moment. In fact, to both of them, I would say, "Stop thinking so much! Just feel!"

You can ruin the present by fretting about the future. Your mind races ahead, worrying about what's going to happen next or even what's going to happen tomorrow on the job. But, as you'll see from the exercises that follow, you can learn how to go with the flow sexually—simply to enjoy the sensual experience and stay in the moment.

A good sexual relationship involves two people—it is a shared responsibility. Even though one partner seems to turn off, the other can benefit from learning techniques to revive desire in the marriage. It is possible to enjoy the sensual experience of affection and physical closeness without having intercourse.

In the next section of this chapter you will find some sensual pleasuring exercises. These are designed to expand your sensual awareness—the appreciation of pleasurable bodily experiences—without engaging in intercourse. From there, you can gradually move toward more sexually explicit activities.

Sensual Pleasuring

The following sensual pleasuring exercises (designed by William Masters and Virginia Johnson) are an extension of activities I've suggested to help you get in touch with your senses for self-nurturing. They will help you deal with your fears and anxieties related to sexual performance and can remove the pressure of performance from the sex act.

These exercises are particularly appropriate for you at midlife, since men at this age are engaged in expressing their newfound affiliative selves while women are asserting new strengths and taking the initiative. In addition, husbands and wives can have individual anxieties regarding sex—for men it might be performance, and for women, pleasing their mates.

Consider these exercises a rest stop on the road to sexual renewal. In fact, during the first stages of this hiatus, you will refrain from intercourse altogether. But you will not refrain from pleasure. Instead, you will concentrate on your sense of touch. The idea behind sensual pleasuring is to introduce slowly and in a graduated way the various forms of touching that occur before intercourse. This can remove much of the anxiety from sex. You are now free simply to enjoy sensual, nongenital pleasure.

It's entirely possible that you might feel silly engaging in these exercises at first. "This is stupid," you might think or "This feels phony." Despite these feelings, stay with the exercises. Remember the value of "as if" behavior. When you act as if something works, eventually you begin to feel and think that it does. Also bear in mind that half the time, you will be doing nothing at all except lying back and learning how to enjoy. (The other half of the time, your spouse will be on the receiving end.)

Taking delight in our bodies can be difficult for many of us, especially if your mind races ahead in future-think as did June's and Adam's. But you deserve to confer the time and attention on your body. It is capable of giving you much pleasure in return. When you learn to relax and receive, you will be well on your way to rejuvenating the sexuality in your midlife marriage.

Your environment is important to the success of the exercise, so set the stage each time before you begin. Be sure you have quiet and plenty of time. In fact, you can agree in advance on how much time you would like to devote to the exercise. Music, low lighting, or scented candles can all add to the ambiance. You will be taking turns as giver and receiver.

Step 1: No Breast or Genital Touching

1. *Lie on your stomach naked.* Your partner gently and slowly massages your back all the way down to your toes. There is no need to rush. You can use lotions or oils if you prefer. Relax. Become aware of your breathing. You should both focus on the sense of touching and being touched.

2. *Communicate.* Tell your partner what you like, what you want changed, and how he or she should proceed. Be specific. This is good practice for assertiveness in your relationship.

3. *Lie on your back.* Your partner will continue the massage in a caressing manner, but he or she is not to touch your breasts or genitals. Fully experience the sensations of being gently stroked.

4. *Change places.* Now it's your turn to massage your partner. Remember that there are thirteen hundred nerve endings in every square inch of your fingertips. Enjoy the experience with the knowledge that there are no demands. This is not to lead to intercourse.

5. *Repeat as needed.* You may repeat this exercise as many times as you wish before moving on to Step 2.

Step 2: Add Breast and Genital Massage and Fantasies

1. ***Keep the rules in mind.*** Remember, there is still no intercourse at this stage. You are still both on your sensuous journey.

2. ***Lie on your stomach.*** Begin the massage as in Step 1.

3. ***Lie on your back.*** Your partner will continue to massage and caress your body, but now he or she will gently touch your breasts and genitals. Body lotions and oils are particularly helpful.

4. ***Communicate.*** Again, become aware of what feels good and what doesn't, and share these likes and dislikes with your partner. You could be surprised by your response. You are changing as individuals and as a couple. As a result of this exercise, you might find that what you enjoy in the way of sexual touch has changed too. Now you have the opportunity to discover anew what feels good to you. Perhaps this is different from when you were first married.

5. ***Trade places.***

6. ***Repeat as needed before moving on to Step 3.***

It is often said that the most important sex organ is the brain. If so, why not use it to enhance your sensual and sexual feelings during Step 2. While lying in bed after your genital touching, you might read aloud to each other a book of sexual fantasies such as Nancy Friday's *My Secret Garden* or Anaïs Nin's work of erotica, *Delta of Venus*. Or you might conjure and share with your partner sexually explicit fantasies you've had. Try creating one together. These, as well as X-rated videos, can be sexual awakeners. Brenda and Jeremy set aside Friday evenings as X-rated video night. Both reported heightened desire for sex in their twenty-five-year marriage after watching these movies.

Acting out your joint or individual fantasies can add to your sensual pleasure. Consider dressing up in a role and acting as the fantasy characters would. This falls into the realm of creativity and fun—both essential ingredients for fulfilling sex.

Step 3: On to Intercourse

1. ***Use what you have learned.*** As a result of Steps 1 and 2, you have garnered much sensual information about yourself and your partner. Now use the knowledge you have acquired during foreplay—the "first act" before intercourse.

2. ***Take your time.*** There is no rush. This is a fresh start, so enjoy.

3. ***Be patient.*** If for any reason either of you feels anxious or pressured, let your partner know and simply return to Step 1 or 2. You will eventually get to where you want to be sexually, but it may take a bit of time. Go easy on yourself, watch the negative self-talk, and enjoy the process along the way.

Remember, you are now making love to someone you know quite intimately. Use this information wisely and well.

Happiness in the bedroom bodes well for you in all aspects of your physical and emotional selves. The wonderful part of all this is that if you have let the sexual part of your relationship go dormant, it is more than possible to breathe new life into it again. Desire is essential to sexual bliss. What is important now is for you to feel motivated to bring this about. Just know that if you think it and if you do it, it will happen!

PART FOUR

The Retirement Years

N O MATTER HOW MANY women are in the workforce today, men are still retiring in greater numbers than women. (This, of course, may change in the future.) The thrust of Parts Four and Five is directed toward couples coping with a husband's retirement. However, many women in the workforce do retire, and based on the role work played in their lives, their retirement may be equally difficult. But retirement may be less problematic for women because they are more accustomed to shifting roles in their lives.

In a 1993 survey of retirees in New York City, 41 percent admitted their retirement adjustment was difficult. Age and status also seem to make a difference—the younger or more prominent the retiree in this study, the more difficult the transition. A man's essential task at midlife—making the move from competing to connecting, from achievement to affiliation—may be one of the most difficult he faces.

Retirement may not change the relationship itself, but it can bring out different aspects of it. For starters, it brings intense closeness. During retirement, there is the potential to spend together the two thousand to three thousand hours a year formerly occupied by work.

And sometimes, familiarity breeds contempt. Personality traits, like Bernie's laid-back attitude, that were initially attractive could, with the passage of years and so much togetherness, become grating. I could have become less tolerant and less patient.

Moreover, traits (such as a husband's perfectionism or a wife's fastidiousness) that were appropriately discharged in the workplace or that you learned to adjust to over the years can become magnified and loom as enormous obstacles. During retirement, they can wreak havoc in your relationship, as when the perfectionist, suddenly bereft of his usual outlets, finds the only thing he can control is his wife, or when the fastidious wife must cope with a husband who, by his very presence, is constantly making a mess!

Yet we rarely acknowledge how much a husband's retirement affects his wife and the marriage. I believe that wives must also consider their husband's cessation of work a major transition in their own lives—not just that of their spouses.

Today we have to take into account the fact that the period following retirement—formerly seen as the little caboose appended to the long train of our lives—may now constitute as much as a third of our existence. Americans are living longer than ever before in history. In the year 2000, there will be close to 40 or 50 million of us over the age of 65. That's about one-fifth of our total population. Moreover, according to the National Institute on Aging, life expectancy in 2040 may reach the age of 86 for men and 91.5 for women.

Not only are we living longer—we're living better. We are healthier, more active, and more vigorous than ever before. We are currently experiencing a revolution in our life cycles. What in the 1950s we used to consider as middle-aged—those dreaded years between 35 and 55 characterized by midriff bulge and graying pates—is shifting fifteen years ahead. Middle age now spans a wider range and can last till we're in our seventies!

In 1995, the average age of retirement was 60. According to the U.S. Census Bureau, by the year 2010, upward of one-quarter of the population will consist of pre- and post-retirement people (age 55 and up).

Research indicates that because of these declining mortality rates and earlier retirement ages, four-fifths of all men who retire do so within a marriage. Marriage is the context in which most decisions about retirement are made and in which most adjustments take place.

Whereas a mere 150 years ago, a husband and wife barely survived the departure of their grown children from the household, often succumbing within eighteen months, today you can expect to remain in your marriage for fifteen to thirty or even forty years beyond retirement. That's a whole second lifetime of possibilities and also of perils. Indeed, new statistical projections suggest that the proportion of older men to older women will narrow considerably over the next several decades. Men's life spans will grow; there will be fewer widows and longer marriages. Read on.

CHAPTER 12

Retirement:
For Better or Worse...
but Not for Lunch

*Most people say as you get old you have to give up things. I think
you get old because you do give up things.*
— Senator Ted Green

LOTS OF QUESTIONS AND ANXIETIES buzzed around my head after Bernie announced his intention to retire. He had no hobbies or interests other than work, and I was concerned—I wondered what it would be like for me, for him, and consequently for us. I thought I had better continue my psychotherapy practice in town even though it was stressful and involved a one-hour commute. At least my work would create a safety zone, a place where I could avoid dealing with the problems I anticipated arising at home.

There were issues that concerned Bernie also. One day he asked me a telling question (which was really a question to himself): "How would you feel if I were no longer a full-time attorney?" He felt he would experience a loss of status. He didn't actually say it, but it was implicit in his question.

"It really doesn't bother me," I replied. "This is your issue, not mine. I don't care whether you're a full-time attorney." What I really wanted was for him to wake up each morning, see the sun coming through the drapes, and say, "Oh my God, what a beautiful day! There are so many choices. I don't know what to do first!" What I really wanted was for him to be happy and fulfilled.

The transition was difficult. Bernie set about preparing his partners. They bought him out of the partnership, and within six months he was out of his suite of offices. As he had promised, he took several of his major clients with him. He planned to work two or three unspecified days a week, as the need dictated.

He moved everything into the house. Appropriating Selena's former bedroom for an office, he installed a brand-new computer, printer, fax machine, copy machine, and additional phone lines—all the latest and the best! I lost the closet (and space for my clothes) to his files. And soon, just as I had imagined, papers began piling up all over. Before I knew it, he had taken over the dining room table, spreading his work around the house.

We talked about Bernie helping around the house. He had never lifted a finger in our thirty years of marriage, but he agreed to prepare his own lunch, wash the dishes, straighten the bed, and take out the trash. Those skills he mastered easily. But, unfortunately, in all of his years as an attorney, he had never conquered typing! He couldn't and wouldn't learn how to use his new computer or any of the other fancy equipment he had purchased. He had always had a phalanx of secretaries ready to serve him. But not anymore.

"I'm sure you're going to help me out," he said, standing in his new office, gesturing vaguely toward his high-tech devices.

My reply: "Get yourself a secretary."

Then, the all-too-familiar guilt trip: "I've been supporting you and the kids all these years, making most of the money, and you're not even going to type an envelope for me?"

How could I say no? I would complain that I was tired after a long day at work, but I would do it grudgingly. Sometimes he would dictate a letter, but I would make mistakes. He became critical. I wasn't as good as his secretary. And so we fought. But I still did it.

He was beginning the game of "Helpless": "I can't do it myself." "I can't find anything." "Do it for me." And so we fought some more.

Then, one night, I had come home from a tough day at work in a pouring rainstorm. Flash floods were imminent. Rivers of mud and water came coursing down from the canyons. You have to live in southern California to understand how scary and life-threatening that can be. My one-hour commute had stretched into two hours that evening. As I dragged my wet, starving, and frazzled self in, Bernie was waiting for me at the door—not with some hot soup, but with a document for me to type.

"Why are you so late?" he asked. "I've got to get this contract out tonight."

There was no dinner. The house was cold and dark. I was so tired, I almost cried. I said, "No."

"What do you mean, 'No'?"

"I can't do it. I'm not your secretary."

Bernie knew that I have a passion for collecting antique mirrors and dishes and exotic masks. So he offered, "What if I buy you an antique mirror each month?"

I said, "No."

"What if I pay you a salary?"

I said, "No. I'm not your secretary, and I don't want to be." This, in spite of my inner temptation to give in again. After all, it had been easier to acquiesce to his needs in the past, but this situation seemed different. I don't know why, but I just couldn't do it. "No!" a new inner voice dictated. "Not this time!" Then, drawing upon my twenty-five years of experience as a psychotherapist, I said, "Let's both think about what would work for us, because this isn't working at all."

And then, after three days, a miracle of miracles—a mutual "Aha!" occurred to both of us. We came together and negotiated what would make each of us happy—after all, it had to be a win-win situation or nothing. We drew up a contract in which I would receive a percentage of the gross billings from Bernie's practice each month. (Some months, I made a lot!) In return, I agreed to type a certain number of pages per week in a timely manner, but he would have to make an appointment with me in advance and let me know what his needs were. Moreover, he was to make suggestions for corrections in such a way that I would not feel criticized or put down. It worked.

But after six months, I canceled the contract and handed my husband a list of six potential secretaries. No matter what, I still wasn't his secretary!

What a Man's Retirement Means to His Wife

There is no question about it. You can have a wide range of emotions at your husband's retirement, ranging from, "I'm thrilled; now we'll have time to travel and be together more," to laments similar to mine: "What am I going to do with a hobbyless husband lying about all the time?"

Indeed, I was dismayed when Bernie announced his retirement, and I am not alone. Several of the women among my happily married retirement couples had similar reactions. One woman told me, "Harry's retirement was devastating at first. It threw us together twenty-four hours a day. All the unresolved things came into focus—either we were going to kill each other or stay together. This period lasted for six months."

And another said, "In the beginning, Mike's retirement was awful. He was always there. I remember saying, 'There's a man in my house,' and he would say, 'There's a woman in my house.' He was always busy cooking or playing tennis. I didn't like having him around so much. I was afraid he would find out how lazy I was, but it didn't seem to bother him. We went through this period of instability for a while."

Research has shown that women are more likely to struggle with negative changes in their home life after a husband's retirement. Your sense of space and time may be physically and psychologically impinged upon; you may experience deep feelings of guilt, anger, entrapment, and fear; you may find the comfortable structure of your life suddenly in shambles. With the kids out of the house, you may believe—and rightly so—that this is your "time to fly," and wonder whether your husband's retirement will spell the end of your hard-fought freedom. You may struggle with how you, your husband, and your marriage can thrive during this stressful time.

Retirement Strategies That Work

A happy retirement marriage does not mean that you never experience conflict. Nor does successful adjustment mean immediate bliss upon awakening the very first morning. Indeed, one interviewee in my study who had earlier contemplated divorce noted, "We did a lot of struggling. We have a photograph album labeled 'Amidst Pain and Happiness.'" The couples in my research on successful retirement marriages had all dealt with the challenges of ill health and loss, yet at this time, their commitment to their marriages and to one another was stronger than ever.

What made them so? The theme that seemed to form a continuous thread throughout the tapestry of their lives was the couples' awareness that time was running out. This perception influenced many of their attitudes and behaviors. In fact, the realization that, as one wife put it, "the days do not stretch out forever" enabled these partners to become more flexible and tolerant. They felt and demonstrated a deep respect for one another in most areas of their relationships. One husband captured the feeling when he said, "It's those little words again—respect and consideration—that just float through everything we do in our marriage." And even if disappointment or anger reared its head during an interview, it was always mitigated by the specter of diminishing time.

Here are some additional strategies that worked for these couples:

- Difficulties did not crush the relationships. Working through crises together strengthened the marriages.

- Many couples did not have all of their plans in place before retirement. As with midlife issues, flexibility and openness were important to the adjustment process.

- The level of interaction with family and friends seemed to have little influence on satisfaction within the marriage as long as both agreed what their involvement would be.

- These couples made a conscious effort to have fewer disagreements. They wanted to spend their remaining years in a more peaceful environment.

- They experienced greater equality in the relationship after retirement. They shared household tasks and decided to appreciate each other more, given the reality of the ticking clock.

- The spouses gave each other plenty of physical and emotional space without imposing demands.

- A sense of humor smoothed the way in many interactions. Humor is a major coping device that enhances communication and minimizes destructive conflict.

The couples in these vital marriages had had problems but had worked through them. They held a shared vision of their relationship and frequently found mutual agreement after talking things out. Ultimately, retirement had had a positive effect on their marriages, drawing them closer.

A Fulfilling Marriage Means
Good Health in Retirement

A successful retirement marriage is not just a question of comfort or happiness; it can be a matter of life and death. Your retirement adjustment can affect—for better or worse—your mental and physical health, and even your longevity. This life-affirming cycle is tied inextricably to the retirement marriage: *a fulfilling marriage is the single greatest predictor of good health for retirees.*

After retirement, a man becomes more dependent on his marriage—and especially his wife—for the self-esteem, social contacts, and rewards that work had previously supplied. While on the job, his status in the competitive pecking order was the primary factor determining his overall contentment with life. But having partially or completely left behind the world of work, he focuses on the marriage for support. It becomes increasingly important to him.

He depends on his marriage for his well-being. In fact, men who have recently lost their wives are at risk of suffering marked deterioration in their physical health. Conversely, married men between the ages of 45 and 64 are twice as likely to live ten years longer than their unmarried counterparts.

Although both spouses affect each other deeply, by and large the husband's mental outlook often has a greater impact on the emotional course of the marriage. That is, if a man is depressed, his mental state will have a more negative influence on his wife than her depression will have on him. A husband's despair can sap the very life out of the marriage, and everyone—he, his wife, and the relationship—suffers.

Those who explore the new scientific field of psychoneuroimmunology—the mind-body connection—tell us that stress, depression, and inactivity can impair the immune system. A depressed retiree sets himself up for all kinds of medical problems. Emotionally, his hopeless mood will rip apart the fulfilling nature of the marriage for him and his wife. Moreover, in a vicious cycle, his despondency may burden and dishearten his wife, which could harm her immune system and result in medical problems for *her.*

But if the husband is comfortable in his retirement, the benefits redound to all. A happy husband contributes to a gratified wife, which makes for a fulfilling retirement marriage. All become winners!

Using the Growth Circle

I've said throughout this book that all marriages consist of give and take. No person can be a healthy "I" without the support of a "You." When it came to the empty nest, Bernie was at first nonsupportive. But he learned, through constant dialogue and listening, to become an understanding and kind teacher who helped me through my own adjustment. When it comes to retirement especially, my research shows that the task of helping falls most often to wives. Women are not only emotional managers in terms of raising emotionally laden issues, but they also set the social agenda and initiate requests for change.

In a perfect world, your husband, finding himself anxious and depressed with the sudden loss of a lifelong role, would "do his own work" and solve his problems without you. But as you know, this is not a perfect world. Besides, he's not the only one having problems. Retirement is considered a major transition in a man's life, but wives must think of it in the same terms. They are as involved in the retirement as their husbands are. And they may also be as threatened and as vulnerable, though, as we'll see, in different ways.

Even the strongest relationships are buffeted by the retirement crisis. When the structure of family life changes dramatically, you as a couple might begin questioning everything you have always taken for granted. Yet today, you have more power and control in the marriage than ever before. You have more choices now, and you can empower yourself with knowledge. I will be providing both of you with the tools to exercise those choices so you can maximize your retirement marriage—to make it the best time in your lives.

As a psychotherapist, I know that people begin to improve their lives when they work with reality—with what *is* rather than with what *should be*. *Shoulds* are toxic. They force you into thinking and behavior that may not fit with reality. And the reality is that many men have not been socialized to adjust well to retirement. Too many pressing issues point toward the need for wives to examine their roles and how involved they are willing to become.

- Most men are singularly focused. Their careers define them.
- Retirement for many means a major loss of identity.
- Not all men are as resilient or as flexible as we would like them to be.

If we accept what Jung has to say—that men become more needful of affiliation and nurturing and more dependent on the marriage as they age—doesn't it seem logical that you as the wife, being in a stronger position at this time in your life, can look at these facts and find a constructive course of action?

- He needs me. He's going through a difficult time, but so am I.
- I'm in a better position now to help him.
- If I help during this time of transition, it will benefit me, him, and us.

No, this won't heap more responsibility on you. I will offer ways for the two of you to work out your issues together, if you so choose. *Choice* is the key word here. You'll find a menu of options. Feel free to take advantage of them according to your abilities and inclinations.

Questions for Growth	**EXAMINING YOUR INVOLVEMENT**
	In Chapter 3 you began to examine your feelings about helping each other through the transitions of empty nest and retirement. Now, both of you examine your specific feelings about help during the retirement phase. This activity will prepare you for your preretirement Relationship Review:
1.	Wives: How involved do you want to become in helping your husband through the retirement transition?
2.	What specific things are you willing to do?
3.	What can you do to take care of your own needs during this time?
4.	Husbands: Do you want your wife involved in lending a hand? If so, to what extent?
5.	Together discuss your individual views.

Form a Relationship Plan

Many of us put more thought into planning a two-week vacation than we do into the years of retirement that stretch before us. Research has shown that the most anxiety-ridden phase of retirement is not the actual cessation of work itself, but the six months that precede it. The retirement transition is one that most of us approach with either exhilaration or dread.

We may have begun financial and health care planning in our thirties. Certainly this has been the traditional way of "preparing for retirement." But the truth is, after retirement, emotional and relationship issues become paramount, and few of us have made provisions for these.

To counteract the apprehension, you as a couple need to construct long-term plans for your emotional health for the next twenty to thirty years. You need a relationship plan as well as a financial and fitness plan. You will enjoy a better quality of life during your retirement years through a satisfying and fulfilling marriage. Just learning that you should expect some adjustments, much the way teenagers are counseled to be patient with hormonal changes, can ease the journey.

In the chapters that follow, you will learn how retirement profoundly affects your marriage. I will suggest strategies to deal with the many issues that can create tension. Finally, we will look toward finding meaning in the retirement marriage.

As we have seen from my study, flexibility and willingness to change are our most important protections; they help us master the crises and transitions we will experience at retirement.

Relation-ship Review	**A PRERETIREMENT RELATIONSHIP REVIEW**
	If you are looking toward retirement in the next several years, then consider the questions below. You might also want to make up some of your own that are specific to your situation. Remember to conduct your Relationship Review in a climate of caring and empathic listening. Be alert to defensiveness on your part, avoid blaming, and stay calm.
1.	What changes do you each anticipate?
2.	How much time together and how much time apart seems comfortable to you? Be specific.
3.	What activities do you anticipate doing individually? Together? How does each of you plan to pursue meaningful activities? Be specific. This may be one of your most important mutual explorations.

4. What space changes do you anticipate in your home? How will you go about providing this?

5. How do you handle disagreements now? Is this working?

6. What changes do you anticipate in the allocation of household tasks? Who does what now? Is this satisfactory, or do both or one of you want some changes?

7. How much time do you devote to family and friends now? Is this acceptable? If not, what changes would you want to make?

As a result of my involvement, the problems in my marriage began to resolve themselves—although as Jung pointed out, "the serious problems of life are never fully solved." We are in continual dialogue, but we are coming along. Bernie has learned to better express his feelings, and our communication has improved. We have worked at respectful and responsive talking and listening. We have learned that in the long run, the truth about what is bothering us is easier to face than avoidance. We sit down with honesty and respect for one another: we communicate, negotiate, and plan. We often take the pulse of the relationship, conducting a Now and Future Relationship Review every few months.

Through my understanding of what the world of work provides an individual and what its loss entails, I have become more accepting of and compassionate about what my husband experienced upon retirement. It has mitigated much of my former impatience and frustration.

And by Bernie's gaining insight into how his retirement affects me, he has become more tolerant and less demanding of me. The foundation has been laid upon which to build the successful retirement marriage that we both desire.

Bernie redesigned his home office. He made a new floor plan and added a second desk so that his papers are no longer piling up on the dining room table. What's more, he has become more active, rediscovering long-lost interests such as tennis and playwriting. He has also joined several organizations. Sure, there's some backsliding, but there's also a commitment to make a better marriage, now that we have the tools in hand. We've enjoyed a personal payoff for all of the thought, energy, and feeling that we've devoted to this issue. And there's a payoff for you, too.

CHAPTER 13

What Work and Retirement Mean to Men

Work sanitizes us . . . ridding us of feelings of inadequacy.
— Roger Gould, M.D.

I SAT DOWN TO TALK ABOUT RETIREMENT with Kenneth late one afternoon in his comfortable California ranch home. Dressed neatly in light khaki slacks and a plaid, short-sleeved sport shirt, this 60-year-old man seemed relaxed and hungry for conversation.

But before I broached the subject of his retirement, I began by asking Kenneth what work had meant to him. "I got a lot of satisfaction from it," he replied warmly. "I was accomplishing something. I was learning. I got to meet interesting people and do interesting work."

Before his retirement, Kenneth had been a systems analyst in the aerospace industry. He began in this field during the 1950s—the heady days of the race to the moon. "What exciting times those were," he added with a smile, "even as late as the Vietnam era. It gave me a chance to use my mind and my education, to do exciting things and visit interesting places. There was always pressure to move ahead. I accomplished something; I experienced achievement!"

He-Is-What-He-Does

Like so many other men, Kenneth's work had meant everything to him. Still, it can be difficult for a woman to appreciate how important a man's work is to his sense of self. As profoundly as the mothering role defines a woman, the intensity and depth of a man's feelings toward his work define him.

It might help to recall the Eternal Mom we met earlier. Irene was bereft at her children's departure. For many men, work may play the same role as Irene's children did in her life. Indeed, a man's world may be split unevenly. Ambition, effort, competition, and achievement may take up a larger share of his physical and emotional life, leaving a smaller portion of his time and energy to be devoted to marriage, home, and children. Some men express their caring and love for their families by engaging in that other world—the world of work. And home can be an infrequently visited refuge from their travails.

You may have opted for far fewer life choices than your wife and, therefore, may have less experience with shifting roles. Frequently, men have played a single role all their lives—accountant, policeman, shop foreman, business executive—and they see themselves more narrowly, defining themselves solely by their work. But just as the empty nest can distress an Eternal Mom, this "I-am-what-I-do" attitude can devastate a man during the retirement transition.

Many of us have been socialized to believe that being a man means working and supporting a family. And, although the women's movement has made inroads into this traditional approach, these days—especially for men who came of age in the 1940s and 50s—the rules haven't changed all that much. Most still equate their selfhood with their status as a worker and provider.

I have found, however, that frequently women don't fully grasp how profoundly important a man's work is to him, and how its loss can engender a crisis. You and your wife may need to be educated about what you are really leaving when you retire from the world of work. The more information on this subject that you both gather, the easier it will be for you to negotiate a successful retirement marriage.

Rehearsal

PIE CHART OF A
HUSBAND'S DIFFERENT ROLES

In line with the adage "A picture is worth a thousand words," create a pie chart to help you understand how much time and energy you devote to different aspects of your life and the many roles you play.

1. List your various roles: worker, volunteer, father, grandfather, friend, and so on.

2. Draw a circle.

3. Mark off the wedges of the pie to correspond to the percentage of time and energy you devote to each role, and write in the roles. This will help you visualize how important your work is to you.

Rehearsal

TRYING ON NEW HATS

Are there any new roles you would like to add? If so, use the following questions to help you:

1. What games did you play as a child? What you enjoyed then will give you clues for the future. Pick one you especially liked.

2. What did you do in the game?

3. How can you apply that to your life today?

4. Share your findings with your spouse.

5. Put together an action plan:

   ◆ What is the goal you want to accomplish?

   ◆ What/who will help you attain this goal?

   ◆ What/who will get in the way?

   ◆ What is your plan of action?

   Later, we will explore your wife's role chart. Then the two of you can compare.

When Work Means Everything

The CEO of a venture capital company, Richard had built his corporation up to $60 million a year in business. "I had worked seven days a week for most of my life," he explained in an interview at his lavish golf-course home. "I was accustomed to being needed and wanted. I always had a lot of people around my desk, the phone was always ringing—I was busy. I felt useful, helpful. I enjoyed it."

Like Kenneth and 75 percent of the men I interviewed for my retirement study, Richard's career gave him great pleasure. As one of my research subjects put it, "The job was the biggest and the best, . . . [and] I thought I was the best in the business."

My interviewees' lives echo those of other successful middle- and upper-middle-class men. Employment enables you to play out a fantasy of heroic accomplishment: you go off each day to slay dragons and defeat bad guys, avert threats, come through in the clinch, and perform feats of skill against all odds. This fantasy helps to give meaning to your daily struggle.

Work furnishes you with many other satisfactions as well, including a sense of community and belonging, an outlet for socializing, structure for your daily life, productive activity, masculine identity, feelings of self-reliance and competence, internal and external recognition, material rewards and money, a good reputation, emotional and financial security, dignity and self-worth, power, status, and meaningfulness.

Work is such a defining feature of men's lives that often men will persist in work or worklike activities even after retirement and when the financial need no longer exists. Consider Richard, the wealthy 70-year-old venture capitalist. He loved work so much that the bottom fell out of his life when he retired:

> I was retired for two and a half years, but I hated it! I had tried to retire several times before, but each time, it lasted only a few days.
>
> Once I retired "for good" at the age of 67, I lost all incentive to do anything around the house. I was crazy—reading all the time. I was depressed. I felt silly and useless—like a failure. My wife and I have different personalities: she's an indoor person and I'm an outdoor person. We didn't have enough things to do together.

I had plenty of hobbies: tennis, photography, bridge, walking. But it wasn't enough. You can play just so much tennis. I wasn't that good, so it was frustrating. I like to be good at what I do. I started to play bridge. I played at several bridge clubs and went to conventions. But I missed being needed; I missed the fun, the jokes, the repartee; I missed the thrill of closing a great deal; I missed holding meetings and taking my staff of young vibrant people on trips; I missed feeling active.

And so, just two and a half years into his retirement, when a former competitor made him an offer he couldn't refuse, Richard went back to work. In fact, he had already begun preparing to reopen his office. One way or another, he was leaving the state of retirement. "All my life, my main motivation was to make money," Richard explained. "Now, it's to feel useful and alive. We could say that my usefulness is now the money of my life!"

Work was too important for Richard's sense of self for him ever to let it go. As another entrepreneur put it, "The business is who I am. Work is my oxygen."

Life Review Is Liberating

In Ingmar Bergman's movie *Wild Strawberries*, Dr. Borg, a man in his seventies, travels from his place of retirement to the city of Lund, where he is to receive the highest honor bestowed on people in his profession. Along the way, he passes the familiar territory of his youth and reminisces about his life. This trip becomes a symbolic pilgrimage. At the end, Dr. Borg has gained wisdom and a sense of integration about his life. He feels that his life was useful and had meaning.

Life Review is liberating and can give you much insight about the meaning of your life. Reviewing the past is often pleasurable and non-threatening. Positive feelings come from taking realistic stock of your life and remembering past achievements and strengths. Reminiscing can turn idle remembrances into constructive review and help you get a better handle on how effective your life has been. Dealing with the past facilitates moving forward. The following exercise could be helpful in reviewing what your work life has meant to both of you.

Rehearsal

REMINISCING ON WORK LIFE—UNFINISHED BUSINESS

In my workshops, one of the most successful couple exercises begins with the wife interviewing her husband regarding past work experiences. The interview process can lift the relationship out of the doldrums and open the door to healthier communication. Invite your wife to participate with you in this activity.

A Word to the Wives on How to Conduct This Interview

1. Arrange for a convenient time and place.

2. Be careful just to ask questions. Your comments can easily cut off communication. Assume you are a reporter who knows nothing about your interviewee, and keep your opinions to yourself.

3. Encourage your husband to respond as fully as possible. Use follow-up questions, such as "Can you give me an example?" to flesh out his responses.

4. Listen. Listen. Listen. It's a form of encouragement.

5. Write down his answers. Remember, you are a reporter.

6. Read back to him what he has said.

7. Confirm that those are his feelings and statements.

8. If a discussion follows, that's fine. If not, drop the subject, but before you finish, thank your husband for a fine interview.

Now, men, for the interview itself. Your wife is to imagine that she is the editor of a company newsletter and that she is interviewing one of her company's long-term employees regarding his memories of his working life. She's interested in his work-related reflections.

The Interview Questions

1. What did you enjoy most about your work?

2. What was your greatest achievement?

3. What do you regret the most?

4. If you had the opportunity, what would you change?

5. Based on your work experience, what advice would you offer your children?

Once you've completed this exercise, turn the tables, and interview your wife about her work experiences.

Men and Retirement

What images come to mind when you think of retirement? The two of you merrily tooling around the country in an RV? That cruise to China you've been putting off? Lazy days on a tropical isle? All are possible, but after you've come back from that big trip—then what?

Retirement is a time when people disengage from work-related roles, activities, relationships, and settings and seek out others to replace those that have ended. It's a restructuring of one's life—and for some, a belated identity crisis. The dictionary defines *to retire* as to withdraw, to become secluded or sequestered. When we describe a person as "retiring," we usually mean retreating from contact with others—reserved and shy.

Just as work can represent meaning, self-respect, identity, a sense of community and belonging, structure, productivity, masculinity, competence, and power, retirement can represent the loss of all of these positive elements. And that's a heavy blow. At retirement, you may feel that you have become obsolete and extraneous—no longer part of the important world of work. You may lean toward being withdrawn, secluded, or sequestered at home. Retirement may feel like a black hole after the initial rush of travel and activity.

Retirement cannot possibly be the same for every man. Your response to retirement will vary with your financial and health status as well as your personality and the way in which you retire.

Research has shown that there is a correlation between personality type and the time of retirement. Entrepreneurs and individuals with Type A personalities who are more aggressive, competitive, quick, and striving tend to retire later than more relaxed, easygoing, patient, and noncompetitive Type B personalities.

Executives and others who wield great power have a harder time retiring. One 62-year-old retiree with whom I spoke was filled with anxiety about his impending retirement. A vice president in an insurance company, he told me of breaking out in rashes and suffering a spell of protracted insomnia when he first began planning his transition. On the other hand, blue-collar workers, who may not identify emotionally with their work, are often grateful for an end to the monotony.

Meeting Basic Needs

We all have basic needs that most likely are fulfilled in the work world, but that may go wanting during retirement. At the most primary level, we have the need for food, shelter, and clothing. Your work often meets these needs automatically. A sudden termination, however, may generate anxiety about your ability to make a living, and even with a planned retirement, the resources for the creature comforts you have become accustomed to may be threatened.

We all need to feel that life is secure and orderly. The structure and salary work brings can provide this for you, and retirement can threaten it. Perhaps you organized your life around your job as a foreman in a factory. You knew when you were supposed to report to work and what was required of you every day. After retirement, you may feel anxious— as if you've lost the safety net of structure you had become used to.

Moreover, because we are all social beings, we need to belong and to feel that others accept and appreciate us. We need to feel connected. This, too, can be threatened at retirement. For instance, you might have hung around with a group of buddies at your job. Perhaps you played poker Friday nights, golfed on the weekends, and socialized with your wives. But after your retirement, maybe you don't see the guys every day. And when you do get together, you feel left out when they share office gossip and common gripes about the new boss. You might fear, "Out of sight, out of mind."

We all have ambition and the desire to achieve and excel, so your ego is also involved in your work. There, you may have sought out opportunities to display your competence for the sake of professional and social rewards. Entrepreneurs and professionals, in particular, can experience great loss of ego status upon their retirement. In fact, as we have seen, they may be unable to tolerate the blow and may return to work.

Finally, work gives meaning to your life. It can provide you with opportunities for growth, creativity, and self-fulfillment. After retirement, you may struggle to find other activities that feel equally worthwhile. But it is possible.

Questions
for
Growth

SEEKING NEW INSIGHT

Analyze the different needs each of you has:

- Food, shelter, and clothing
- Security and structure
- Social interactions and belonging
- Ego gratification and status
- Fulfillment and a sense of purpose

Discuss with your spouse whether and how work had fulfilled those needs and where you are now, retired (or not). How are your needs, and your spouse's needs, being met? Discuss ways you can each fulfill your unmet needs in the future.

Managing the Stages of Retirement

Your perception of retirement may change even while you're in the midst of the process. Many retirees pass through several phases on their way to full retirement. Their feelings about the process evolve as they tackle each phase. My observations of and conversations with my client Ted, a gregarious, affable district salesman for a shoe manufacturing company, can help you understand what might happen to you.

The Remote Phase

Still a year or two in the offing, the cessation of work seemed a faraway event to Ted, one that posed little threat. He and his wife, Dottie, dreamed about retirement and talked it over with their children and friends. He poked fun at his retired neighbor, Harrison, who seemed to hang around the house all day, bickering with his wife. The Preretirement Relationship Review in Chapter 12 would help Ted and Dottie envision what his retirement might look like.

The Near Phase

The proximity of retirement can be extremely stressful to you. The mere act of setting the date, confirming that retirement is no longer an abstract notion, can bring on a crisis. It may threaten your sense of self and well-being.

That seems to be what happened to Ted when he put in for retirement. The economy was slowing down, and at 64, he had survived a mild heart attack and coronary artery bypass surgery. It was time to get out, so he asked his district manager how to get started. He was fine at the office, but as soon as he got home, his pulse started racing.

"I was afraid I was going to have another heart attack," he said. "I was so worried, it made me a nervous wreck. I thought, 'Hey, you're never going to work again. You're never going to earn a salary again.' For weeks after that, I would lie awake in bed nights, worrying about finances. I was totaled by the uncertainty and the prospect of change." The ribbing he had given Harrison suddenly became a reality to Ted—and it scared him.

Questions for Growth	**WHAT'S ON YOUR MIND?**
	If you are not yet retired but are nearing it, what issues concern you? List them. If you can, open up to your spouse and share your concerns. Get a dialogue going.

The Retirement Event

Sometimes there is a party or luncheon. Speeches are made, the proverbial watch presented, and the first blush of freedom is felt. Ted related the warm feelings he experienced from the retirement party thrown by his boss and staff. He loved being the center of attention and was bowled over by the testimonials and gifts.

Questions for Growth	**THE RETIREMENT EVENT**
1.	If there was an event to mark your retirement, were you happy with it? If not, what was missing?
2.	If you're not yet retired, what would you like to have happen?

> 3. If you've retired without an event, how do you feel about it? Think of an ideal celebration. See how you can incorporate some of that ideal into your life right now.

The Honeymoon Phase

This is a feeling of euphoria that comes from the realization that you are free to spend time as you wish. For men who have retired voluntarily and who have sufficient financial reserves, this phase can last much longer than six months.

Dottie had a three-week vacation coming, so she and Ted took a long-delayed trip to England. After they returned, he visited their out-of-state kids for several weeks. He slept late, played golf, and read a couple of best-sellers he had been too busy to look at while he was working.

Questions for Growth	YOUR HONEYMOON PHASE
1.	Did you enjoy a honeymoon phase? What was it like? How long did it last?
2.	Can you bring some honeymoon elements into your life right now? Which ones?

The Disenchantment Phase

Some men experience a period of emptiness, depression, and disappointment following retirement or the honeymoon phase. Ted was one of them. After five months of sleeping in, golfing, and traveling, he missed the camaraderie of his fellow workers; he missed conducting sales meetings. Dottie hadn't retired yet, so she was gone every day. Most of Ted's other friends were still working. The few who had retired busied themselves with their own lives. Ted became depressed.

Questions for Growth	**TAKING THE "DIS" OUT OF DISENCHANTMENT**
1.	If you're going through or have gone through this phase, what are you feeling?
2.	What activities are you missing?
3.	Discuss these issues with your wife. Keep talking. You're getting ready for the reorientation phase.

The Reorientation Phase

During this stage, disenchanted men will take stock of their current situation, pull themselves together, and decide what they really want to do with the rest of their lives.

Ted and Dottie had a long talk about how he could brighten his mood. She had asked friends at work whose husbands had also retired what their spouses did. They suggested checking out volunteer agencies to see what kinds of activities were available. Ted enjoyed teaching children, so that was a possibility. He also loved early California history. He contacted some of his retired friends, and began to see that he could make plans for the future.

Questions for Growth	**WHAT WILL I DO WITH MY TIME?**
	In the Reorientation Phase, you take stock of the situation, pull yourself together, and plan. Meaningful activities are a major consideration.
1.	Identify with your spouse, if possible, the activities you engage in now that you would like to continue.
2.	Brainstorm new activities that you would like to try.
3.	Make some plans to begin doing the new activities that interest you most.
4.	Think about establishing a new routine. How would these activities fit into that new routine?
	(See Chapter 16 for an in-depth exploration of meaningful activities.)

The Stability Phase

Eventually, a retirement routine is established, and retirees find stability. Ted discovered that he could volunteer in the local elementary school twice a week. He took the kids on field trips related to California history. He joined a gym, and created an exercise routine that was beneficial for his mental and physical health. And he got together with his retired friends more often.

Questions for Growth	**WE'RE ALWAYS CHANGING**
	Even though you've established a routine, it is inevitable that life circumstances will change and cause you to make some adjustments. Take stock of your activities every few months. Are they meeting your needs? If not, plan some new ones.

A gentler way to leave the workforce might be through a phased or partial retirement in which you gradually reduce your workload and salary each year until complete retirement takes place. Phasing softens the blow as you slowly become accustomed to your new routine and lifestyle.

Creating a Retirement Ritual

There is great value in having a meaningful retirement ritual to mark this rite of passage. Earlier I noted that few, if any, rituals exist for the emptying of the nest, and I advised you to create your own if that would feel helpful. There are, however, socially sanctioned rituals for retirement. The dinner, the watch, the testimonials—we all know how the stereotypical celebration of retirement should occur.

There is no one way to celebrate retirement. Some individuals receive lavish parties and gifts, others do not. Sometimes one person is recognized, sometimes a whole group. And, most often, the speeches review past accomplishments rather than focus on the new phase of life the retiree is entering. For some, the event itself can feel anticlimactic, however, and the gestures can be devoid of meaning.

Anthropologist Joel Savishinsky at Ithaca College reports on an informal retirement ritual for an administrator at a small nonprofit agency that was exceptionally meaningful to the female retiree. Such a ritual might also feel great to a man.

> The retirement event created by Alice's staff, her board of directors, and the agency's volunteers included a dish-to-pass supper, the presence of Alice's adult children, a dance band featuring several of her colleagues, a song composed in her honor, and several speeches—brief but rich in detail—recounting episodes from Alice's career and highlighting qualities of her character. There was also a memory book in which most of the six dozen people present wrote at some length about their feelings for Alice. Finally, there was a gift of a hand-carved easel, reflecting people's awareness of Alice's intention to focus her energy on her great passion, painting, once retirement began.

All of this served to enhance Alice's self-esteem at retirement. It gave her the sense that "my work had not been in vain, that I wasn't as incompetent as I feared I had become." The main reward, then, as Dr. Savishinsky saw it, was not the easel, beautiful as it was, but rather "the gift of reassurance and self-worth."

Unwelcome Retirement

The circumstances of your retirement often have much to do with your adjustment. Downturns in the economy, plant relocations and closings, mergers, downsizing, and bankruptcies have greatly affected the workforce and have encouraged early retirement. Moreover, many workers in their fifties and sixties have been given a golden or leaden handshake because of technical obsolescence or because their employers were seeking to fill their positions with younger workers who had lower salary requirements.

In a recent *Wall Street Journal* article, it was reported that late-middle-aged males are particularly vulnerable to being downsized. Older workers who have lost their jobs have the hardest time finding new ones. And, fearing it too late to start over, they often simply retire early. Sadly, early retirement can be abrupt and disorienting.

Men in this position can feel betrayed and enraged. They may be financially unprepared to face years of idleness. They may turn to alcohol and sink into depression as they struggle to cope with feelings of inadequacy and despair. Even former U.S. presidents are not immune. In a *Los Angeles Times Magazine* article on George Bush's retirement after his loss to Bill Clinton, Martin Kasindorf described Bush as a "restive soul simmering with emotions," and used adjectives such as "querulous" and "sulky" to suggest Bush's postretirement state of mind.

In *Everything to Gain: Making the Most of the Rest of Your Life*, Jimmy Carter reveals just how dreadful his early (and unwanted) retirement experiences were:

> Rosalynn and I were alone; our large official retinue of White House staff members and political associates were traveling back to Washington or to their former homes. It was deeply discouraging for me to contemplate the unpredictable years ahead.
>
> Only later would we realize that many people have to accept the same shocking changes in their lives as we did that winter: the involuntary end of a career and an uncertain future; the realization that "retirement" age is approaching. . . . And in our case, all this was exacerbated by the embarrassment about what was to us an incomprehensible political defeat and also by some serious financial problems that we had been reluctant to confront.

The jolt of such a sudden, forced, and unbidden retirement can be hard on anyone. Organizational psychologist Vance Caesar talked with me about how poorly executives who have been forced into early retirement fare. "These men generally have a lot of shame," he explained one afternoon. "They're ashamed of being kicked out of the company they were married to. It's like a divorce, and they're the ones being thrown out of the house. They have no power. Outplaced, terminated executives feel like losers. Not only have they lost the race—they haven't even been allowed to complete it. In almost all cases, these men feel they didn't do enough with their careers."

This is not only true of executives. An interesting discussion of retiring policemen noted that many remain on the job past retirement age because they have difficulty relinquishing their identity as well as their symbols of authority, such as the uniform, badge, and weapon. Another key factor in their staying on is related to their feeling that they have not made a lasting impact on their community, especially when criminals they have put behind bars are released after a short incarceration.

Similarly, some of the aspirations you have held for your career may never be realized upon retirement. Time has run out. It can be as difficult to relinquish hope for career fulfillment as it is to give up the dream of true love.

Crisis and Constructive Change

A crisis is a period of instability and uncertainty wedged between periods of relative calm. Forced retirement is an imposed change that can bring on a crisis. It is an unexpected, undesirable situation over which you have little or no control. All change is accompanied by at least some turmoil and stress, but downsizing can lead to great distress and even depression.

James, one of the participants in my study, was a loyal middle manager who had worked for thirty-five years at the same toy-manufacturing company. He was a placid, easy-going guy who went on for years believing that the company would always be there for him. He anticipated that at age 65 he would choose his own retirement.

But the business climate in southern California did not support that expectation. At the age of 56, James was suddenly terminated. The shock sent him into a depression. He would stay in his room all day, coming out only for meals. He moped at the dinner table. Two of his unmarried children were still living at home, and the situation was painful for everyone.

James's wife, Robin, was an outgoing, take-charge lady who held a part-time sales job in a clothing boutique. She decided the family couldn't go on this way, so she called for a family meeting.

As soon as everyone sat down together, 20-year-old James Jr. turned to his father and said, "Dad, we're upset. You're depressed. This is hard on you, but it's also hard on the rest of us."

"Yeah," chimed in daughter Jennifer. "Come on, Dad. You've got it in you. Mom loves you. You've got our love and support. Do you remember when you were a kid and you went to live with Aunt Sue? What did you do to help yourself then, Dad?"

James, surrounded by his loving family, recalled the crisis in which both of his parents were killed in a car accident. He remembered how, even though he was only 16, he had pulled himself together and gotten through it. He reminded himself that he was a survivor and that he could do it again.

To help the process along, James began keeping a daily journal. As he would recollect what he had done as a 16-year-old, he would slowly slide into his present situation. The journal initially was a tool for remembering his strengths, but eventually it grew into an anchor. He would use it to plan his days. He had always loved bicycling, and soon he became involved in a riding club. He remembered a long-lost interest in gardening and started a vegetable patch in his yard. Soon, he used his journal to plan trips with Robin on her days off.

The action orientation and the Protestant work ethic of Western culture that equate productivity with self-worth do little to prepare a man for the sudden transition of downsizing. Withdrawing from the work world is a major life adjustment that can be emotionally and physically destructive if you are unprepared for the transition. It's difficult to let go of what you know and endure the Nowhere Place of the in-between stage until you have latched on to a new reality.

But crisis can lead to constructive change. You can emerge from such a disaster with enriched self-awareness. As with James, suddenly losing your job can help you identify your coping style and tap into previously unrecognized strengths. Indeed, such a crisis can awaken your survival instincts.

Questions for Growth

YOUR PERSONAL COPING CAPACITY (PCC)

In Chapter 10, you looked back on the earlier years of your marriage for coping strategies you used when presented with a problem. Now do the same, but this time, like James, go back and examine difficult times in your life aside from your marriage. How did you cope? Write your answers in your journal. Now you have a record of your PCC, or Personal Coping Capacity. Use it! This is an especially important time to share information with your spouse.

Assessing Your Life's Work

Many men use their retirement transition to look back on their work lives and assess what they have achieved. And some ask themselves, "Was all that toil and turmoil worth my life's blood?"

Leaving work without a sense of accomplishment can deal a man a double blow. He may experience the loss of self-esteem, structure, and identity that all retirees face, but in addition, he may become stuck in anger or lost in depression. He enters retirement with a sense of unfinished business.

Aerospace systems analyst Kenneth was typical of the men who find themselves in this situation. For the first fifteen or twenty years, work was great for him, but more recently, it had lost much of its fascination. In his words:

> Work got routine, boring. There were cutbacks. And after the company was bought out in the late 1980s, the corporate climate changed drastically. It became rigid and no longer allowed for individual personalities or thought. My supervisors were into the bottom line. We were always in conflict.
>
> They offered me an early retirement package, and I accepted it, but then I got cold feet. . . . After a month, I asked them to rescind my request, and they agreed, but things went downhill at work after that. There was no challenging or interesting work. My supervisor gave me a lot of aggravation. There was one project that had my name on it, but they wouldn't let me do it. I must have ruffled some feathers. I'm outspoken, and I didn't tell them what they wanted to hear.
>
> I had foot surgery just before I retired. I guess you could say that I started off on the wrong foot. I didn't start on an active plane.

Although his retirement marriage differed from those of most of the men in my study, his work experience did not. Of the 75 percent of successfully adjusted men I researched who said they had enjoyed their careers, 40 percent complained that they were dissatisfied with it in the end. It had become tedious and stressful to them. And some men simply don't love their life's work. If they feel disappointed and unfulfilled in this arena, they may have many complex reactions to retirement, as Kenneth did. Despite his sense of accomplishment during the early years, Kenneth expressed many regrets as he looked back at his career.

> I feel I could have done a lot more. I wish I had made more of a name for myself. I wanted to leave a mark, to publish papers in the field, to contribute new knowledge. But that was a choice I made after I finished my master's degree at Cal Tech. I went into industry instead of academia. Part of me wanted to be a professor, but financial reasons dictated my direction. Also, I'm not sure I had the ability to do outstanding work. I should have pursued a Ph.D., but I was burned out when I finished college. . . . The things I regret doing, or not doing, bother me enormously. It's paralyzing.

Kenneth's unhappy termination and his many regrets have made for a difficult adjustment. However, dissatisfaction with work does not always predict a rocky retirement. As one respondent in my research put it, "Being unhappy at work was a wonderful preparation for retirement." This man couldn't wait to be "out of there!"

Questions for Growth	**REVISITING YOUR REMINISCENCE ON WORK LIFE**
	Earlier in this chapter there was an exercise on reminiscing on your work life. If you completed it, review your answers again. Ask yourself one final question: Was it worth it? Explain.

Retiring from Retirement

Some people, due to their economic needs, temperament, or desire for challenge, view work as central to their lives and, as did Richard, the venture capitalist, choose never to retire. Work can help to boost your morale. It can help you feel needed and important again.

In fact, if you're not already retired and know you want to continue working, consider creating a shadow career—a new career different from the one you have now—that uses your skills, interests, and lifelong experience. For instance, Paul, a retired high school counselor, loved flying. He got his pilot's license in his thirties and flew every weekend he could. He knew he wanted to do something with this skill after his retirement so he started teaching that which he loved best. He now works about half the time he used to and makes more than enough money. Such a shadow career might require planning, brushing up on old skills, or reestablishing your credentials before you begin.

Overcoming the Myths and Stereotypes about Aging

If you have already retired and then tried to go back to work, consider that returning to the workforce can be challenging because of the stereotypes and prejudices that may be imposed on you. These myths constitute ageism—prejudice against older people—and they definitely exist:

Myth: Older people don't produce much. They just want to leave the workforce and congregate in retirement communities.

Reality: Mandatory retirement and downsizing have forced many willing and capable workers out of jobs and, in a more subtle sense, discouraged them from seeking new employment.

Myth: Older employees are not as reliable or flexible as their younger peers.

Reality: Studies have shown that although older workers may take longer than younger people to learn new information, they often retain it longer. Statistics also support that older workers are absent less and have fewer accidents.

Myth: Older people become rigid in their thinking.

Reality: Adaptability and flexibility are lifelong traits and have absolutely nothing to do with age.

Myth: Old people are all the same.

Reality: Those who are middle-aged and above are the most diverse group socially, economically, and psychologically.

When you go for a job interview you may confront ageism, if not outright, then subtly. With a positive attitude, provide illustrations from your life to counter these myths. You might say, "I love backpacking and just returned from a two-week trek in the Sierras." Or, "In my last position I didn't take sick leave for three years running." Or, "At Acme, I initiated a new marketing strategy since the old way was unproductive."

Questions for Growth	**GETTING BACK INTO THE WORKFORCE**
	If you're considering reentering the world of work, you may find the answers to these questions helpful:
1.	Know yourself first. Ask yourself, what are my goals, needs, and desires? Feeling useful? Meeting people? Overcoming challenges? Additional income?
2.	Where are the good jobs?
3.	What skills and experiences do I have to offer?
4.	Do I want to work full-time, or would I rather work part-time and have more time for family, friends, and individual pursuits?
5.	How much responsibility am I willing to take on now?
6.	Will I need to retrain for what I want to do? Where can I get this training?

If your qualifications are not in demand or the job market is limited, it may be necessary to readjust your sights. Just as flexibility adds so positively to your retirement marriage, it also contributes greatly to your job search. Know that it may take many months before you find the right fit. You might expand the market for your skills by updating your qualifications. Retraining is a good way to do so.

Training programs are funded by federal and state governments, and the Private Industry Council allocates funds for on-the-job training programs. If you don't qualify, consider short-term adult education programs at local high schools or certificated programs at junior colleges. These are usually low in cost. Another option would be to go into business for yourself, market your skills, and become a consultant.

In all this you will need a positive attitude, flexibility, and emotional support from your spouse. Do not undertake this search unless both of you discuss what you want first and work out strategies for mutual support as well as strategies to confront the job market. "I," "You," and "Us" are still very much in play in all your endeavors, whether or not you are working.

Rehearsal for Women	GIVE YOUR SPOUSE EMOTIONAL SUPPORT DURING HIS JOB SEARCH

If you're sensitive to your partner's needs during his new job search, it will greatly benefit your marriage. But remember to take care of yourself and your needs too.

1. Be a good sounding board; listen to your spouse's hopes and concerns.

2. Be alert for highs and lows in his moods. If he's depressed or seems to drink excessively, steer him toward healthier coping. If his situation is severe, professional intervention may be necessary.

3. Set aside special time (maybe once a week) to review how the search is going. By doing this, you limit your spouse's need to explain and your tendency to become overly involved to the exclusion of other activities.

4. Money can loom high on the list of concerns. Together negotiate ways of constructing a livable budget—one that reduces the pressure on your spouse. Stay calm and rational regarding finances.

If you let it, retirement can be a second chance—an opportunity to do something new with your lives. Coming to terms with retirement means accepting the past and having a sense of the future. It means letting go and moving on. In successful retirement marriages, wives work with their husbands so that together they can move on to the next phase of their lives. They work together and grow together in the marriage. Consider retirement as an ending (as in the transition process), but also as a new beginning.

If you retire without meaningful activities to fill your needs, you are in danger of becoming depressed, resentful, or just a grumpy old man. But in my study, I found many couples who exemplified the ability to look forward and who possessed a great deal of flexibility. Their answer to the losses inherent in retirement was to find other involvements and activities that fulfilled their needs. You will discover many of their ideas plus additional exercises to help you satisfy unmet needs throughout the rest of this book.

CHAPTER 14

What Work and Retirement Mean to Women

When you're following your energy and doing what you want all the time, the distinction between work and play dissolves.
—Shakti Gawain, *Living in the Light*

IN EARLIER GENERATIONS, WOMEN at midlife would volunteer and become active in women's organizations after their children left home. Today, they continue working, go back to school, or start new careers.

Still, some of us hold the mistaken belief that work is less important to women than it is to men and that women are not as committed to it. This may be because some women have had less continuity in their working lives, stopping at different points to raise children and deal with other family responsibilities. But the fact is that many married couples approaching retirement are dual-wage earners. (According to the Bureau of Labor Statistics, in 1995, 72 percent of married women aged 45 to 54 were in the labor force, while 45 percent of married women aged 55 to 64 were.) Just as with men, work and retirement have profound meaning for women.

Working women are usually more satisfied with their lives than their stay-at-home counterparts. Not surprisingly, they have less positive attitudes toward retirement. As with men, work has become the stage upon which they play out their need to achieve status—a stage that society did not provide elsewhere.

As I mentioned above, however, women's paid work activities move in more irregular patterns. In both working-class and middle-class intact families, the general pattern is for a woman to work for a short time after she finishes high school or her undergraduate degree. She stops to marry and have children, but as they grow, she resumes part-time work to supplement her husband's income. And when the children leave home, she may go back to school, get some training, or take a full-time job.

Married professional women experience different career patterns. In fact, four paths are common:

1. **Regular.** The woman pursues her career immediately after graduation with no interruptions throughout her married life.

2. **The interrupted career.** The woman begins as above but stops for several years for child-rearing. Later she resumes her career.

3. **Second career.** She starts a new career after the children leave.

4. **The modified second career.** She starts her training while the children are still at home but often works full-time after they leave.

Even though there is less continuity in their working lives, women often do return to and stay in the workforce for numerous reasons. Financial advantage can be one of them. For instance, a woman who reenters the workforce at 45 and earns a salary of $30,000 can expect Social Security benefits of $535 if she retires at 62, but she would collect $1,102 in benefits if she waits until age 70 to retire.

Money isn't the only factor influencing women to return to work. Other motivators include alleviating loneliness or boredom, building friendships (especially important to women), and looking to fulfill newfound interests.

Even though this new entry or reentry into the workforce can be revitalizing to a woman, if she is needed at home to care for an ailing husband or parent she may be expected to quit and tend to family needs first.

Rehearsal | PIE CHART OF A WIFE'S DIFFERENT ROLES

Women play many roles in their lives. Earlier, I asked your husband to construct a pie chart of the different roles he plays. This is your chance to do the same.

1. List the many roles you play in your life.

2. Draw a circle.

3. Mark off the wedges of the pie to correspond to the percentage of time and energy you devote to this role, and write in the roles.

4. Now, compare your chart with your husband's. Discuss the differences. Does this lead to any new insights?

Rehearsal | TRYING ON NEW HATS

Are there any new roles you would like to add? If so, use the following questions to help you:

1. What games did you play as a child? Pick one you especially liked. What you enjoyed then will give you clues for the future.

2. What did you do in the game? Who did you play with?

3. How can you transpose that to your life today?

4. Share your findings with your spouse.

5. Put together an action plan:

   ◆ What is the goal you want to accomplish?

   ◆ What/who will help you attain this goal?

   ◆ What/who will get in the way?

   ◆ What is your plan of action?

Women and Retirement

As we have seen, you may have more options as to how you organize your life: you may have sacrificed work for marriage and children, marriage and children for work, alternated your focus, or juggled all three. You may hold many roles at once, sliding into varying functions as a wife, mother, employee/employer, friend, empty nester, caregiver, volunteer. And generally, even if you have devoted yourself to a career, you may have social networks in place outside your work life. If things are going poorly in one arena, you may have several others to turn to for positive self-esteem.

The fact is, you have probably experienced many mini-retirements from your various roles along the way, as when your children went off to college or when you relinquished care for an elderly parent who died. It is safe to say, therefore, that retirement may pose a less devastating blow to you than to your husband.

However, many wives in my research have expressed negative expectations about their impending retirements. Consistently, they voiced fears of potential loneliness, boredom, feeling unappreciated, and generally being at loose ends. As one respondent explained, "I don't think I could be as happy if I retired. I don't have hobbies. I would drive my husband crazy. I need the structure!"

My findings certainly contradict popular notions that retirement is a problem for men only. In fact, retirement can be seen as devastating to some and mixed for others. Only a few anticipate it positively. Most said that unattained goals, high job satisfaction, financial insecurity, and good health were reasons for their negative expectations.

Another study found that a person's health and the family's finances were less important to a woman's adaptation to retirement than the adjustment to retirement of her spouse. This finding speaks volumes on the importance of both partners' adapting successfully and supports my conclusions that active retired husbands with high morale make an especially positive contribution to the retirement marriage.

You Work, He Doesn't

It used to be that a husband retired to spend the rest of his days with a wife who had been a homemaker for most of her life. Today, however, wives are beginning or continuing to work long after their husbands retire. And their numbers are growing. A University of Michigan study of 813 married women in their fifties and sixties whose husbands were retired found that 45 percent of these wives still worked—most full-time—and their numbers have climbed from 36.3 percent in 1980. Add to this the fact that the number of men in the workforce is declining—in 1980, 75.4 percent of married men aged 55 to 64 were working, whereas in 1996, it was down to 70.2 percent—and you will find that roles are reversing when it comes to labor force participation in this age group.

In 1994 I conducted a study dealing with the wife working while the husband was retired. I called it "She Works/He Doesn't." The wives in my study offered the following benefits of their continuing to work:

- The social aspects—being with people
- Productivity
- Heightened self-esteem from accomplishments at work
- Earning power
- The challenges that work provided
- An end to boredom: "Having somewhere to go and something to do"

Only three out of thirty women mentioned getting away from their retired husbands as a reason to go to work!

In most cases, a wife's working had a positive impact on the retirement marriage. The overall feeling was that if a woman felt fulfilled and generally pleased with herself and her work, that would filter, in a positive way, into the marital relationship. In fact, many respondents made comments such as, "If I'm happy then he's happy." Or, "I'm a fulfilled person so my marriage is better than ever." And, "We're not joined at the hip twenty-four hours a day, and that's good!"

Some even suggested that their marriages improved with their husband's retirement and their continuing to work. "My husband's retirement has been an advantage for me," one woman told me. "He's taking over things I didn't want to do anymore. He really enjoys doing all the marketing and cooking, and it's a relief for me. He's more relaxed, and I can play more."

In almost all instances in my research, husbands shared in the household tasks. A recurring theme among respondents was "I don't care if I ever cook again. I'm thrilled my husband has taken over the kitchen!" And, "It's his kitchen. I cooked for twenty-five years and that's long enough!" Several, nevertheless, voiced some resentment regarding their husband's intruding on their shopping and cooking domains. "He has control now," one woman told me with some chagrin. In spite of this, however, these wives said they were willing to relinquish the chores because work took so much of their time.

Research has shown that a husband's helping with housework is vital to a couple's happiness, especially if his wife works and he is retired. For example, in a study of two thousand married men and women regarding their retirement marriage, the lowest level of satisfaction was reported by working wives of retired husbands, and the reasons cited for this dissatisfaction had to do with the husband's lack of participation in household tasks.

PART FIVE

Managing Shifting Needs in Your Retirement Marriage

A S YOU CONSIDER HOW TO MAKE a smooth transition, know that in addition to the Seven Marital Themes, activity, diversity, and connection are important to you individually and as a couple.

♦ *Activity.* The couples in my study took part in many activities—especially the husbands, who often engaged in three to five hobbies. These contributed to filling basic needs and gave meaning to their lives.

♦ *Diversity.* It's essential to have a mix of activities and people in your life. Keep in touch with people of various age groups, economic backgrounds, ethnicities, and religions. Create a balance in family, community, social contacts, meeting your physical and spiritual needs, couple life, learning, and your own individual pursuits.

♦ *Connection.* Being linked to others brings deep meaning to our lives.

Keep in mind however, that all of these issues are often played out against a backdrop of differences in how you and your spouse view your retirement marriage. Each marriage is, in fact, two marriages: the wife's view and the husband's view.

Several studies of couple's attitudes toward a husband's retirement have found that wives often hold a more negative perception of the various issues affecting the marriage than their husbands, who generally report a more positive perspective. In contrast, the couples in my study concurred in their view of various aspects of their retirement experience. Mine was a different population, however. These were couples who identified themselves as happy. The expectation was that they would agree on many aspects of their relationship, and they did.

In general, high expectations are a good thing. Teachers who expect more from their students usually get it. Partners who have higher expectations of each other tend to get them met too. It's an "if-you-expect-it-it-will-come" mentality. But I believe that in the long term, especially in retirement marriage, you need to revise your expectations. Keeping up unrealistic expectations harms the relationship and prevents your moving on. Remember the unchangeables.

Are you really expecting your spouse to change after thirty-five or forty years of marriage? Perhaps you can't change his or her behavior, but you can change your attitude toward it. Yes, I'm recommending a revision of your attitude toward acceptance. It was evident that this shift in attitude occurred in the marriages I studied, and the relationships were all the better for it!

CHAPTER 15

Turf Tiffs, Time Zones, and Chore Wars

It is one of the most beautiful compensations of life that no man can sincerely try to help another without helping himself.

—William Shakespeare

Dear John:

For six months I have been meaning to write this letter, but after today's scene at the market it can't wait. We've been married for thirty-eight years now, and I thought I knew you. Not so. Since your retirement, I find I am living with a different man, one who is driving me crazy.

Frankly, darling, I don't think you're aware of how you have changed and how the many things that are happening at home are driving me up the wall. Let me enumerate:

1. Every time you come to the market with me, you tell me what I can and cannot buy. I suspect you're probably trying to be helpful, but understand that for thirty-eight years I have done the shopping; I know how to pick quality items for the lowest price. Today when you made a big scene over the price of

tomatoes, I almost died from embarrassment. I'm not one of your clerks at the office.

2. I like to work in my sewing room at night, but you've decided to go in there during the day, push my sewing aside and pile up my table with your papers—I want my space!

3. I have my piano lessons two nights a week. It has been that way for a year now but you get that forlorn look every time I walk out the door, and do I ever feel guilty. I don't like that feeling. You never used to care—in fact, last year you encouraged me to take lessons.

4. You promised to share some of the housework now that you're not working and I'm still in the office full-time. Actually, John, you vacuumed and took out the garbage for one week—that was it. The other night I tripped over the garbage can, and trash spilled all over the kitchen floor.

5. When I suggest that we go to see the grandchildren or even go out with friends, it's always "NO!" Frankly, I'm frustrated.

I can see that your retirement has not been the happiest time in your life, but we're having problems. Don't you think we should talk?

With love . . . still,

Your wife

No question about it. John's wife felt that her space was being impinged upon and her efficient running of the house questioned; she felt guilty for pursuing her regular activities, overwhelmed with responsibilities for housework, and saddened by her husband's general dependency and depression. This letter represents a composite of the comments I have heard from many wives who have come to my "For Better or for Worse . . ." retirement workshops. Managing the shift from work to home turf is truly a challenge, but one that can be overcome.

The couples in my study of successful retirement marriages held a distinctly different view. Here is a typical response:

It's the togetherness. I've never been happier in my life, and I know he's the center of that. It's almost too good to be true. This is my nirvana. He's home, and I have my children and my grandchildren here. My cup runneth over!

Apparently, this couple was doing something right. In the remaining chapters, I will highlight many of the findings from my study of successful couples such as this one. I hope that their actions, feelings, and views of each other and their marriage will help point the way toward a more fulfilling marriage for you.

Turf Tiffs

Many of the women in my workshops have asked me, "Betty, how can I maintain my privacy and still be intimate with my spouse?" In reality, they are wondering, How do I rebalance the "I," "You," and "Us" now that he's home?

Wives of retired husbands often describe their experience in terms of impingement, which refers to someone moving into their space, or trespassing. We all have a deep-seated human need to maintain zones of solitude—areas labeled "Private"—for our psychological as well as physical well-being. This personal space helps to protect our integrity, our sense of self. If the "I" feels impinged upon, the "You" and the "Us" will fly right out the window.

Many unhappy wives in my workshops feel that their husbands' retirement has impinged on their domain, limited their privacy, and disrupted their routines. As one woman told me, "I resented his being home. This was the first time in my life that I could do what I wanted." Research studies have shown that women often feel they must reorganize their routines to accommodate their newly retired spouses.

Traditionally, the wife's domain has been the interior of the house, while everything outside—the garage, garden, lawn, and automobiles—were considered under the husband's control. But more than ever as we move into our retirement years, we understand that this notion of "my house" and "your garage" will not work. Space issues must be renegotiated at this time so that the marriage is not mired in turf wars. Indeed, one of the paramount tasks any wife faces is the incorporation of her husband into the activities of the home.

What can we learn from the successes of the well-adjusted couples in my study? Some prepared in advance by allocating bedroom space for offices and other private areas. One couple converted two of their four bedrooms into individual offices. They claimed to have so much space, they had to check on each other periodically during the day to see who was home. "We respect each other's privacy," the husband said. "If she sees me involved in something, she leaves me alone and I do the same for her." Another couple shared a home office. "We have a similar way of doing things," the wife told me. "There is a lot of clutter, which is fine for both of us." Another husband created his own computer room. That greatly helped both spouses and allowed the wife to pursue her own activities without guilt.

When couples did not plan for any physical changes in the house, there was still a sense of "not stepping on the other's toes," of respecting each other's need for privacy. And most of these couples were aware that the physical changes brought about by the husband's retirement did not affect their general comfort with each other.

Sometimes, however, circumstances dictate other responses. The following account dramatically illustrates how, with her husband's serious illness, one wife decided to become more accepting of the impingement on her space and how she paid more attention to the "You" in her relationship:

> After my husband's illness was diagnosed, all my space and privacy left. With all the visits to the doctors, we were together day and night. We were always in the same room at the same time. Sometimes I felt like I was smothered. This created a lot of conflict because I didn't want to leave him; I was so fearful that I would regret it. We eventually worked this out and now have our own spaces where we do our own work. What helped was some brief counseling and both reading every self-help book we could get our hands on. Now, I think about the value of the person rather than my separate likes and dislikes.

Nevertheless, all of these middle- and upper-middle-class couples owned their own homes, and except for two, none had anyone else living with them. Their houses had from three to five bedrooms and, in most cases, plenty of room to spread out. This suggests that adequate space could be a prerequisite for avoiding the feeling of impingement after retirement.

CREATING BLUEPRINTS FOR UNDERSTANDING

In order to avoid "turf tiffs," you need to engage in "turf conversations." Do this exercise separately first, and then share.

1. *The way it is.* How are the rooms divided in your house now? Do the two of you use all the rooms equally? If not, which rooms does one of you use solely and which do you both use? On a sheet of paper, draw a simple diagram of all the floors in your home, marking off each room, and label each as: "wife," "husband," or "both."

2. *The way you want it to be.* On a separate sheet of paper, make the same diagram, but this time ask yourselves: What is my ideal setup? How would I like the rooms to be used? Label them. If you plan on adding a room, draw it and designate who will be using it.

3. *Share your drawings.* Discuss what changes, if any, you would each like to make. Use your communication and negotiation skills to come to an understanding of how to reorient your joint and separate spaces.

Time Zones

> We were thrown together twenty-four hours a day—I was jumping out of my skin. Every time I saw him, everything he said annoyed me. I wanted to run out of the house screaming!

In retirement there is often less you and me and more us and we. Togetherness can be wonderful, but not when it's constant and you have no time for yourself. Studies have shown that the diminished freedom of movement and time affects wives of retired husbands more than any other problem. This is true especially of wives who work part-time or not at all. They often feel honor-bound to interrupt their own routines and be available for their husbands. If they take time for themselves, their spouse's sadness, anger, and hostility might surface, and that could prompt guilt and resentment.

Sometimes you can create a closed system that involves just the two of you. This encourages survival but not the flowering that would exist if you maintained a Growth Circle in which you both allowed for change and incorporating others. A closed system can emerge from feelings such as "Nothing is forever; we may not have many years left together," "All we have now is each other," "For the first time my husband really needs me," "No matter what happens we can still rely on each other," or "We're terrified of being alone." Two people grasping each other so tightly do not support each other, however—they smother.

Avoid the Dance of Guilt

Just like having personal space, time on your own is essential for your well-being. In fact, the sense of being stifled usually causes one of the spouses to rebel or start a fight. This can result in guilt. In most instances, guilt takes two: the instigator (the person feeling rejected) and the accused (the one who needs more space). If you are the accused, you can stop the process cold by refusing to feel guilty. Many times it's as simple as that. Try as hard as he can, your husband can't make you feel guilty without your cooperation. Saying no can be the ultimate self-care. So, say no to playing this negative game.

What is your role now—caretaker; martyr; deserter; guilt-ridden, angry woman? Actually, none of the above if you don't want it to be. Consider the following scenarios about taking time for yourself:

Scenario 1

Sally: How do you feel about my meeting Nancy tomorrow for a day at the museum?

Arthur: *(looking sad)* Weren't we going to the beach for lunch?

Sally: *(feeling guilty and lying)* Oh no, I thought that was Wednesday.

Arthur: *(with resignation)* Oh, all right. Go . . . have fun. I'll read.

Sally: A. *(disappointed, angry, and martyred)* I don't want you to be alone. Since I promised you tomorrow, I'll stick to my promise.

B. *(avoiding, lying)* Come to think of it, I'd rather go
with you tomorrow.

C. *(guilty, guilty, guilty)* I'm going!

Scenario 2

Sally: Arthur, I'm meeting Nancy tomorrow for lunch and the
show at the museum; I'll be home by five.

Arthur: *(looking sad)* Weren't we going to the beach for lunch?

Sally: *(calmly)* We started to talk about it, Arthur, but we never
decided. Nancy located some hard-to-find tickets, and I really
want to see this exhibit. Let's have a special day on Wednesday.
We'll plan it together over dinner tonight.

Arthur: *(brightening)* Sounds good.

In the first scenario Sally was asking permission based on her feelings of guilt, anger, and entrapment. She and Arthur became embroiled
in an unproductive exchange in which she was playing "I'll give up my
good time and be a martyr, but I'll be angry and resentful" to his "Poor
me; take care of me. Can't you see I need you?" As Scenario 2 points out,
however, it's unnecessary to replay that old tape. Sally took charge. She
let her desires be known, but she was also aware of Arthur's feelings. She
took care of the "I," the "You," and the "Us." There was no need for
lying, guilt, or anger. Arthur, of course, knew how to push Sally's guilt
buttons, but she had learned how to be assertive and resist the pressure.

If your husband accuses or blames in the name of love, putting you
on the defensive in terms of where you are going and what you are
doing, you can still go on with your plans; you don't need permission. If
he rants and raves, move to another room. If he continues, you may
consider confronting him assertively and honestly. You might say: "I
can't stand your bossiness. It makes me unhappy. What can we both do
to make this situation better?"

Use the conflict resolution guidelines in Chapter 9. However, it's
important for you to remember: It is beyond your capacity to be everything, to replace all that your husband has lost by retiring.

Other Useful Strategies

When I asked the couples in my study about what strategies they used to
help in their comfort level with the matter of time, they suggested the
following:

◆ "We just tell each other where we are going, and if I'm late I pick up the phone and call. We're considerate of each other's time."

◆ "We spend more nights apart now because each of us goes to the condo alone. The condo represents rejuvenation to me, and he tells me it's variety for him. It really helps us keep our individuality."

◆ "We each have our own activities during the day and get together at night. Now, we play more bridge together, which has greatly helped our communication!"

◆ "We work together one day and one day we work separately at the bookstore. There's a new balance; I never feel lonely. It's wonderful how we fell into this perfect balance with time."

Paradoxically, the prospect of spending a great deal of time together over the years can ease the conflicts in long-term marriages. All of that togetherness can create the need to cooperate, negotiate, and just generally get along for survival's sake. This may be a time for both of you to mellow out.

Rehearsal | TIME CARD FOR SUCCESS

This is another exercise for the two of you to do first separately and then to share. On the basis of each day starting at 8 A.M. and ending at 10 P.M. (14 hours), fill in the following chart or make a copy of it, noting how much time you spend together each day, and how much time you spend apart:

Day of the Week	Time Together	Time Apart
Monday		
Tuesday		
Wednesday		
Thursday		
Friday		
Saturday		
Sunday		

TOTAL HOURS: Together _____   Apart _____

Add up the number of hours you are with your spouse and the number of hours you are independent (at work, having alone time, or with others). Are you happy with the alone and together time? If not, what would you like to change? Now share your list with your spouse. You may find it interesting to see how you have each evaluated the time you spend together and separately. If either or both of you are displeased with the time aspects of your relationship, negotiate for some changes.

Chore Wars

She said: "I felt he was too young to retire and that it was unfair that he did nothing while I worked."

He said: "I started to do some cooking and more housework. That made for less tension, and the relationship started to smooth out a lot."

The comments above speak to the fact that working wives are more upset with their husband's retirement when the men shirk household tasks. Unfortunately, the ideal may rarely be reached. Previous research has found that regardless of whether the husband and wife retire or just the husband (with the wife still on the job), men maintain the same level of involvement in housework after retirement as before. That is, in general, they don't do much.

However, in my study of happily retired couples, 60 percent of the husbands helped more with chores. One wife told me: "I did everything before my husband's retirement. After he retired, he took over shopping and meals, and he loved it. I was still working, so I enjoyed coming home to a prepared meal. Sometimes though, we try to push off the cooking and shopping on the other person. At first he didn't know where the kitchen was; I think all of this has been an adventure for him."

Forty percent of the couples in my study, however, reported no change after retirement. In some cases where there was a traditional marriage, the wife continued to do the housework and accepted it as one of her duties. In other cases, the husband had always helped and continued to do so. As one husband told me, "We always shared the housework. I would bathe the kids, feed and play with them. My son does the same with his kids. I don't know, maybe I was a good role model as a father."

In analyzing the strategies these couples used to deal with changes in housework, the theme that emerges is caring and cooperation. This attitude drove the couples' behavior. As one husband told me, "I have a change in attitude. I used to believe it was 50–50; now I believe it's 100–100. You see something that needs to be done and you do it."

The importance of a husband's participation in household tasks cannot be overstated. It is one of the major contributors to a sense of well-being and fulfillment in a retirement marriage. It also demonstrates the husband's willingness in changing roles—something that serves him well as he ages. In fact, wives whose husbands share in these chores report more positive feelings regarding their men and feel there is more equity in their relationship in general. So, husbands, you can see that helping with the housework is a smart move! As one husband told me, "I filled in the time I missed from work with taking over many of the household duties—shopping, cooking, vacuuming, and doing some house repairs. I help with the heavy things because she has a bad back. I know she appreciates my help."

In my research, the household tasks most often performed by husbands, in descending order of frequency, were loading and unloading the dishwasher; taking out the garbage; vacuuming, washing floors, and moving heavy items; shopping; clearing dishes from the table; and cooking.

The happy couples in my study agreed unanimously that their marriages were equitable—there was a sense of fairness—and this emerged from the sharing of household tasks. One couple, for instance, felt they were also having more fun. "Thirty years ago there was great inequity," the wife told me. "Now we both feel it's 50–50. Sometimes we act like children, we play little games; whoever is first out of bed has to get the paper, . . . it's really fun. We don't resent the other. Life should be fun."

Another wife equated her changing views of equity with the shifts in society:

> I was indoctrinated to believe that fairness was a woman doing 95 percent of the chores. This was the way of the world, despite my college education and my psychology courses. It bothered me, but I did it anyway. I even made all my own

clothes. In those days who would consider that a husband should do anything around the house? But I was ahead of my time. In my mind this wasn't the way it should be. I accepted it physically but not mentally and just shoved it aside. Now, I don't shove it aside because I've realized that the world has changed and so have I. I'm not the person I used to be, and our relationship is better for it. We really share now.

Rehearsal

NAVIGATING HOUSEHOLD CHORES

Who does what in your house? Are you pleased with the arrangement? If not, it's time to talk and negotiate.

1. Arrange for a special time to talk about these issues. Listen to each other, be respectful, and be careful about demands.

2. List all the household chores, both inside and outside your home.

3. Analyze your list. Draw two columns, one marked "Husband" and the other marked "Wife," next to your list. Each of you can write "okay," "don't mind," or "hate" next to each of the chores.

4. Parcel out the "okays"—they're easy.

5. You'll now have to negotiate your "don't minds" and "hates." Make offers and counteroffers. Use the following strategies:

   ◆ Take turns doing unpopular chores.

   ◆ "Tit for tat." Barter and trade. You might say, "I'll do the vacuuming (which you hate) if you'll wash the car (which I hate)."

   ◆ One of you does it all one week and the other does it all the next week.

6. If you still disagree, review your list. This time, discuss your relationship and what is important. Stress that the

chores are an expression of working together for the benefit of both of you.

7. After you've reached an agreement on who will do what when, chart it and post it. This can defuse misunderstandings.

8. Review your arrangement on a regular basis, maybe once a month.

CHAPTER 16

Meaningful Activities

We must forget what is behind. If we cease to originate, we are lost. We can only keep what we have, by new activity.

—William Ellery Channing

EIGHT MONTHS HAD PASSED since Gene's retirement. He and his wife had taken their ideal vacation; he had read all the books that had languished on the shelf for years; he had created his dream garden; and now, he looked around and thought, "What next?" He missed the phone calls from other salesmen, the lunches with his co-workers, the excitement of closing a big deal. There was definitely something wrong.

The activities in which Gene was involved were not meeting his needs. His need to belong and his sense of self were especially challenged since they had generally been met in the workplace. Yes, gardening allowed Gene a measure of creativity, but who was around to recognize and appreciate it besides his wife? Clearly, he wanted more.

According to many studies, meaningful activity is good for your health. Research by the MacArthur Foundation into successful aging found that those who continue to engage in productive activities are physically and psychologically healthier. In my study of fulfilled couples, retired husbands were somewhat more involved (with three to five hobbies each) and had more varied interests than their wives. This underscores one of the study's findings: active husbands with high morale contribute positively to the successful retirement marriage. To paraphrase Mae West, "It's not the man in my life, it's the life in my man" that seems most important. Engaging in meaningful activities promotes the well-being of the individual, and consequently the marriage benefits.

Activities for Self-Fulfillment

The following are general activities that can provide meaning in your life:

- ◆ *Self-expression/personal development.* Creative crafts, gardening, writing, playing an instrument, acting.
- ◆ *Participation.* Volunteering within the community at hospitals, libraries, schools.
- ◆ *Recognition.* Being of service, sitting on a nonprofit board, running for political office, becoming head of an organization. Feelings of accomplishment and the ability to influence others affect our lives enormously.
- ◆ *Adventure/new experiences.* Traveling, swapping homes, revisiting your birthplace, trying new activities, taking risks.
- ◆ *Learning.* Community, technical, and junior college classes, as well as your local university; learning-in-retirement institutes such as Elderhostels; senior centers.
- ◆ *Contemplation.* Meditation, walks in the woods, listening to music, peace and quiet.
- ◆ *Pleasure:* Being with friends, having fun at whatever one enjoys.
- ◆ *Relaxation and recreation.* Sports of all kinds. Unfortunately, the television is the most frequently indulged-in form of recreation.

Questions for Growth	**WHAT DID YOU LOVE TO DO?**
	The work ethic still predominates in our culture. We even have less vacation time than workers in many other countries. When you work so hard and long, it's easy to lose sight of what you used to love or look forward to doing. Retirement offers you the opportunity to rediscover what really turned you on.

What will you do with so much unstructured time now? How can you carve out some meaning in this new phase of your life? In the mode of kind teacher and willing student, take turns interviewing each other. Ask the following questions:

1. What were you interested in when you were 15 or 20? What activities or hobbies were you most enthusiastic about?

2. Name at least three activities—sports, skills, crafts, work, studying a musical instrument or a foreign language— that you always wanted to do.

3. Here's a heavy-duty question to put you in touch with the march of time: If you knew you had just three years to live, what would you most like to do in the time remaining?

Your answers will give you a composite of what you really value—of what constitutes your passion. Think about doing at least one of the activities that you loved years ago.

Try Volunteering

Nate worked in the construction industry for thirty-seven years. He managed a crew of 150 and derived great satisfaction from building beautiful homes and working with excellent craftspeople, with whom he always maintained good rapport. When his company merged with another, he was let go. Understandably, he felt cast adrift. At 59, he was still strong and capable, and hardly ready for retirement. When he found other work in his field with lower pay and responsibility, he became dissatisfied to the point of depression. Work no longer held fulfillment or meaning for him.

Nate loved to play tennis. Seeing how unhappy he was, his wife, Janice, suggested he teach other children to play tennis just as he had his own kids. He contacted a youth organization on the east side of town where there were economically disadvantaged families and offered free instruction to any youngster who came to the tennis court. Word got around that he was a patient and skilled teacher, and more and more children joined his classes. Eventually, he expanded his reach and began teaching physically and mentally challenged kids as well.

Soon, the demand became so great that Nate quit his unfulfilling job. His finances were in relatively good shape, and he was getting so much out of teaching. "I love working with kids," he told me. "They are so appreciative. I feel like I'm back again at my old job—doing something I love and being appreciated for it."

Volunteering is a wonderful way to engage in activities that fulfill your needs and help others. It offers you the opportunity to:

- Create structure, purpose, and meaning in your life
- Make new friends
- Develop new skills
- Use your inherent talents
- Work with a respected community organization
- See positive results from your efforts

You could volunteer if you have an interest in solving a particular problem (such as helping battered women or eliminating illiteracy), have a special skill as Nate did, or if you've had negative experiences in the workplace and want to offset them with positive volunteer experiences.

Jerry also found satisfaction in volunteering. He had been the manager of the produce section of a large supermarket for many years. He had enjoyed donating day-old vegetables to neighborhood groups for the needy. When he retired at 68, he, too, was at loose ends. He read a lot, swam, and exercised at the gym twice a week with friends. But it wasn't enough. He had enjoyed his work immensely, and these leisure activities did not fill his need to interact with people, manage projects, and feel that he was doing good.

Shopping one day at the market, he ran into the director of one of the neighborhood charities that had benefited from his giving. She told Jerry how much he was missed and how his donations had helped the agency in times of need. A light went on in Jerry's head. He contacted his former boss and, through him, other stores in the grocery chain that were willing to cooperate and give food to the needy—food that would otherwise be discarded. Other food chains cooperated, and soon Jerry found himself collecting large amounts of food. He asked a friend to donate an old warehouse where all the supplies were stored. Religious groups, homeless and battered women's shelters, and soup kitchens came to this warehouse each day to pick up food.

"I gave away over four million dollars' worth of food last year," Jerry told me proudly. "That's a lot of food, and it takes up most of my days. You can see all the plaques on my walls, the letters from grateful people. Yes, they are important, but even if I didn't get one plaque or one letter, I would still be so happy. The most important thing is that I get so much satisfaction out of what I'm doing. I love to help people; it makes me feel good. I'm not one to express myself well. I just know that this giving fills my days with so much meaning. It gives me a reason to get up every morning."

Both Nate and Jerry exemplify the enormous rewards of giving through volunteering. Their generosity made their lives meaningful; they felt needed and could see the benefits of their giving—payment enough.

Life takes on meaning when you can give back to others and also when you can reflect on your past and see that what you had to offer was valued. Volunteering is certainly an avenue to explore for self-fulfillment during retirement.

AARP has a national volunteer referral service, the Volunteer Talent Bank. You put your name, skills, interests, time availability, and location in their data bank, and they match you with appropriate volunteer opportunities. Call 1-202-434-3219 for a registration packet.

RSVP (Retired Seniors in Volunteer Programs) has offices in most U.S. cities. After an initial interview, this organization will match you with programs throughout your community. You might work with children, management, mentoring, tutoring, food banks, and much more, according to your skills, interests, and free time. This program is designed to meet community needs in schools, hospitals, libraries, day-care centers, and the courts.

SCORE (Service Corps of Retired Executives) is a national network sponsored by the Small Business Administration. Retired executives counsel those starting up their own businesses. Your lifetime of business experience can be put to good use. You can contact SCORE through your local chamber of commerce.

There are also senior and recreation centers and libraries that provide volunteer opportunities. Or you might be interested in programs that train paraprofessionals as counselors for those in the community who can't afford to pay for services.

Check the phone book. Look under Elder Services, Volunteer Opportunities. Elder Care Locator is a way to find community assistance for seniors. It will put you in touch with local or state area agencies on aging for volunteer purposes. The toll-free number is 1-800-677-1116. Of course, there's always the library. Your reference librarian will have many resources for you.

Some cities have Leisure Counseling services. These are private agencies or individuals who can help you identify your skills and interests and point you toward volunteer opportunities in your community that could really put your expertise to use.

Rehearsal	**MOVING TOWARD MEANINGFUL ACTIVITIES**
1.	From the "What Did You Love to Do?" exercise, make a list of those activities that you really loved as a youngster.
2.	Looking at the resources mentioned earlier, pick several agencies. Call and inquire about steps to take that would use your talents. It's a great beginning.

Activities for the Two of You

What about activities that have meaning for the two of you? The happy couples in my study visited grandchildren; socialized with friends; traveled; entertained; attended church or synagogue activities; read together; went to the movies; played cards; attended the theater, concerts, and classes; led groups; danced; worked on home decorating projects; and cooked together.

One couple established a new business together based on their mutual love of books. "We always wanted to own a mom-and-pop bookstore," Doug told me, "one where local people could come and chat, where we could offer groups to talk about the books that our customers read. It wasn't easy getting the money together or finding just the right location, but we stayed with our dream, and now it has come true."

In a recent issue of *Fortune* magazine, James Conaway profiled five retired couples who initially thought they would take it easy, travel some, and just settle into their new routines when they left the world of work. That didn't happen. Instead, these couples had that all-important communication—what I call a Relationship Review of what was most meaningful to both of them—and then set new goals for themselves. They are now all relishing their achievements.

One bought some land in California's Napa Valley and started a small vineyard. It was a struggle, but now they are enjoying their new lifestyle with beauty all around them and the opportunity to see their nine grandchildren on a regular basis. The wife of another couple pursued her childhood passion of fly-fishing. She began teaching it to other women, making presentations at trade shows, and publishing a newsletter. Eventually her husband got involved in this new career. Now, they are both enjoying this activity, getting out in nature and meeting many new and interesting people.

Questions for Growth	**WHAT DO WE ENJOY DOING TOGETHER?**
	Just like the couples mentioned earlier, you too might develop a meaningful "new career" that you enjoy engaging in together. Discuss the following:
1.	Review your individual lists of interests compiled for the last two exercises.
2.	Are any of your individual interests similar to those of your spouse? Identify your common interests and goals.
3.	Pick two or three that are the most interesting and feasible for the two of you to engage in together.
4.	Look at ways to make at least one of your choices a reality.

The Importance of Family and Friends during Retirement

Do not protect yourself by a fence, but rather by your friends.

— Czech Proverb

KEEPING BUSY IS NOT THE BE-ALL and end-all of successful retirement. The feeling of connectedness to others is essential to your lives and your marriage. Many studies reaffirm the buffering effects of positive social ties on the negative daily events that affect our lives. And the MacArthur Foundation found that regular physical activity, resiliency, and continued social connections contribute to successful aging. Emotional support from family and friends contributes to a better self-image and also results in better physical functioning and lowered blood levels of stress-induced hormones that can promote disease.

Your marriage can benefit from outside relationships. For example, Jane's husband, Lee, suffered from diabetes. He had to adhere strictly to his diet, exercise, and medication regimens in order to remain stabilized. Lee engaged in a lot of self-care, but his illness also required Jane's time and attention. Her close friendship with Clara helped to ease some of the stress she experienced as a result of the many demands Lee's illness had placed on her individually and on them as a couple.

Approximately 60 percent of the couples in my study said they were very involved with their immediate family—children and grandchildren. Many saw or spoke with them on a daily basis. Even though some couples claimed they were equally involved, by all appearances, the wife, more than the husband, maintained closer connections with the immediate family.

As one wife explained, "We see our family all the time. Our home is the center of all the family's entertainment." And a husband reiterated, "I've always been the disciplinarian. I'm not involved the same way my wife is; I'm more involved with the decision making in regard to the kids. Actually, I did more with my children before retirement because I had more money then."

Sometimes however, the wives in my study, in their eagerness to be all things to all people, felt pulled in too many directions. One woman told me:

> I had too many demands from my children and my grand-
> children; it took time away from my husband. I was trying to
> walk a fine line between being there for my husband and my
> children—making everybody and me happy at the same
> time: that was my goal. I would say to myself, "Mommy has
> done this for years; Mommy has fought the good fight in her
> career and was happy doing that and now it is my turn."
> That is probably my biggest problem—trying to make every-
> body happy; it's a battle, and I'm winning it!

About one-third of the husbands in my research interacted with their families more since retirement. As one man told me, "I'm passionately in love with my kids. Since I've retired, I'm spending more time with them during the day and also traveling with them from time to time."

In contrast, however, 40 percent stated they had moderate to little involvement with their immediate kin because their children lived out of town or because there was some trouble with the relationship. In some cases, my research subjects expressed sadness about their noninvolvement but, by all appearances, this did not seem to greatly affect their adjustment to retirement or the quality of their marriage. If anything, they appeared to exhibit more reliance on each other and widened their circle of friends with no apparent damage to their marital satisfaction.

It's a Two-Way Street

Your grown children can be affected by your retirement as well, especially if you relocate to another city. In that case, you could call them *retirement orphans*. Your kids may simply miss you. They may want the generations nearby—it gives them a sense of continuity—and may lament the fact that their children will have less frequent contact with you. Your departure could also put them more in touch with the reality of their own aging. They could even become angry. "You're reneging on the two lasting things you can give us," they might say. "Our 'wings and our roots.' You're shaking our roots; we're supposed to leave—not you!"

As with all issues involving you and your children, it is essential to communicate your feelings with a large dose of reassurance that the family will remain intact—with more miles between you, but intact, nonetheless. Some families use e-mail to stay in touch; others plan periodic family vacations.

Questions for Growth	**DO YOU HAVE RETIREMENT ORPHANS?**
	Think back to the empty-nest period when the kids left.
1.	How did you feel then? If you were sad, your grown children may share those same feelings now if you take off for a warmer climate or move to a retirement community.
2.	What can you do to help mitigate those feelings?

That Special Relationship: Your Grandchildren

One of the most nourishing ways to reach out in your retirement years is through involvement in your grandchildren's lives. Our drive for grandchildren springs from our wish for immortality—the notion that somehow our lives will continue through the lives of our offsprings' offspring.

In 1970, Dr. Arthur Kornhaber initiated the Grandparent Study, and it's still ongoing today. To date, he has found:

◆ The grandparent-grandchild bond is second in emotional importance only to the parent-child bond; grandparents and grandchildren affect each other's lives deeply.

◆ Many grandparents do not repeat the mistakes they made with their own children. Even parents view their own parents as being better with the grandchildren than they had been with them.

◆ Grandparenting provides many retired couples with meaning and joy.

◆ Grandparents can enhance their grandchildren's lives. Grandparents are allies; they can be more tolerant and accepting, and less judgmental, than parents. They provide a larger loving support network. Through interactions with their grandparents, children learn respect and compassion for older adults.

◆ Parents benefit greatly when grandparents are involved with their families. Grandparents are positive buffers. They spend quality time with the children, and parents take comfort knowing their children are well cared for and safe.

◆ The fit of temperament and personality between grandparent and grandchild affects their relationship for better or worse.

Ninety-four percent of older Americans with children are grandparents, and half of all older adults with children will become great-grandparents! Moreover, today one quarter of all grandparents report they have primary responsibility for taking care of their grandchildren.

It is also true that you may look for meaning in your relationships with your grandchild as other areas of role performance close to you. In fact, this is your opportunity to refill the empty nest, but in a different context. Meaningful relationships with your grandkids often require minimal obligation and responsibility yet provide a sense of renewal.

Anthropologist Margaret Mead wrote that when grandparent and grandchild are together, the past and future merge into the present—a generational continuum. According to recent research, 82 percent of grandparents say that they are the primary means for passing along family traditions. Our children and grandchildren can give our lives deep meaning. They are our gifts of ourselves to the generations.

In my study of fulfilled retired couples, 88 percent had grandchildren—from two to eight each, with an average of four per couple. Of all the joint activities these couples engaged in, visiting the grandchildren was the most popular, more so than socializing with friends or traveling.

Even though wives traditionally have more contact with children and grandchildren after retirement, close to 40 percent of the husbands in my study began to interact more through visits, baby-sitting, and phone calls. As one grandfather said, "I get a kick out of baby-sitting the kids—they're so much fun; I'm much more involved with the family since I retired." This supports the idea of older men needing more affiliative contacts. Becoming involved with grandchildren is one way to fulfill this need.

Grandmothers are traditionally more connected to the grandchildren, but they have been socialized to fulfill this role. It doesn't have to be that way. Everyone misses out when grandfathers are excluded—they are role models too. Boys and young men need relationships with older men. This is true for girls and young women as well. They, too, can benefit from meaningful relationships with their grandfathers.

Maybe when your children were young, you didn't have enough time or didn't take the time to interact with them. If you are a grandfather, now is a wonderful opportunity for you to be a teacher and a leader and to explore another part of yourself. But beware the myths that surround grandfathering:

- Child-rearing is woman's work. They always do it better.
- Grandfathers are less interested in child development.
- Grandfathers don't know how to take care of children and are insecure in such a role.
- Retired grandfathers pay more attention to their own hobbies and are not interested in being with the kids.

These are not necessarily true. As one husband in my study noted, "Having your grandchildren around is a total ego builder; they give you so much love."

Fifty-seven percent of grandparents say they baby-sit regularly. Yet, you may feel torn between your need to be with your grandchildren and your need to take care of yourselves and have your own lives. Our grown children often want us to help with child care. How much time should you devote to it?

Generally the best rule of thumb is to base your commitment on the kind of involvement you want and how it fits into your life, not on how your adult children conduct their lives. Some involvement guidelines:

- Set your own priorities. Child care may be high on your list or it may be low.

- Listen to your children's situation and describe your own.
- Make it clear when and how much you wish to be available.
- Put your own intentions first but be aware of special needs, emergencies, or other factors.
- Wait until your kids ask you to help.

You may sometimes disagree on how your children are raising the grandkids. Good communication is essential for good relationships. If you feel it important to speak to your grown child about the welfare of your grandchild:

- Express your opinion once and then back off.
- Speak calmly and rationally.
- Respect your adult child's opinion.
- Be careful not to make your adult child feel like a bad parent.

Questions for Growth

A PLAN FOR INVOLVEMENT WITH YOUR GRANDCHILDREN

Both of you can further your enjoyment of your children and grandchildren by discussing the how, what, and when of your grandparenting. Ask each other the following questions:

1. What kind of relationship do I/we want with my grandchildren?
2. What traditions do I/we want to pass on?
3. How much time do I/we want to devote to them?
4. What activities would I/we enjoy doing with them? What do I think they would enjoy doing with me/us?
5. What activities would not be enjoyable?
6. How do I/we feel about baby-sitting? How much are we willing to do?
7. How will we make arrangements to spend time with them?
8. What would be the most fun for me/us/them?
9. How can I/we help with their growth?

Diversify Your Relationships
and Friendships

Your friends are also essential to a happy retirement marriage. Diversifying your relationships helps you to adjust. A protective shield of friendships—a people support system—can be as important as a good financial and health plan at this time in your lives.

Roughly 65 percent of the couples in my research spoke of the importance of their friends, with a considerable number stating that they were more active with couple friends since the husband's retirement. As one wife told me, "We're very involved with our friends. I see my women friends during the day and my husband has a few friends that he sees during the day, but at night we see a lot of our couple friends now." A few expressed the idea that friendships helped fill the gap they experienced from a lack of family involvement.

Friends can stand you in good stead. It's possible, for instance, that interactions with your adult children can have a negative effect on your morale or self-esteem. After all, your family relationships are bound by obligation and are virtually permanent, whereas friendships are based on mutual choice; they can be ended if they prove unrewarding. Interactions with your friends are more likely to enhance your self-esteem because friends reflect back a positive image of yourself. That's why you chose them as friends in the first place!

Despite the fact that many of the happily retired couples in my study depended on their friends, about 38 percent noted that their relationships with friends had diminished since retirement. With the increased time together, retirement caused these couples to move toward more exclusivity with each other at the expense of friendships.

Did their marriages suffer as a result? Apparently not. The couples enjoyed being together. They perceived their spouses as their best friends. As one woman told me, "I don't have buddy-buddy friends; I never have. My husband is my best friend. We go out with other couples, but we really don't need to. We're more constant companions since retirement."

These couples, regardless of whether they had positive experiences with close family ties, found a way, through their commitment and their love and respect for each other, not only to endure, but to succeed at one of life's more difficult tasks—forming a close, fulfilling, and enduring relationship.

Your Relationship Protection Plan

Even though a portion of the couples in my study claimed their relationships with their spouses were sufficient to the point of less involvement with family and, in some cases, friends, life brings us many surprises. You never know what is looming around the bend: deteriorating health, changes in the structure of your family, the potential loss of a spouse or friends can leave you reeling. We're all vulnerable. Our needs for mature companionship become clearer as we endure these changes and losses.

Constructing a Relationship Protection Plan will put into sharp focus which relationships provide emotional, physical, spiritual, and financial support for you. These are the people who will be there for you in times of need. Each is a block of security that forms part of a protective shield against the difficulties that are likely to confront you in retirement and as you age. Doing this exercise could cause you to place more emphasis on the human side of your life.

Also bear in mind that:

- The people you will be listing are those who will be there for you. They would voluntarily come to your aid. But there are no guarantees. That's why I'll be asking you to identify ten to twenty individuals. Having more than that can cause you to neglect some important relationships. Moderation is important.

- You may find there are some people you have neglected and want to include, or you may want to enhance your relationship with someone you've overlooked, or let go of an unproductive one.

Rehearsal | **CONSTRUCT YOUR RELATIONSHIP PROTECTION PLAN**

Part 1: Assemble the Building Blocks

1. List your closest friends, relations, and helping professionals. Between ten and twenty is a good number. People of all ages should be represented.

2. Are you comfortable with the depth of the relationships you have with each of these individuals? Can you rely

on them to be there for you? (If not, don't include them. If you have pets in your life, include them as well.)

3. Decide whether you can spend enough time to keep these relationships alive and active.

4. Will you neglect old relationships if you take on new ones?

Part 2: Construct the Wall

Using the names you've listed in Part 1, draw a wall of bricks and fill in the bricks with your ten to twenty names. Remember, you are at the center of the foundation; those whom you put closest to you represent your most treasured relationships.

This exercise is best done individually at first. After completing yours, share it with your spouse. Every plan will be unique. Let your partner know whom you consider important enough to include. This could raise some eyebrows, but remember to be tolerant of each other's choices; go with the flow and lighten up. Humor is always helpful. You might want to create a joint Protection Plan, as well. This wall of protection can act as a form of insurance for your future. Now consider the following:

◆ You will be able to see clearly who is important and who is difficult or no longer important in your life.

◆ When you lose people through moving or illness, you will certainly miss them, but it's important to form new connections. Bear in mind that it is your responsibility to keep watch over your stronghold.

◆ You may consider bringing different kinds of people into your life—younger people, for instance, or maturing grandchildren.

◆ Review your Protection Plan from time to time, and update it as needed.

CHAPTER 18

Sex and the Retirement Couple

To see a young couple loving each other is no wonder; but to see an old couple loving each other is the best sight of all.

—William Makepeace Thackeray

SEXUAL RETIREMENT? IT AIN'T necessarily so. Older people can have active sex lives, and many of them do. Besides, a healthy enjoyment of sex has much to recommend it at retirement time.

Earlier, we looked at sexual issues during midlife. Now let's see how to enhance your sexuality as you age.

Sex can be an antidote to pain. Many of us feel that our only remaining physical joys involve eating and drinking. But weight gain and alcohol abuse can produce unhealthy results.

Have you given up the bedroom in favor of the kitchen? Maybe it's time to wander back into the bedroom. Sex remains one of the healthier ways to deal with aches and pains as you age. The knowledge that you have the capacity for sexual activity and the resulting good feelings it brings are very reassuring.

Sex can be a wonderful and safe form of exercise. Exercise is essential to people of all ages and is especially important as a contributing factor in healthy aging. However, you can overdo it. But not with sex. Generally, the only time you will hear of an injury during sex is in a joke or if someone falls out of bed in his or her eagerness to get down to business! Sexual activity is the aerobic equivalent of walking three blocks or climbing two and a half flights of stairs. During intercourse, you use all systems of your body. Indeed, sexual activity contributes to your good health.

Sex can promote and sustain a positive body image. Your midlife body is changing, and as you experience the retirement years, you may acquire yet more unwanted wrinkles, gray hair, and bulges. This can have a real impact on your self-image and your sense of being desirable. But to be sexually active means that someone finds you attractive. Touching, embracing, and making love are highly self-affirming. They restore your self-confidence.

Sexual activity can help you deal with daily stresses and anxieties. "Lose your mind and come to your senses" is an apt saying, especially in the realm of sex. The more you can give yourself up to the sensual experiences of sexual activity, the less your concerns for health issues, your grown children, and all other anxiety-provoking problems you may face daily. Sex helps you cope with life's challenges in a more productive way. A healthy, loving sexual/sensual relationship is immensely reassuring and gives you and your spouse the courage to face whatever lies ahead.

Sexuality and Ageism

Intergenerational understanding and respect can be enhanced when young people recognize that older adults are not only sexually interested, they're also sexually active. It helps them understand that the gray-haired grandma baking cookies and the wizened granddad rocking in his chair are stereotypes that inadequately represent the over-60 set. All of us, young and old, share fears, enthusiasms, and enjoyments in regard to sex. This understanding debunks some of the myths surrounding the aging population.

In relation to attitudes regarding sex in men and women over 60, a recent study found that 53 percent strongly felt that sex was vital to their marriage. This rose to 70 percent of those who had sexual relations at least once a week. Older adults believed the sexual bond in marriage to be more important than did younger people. This finding may be surprising, since many of us buy into the myths of aging, which suggest that sex is interesting only to the young.

Studies confirm that if you enjoyed a full sexual life in your earlier years, you will probably keep on doing so as you age. Physical health—staying active, exercising, eating right, and getting enough sleep—is important for continued sexual satisfaction. So is maintaining a positive self-image, which includes attention to grooming and appearance. All of these factors contribute to your sex appeal and to a healthy sex life.

Problems during the Retirement Years

Previously, I discussed the physiological changes in relation to sex that take place in men and women at midlife. The standard "penis in vagina" so prevalent in the earlier years of the marriage is not necessarily to be expected now. Changes in responsiveness continue.

During the retirement years, a man may need more time for his penis to become erect, and he may require more direct physical stimulation. A woman's vagina, especially with inadequate estrogen, can lose some elasticity and shrink. "Use it or lose it" is true to a certain extent. Regardless of age, however, men and women are still able to have orgasms but generally of less intensity than when they were younger.

Physical illnesses such as diabetes or a heart condition can also interfere with sexuality. But these don't necessarily have to be limiting. There are ways to work with these illnesses—accommodations you can make in your lovemaking that can circumvent these obstacles. Be sure to communicate with your partner honestly and be willing to experiment with what works.

In the case of heart conditions, gather information together from your physician about sexual activity. Learn your tolerance for exercise. After all, sex is a physical activity. Resuming sexual activity as soon as is safe after a heart attack can help alleviate anxiety.

Arthritis is one of the most common medical conditions of aging. But you'll be happy to know that the range of motion involved during sex is good for arthritis. Not only are you moving the affected joints, but the sex act itself could stimulate the body's release of cortisone, which is often prescribed for the treatment of rheumatoid arthritis.

Medications can also disrupt sexual functioning: more than two hundred medicines have been identified as having sexual side effects.

Some blood pressure pills and antidepressants are notorious for this. If you are having problems, consult with your physician about all of your prescriptions. Perhaps the doctor can lower your dosage or change to a different drug that does not have side effects.

And, although not a physiological issue, the potential for the two of you to spend endless hours together during retirement can have a positive or negative effect on your sex lives. Some couples relish the closeness while others find that the constant presence of the other lessens their desire. In that case, it is important to have time alone. "Absence makes the heart grow fonder"—an axiom that has endured because it captures the truth.

Make Love, Not Sex

All in all, "making love" is an appropriate term to use at this stage of life, rather than "having sex." What is essential is that you relate, that you touch, caress, fondle, feel love for, and feel loved by, your spouse. These activities help affirm you as sensual, sexual beings. A couple in my study illustrates the value of lovemaking as well as the changing views of men and women as they age—the crossover in attitudes:

> *Eva:* The sex is good now—better than it has ever been. By sex, I don't mean just intercourse. I mean everything that goes on before we go into the bedroom and what goes on while we're there. We have so much time to really savor each other. There isn't that mad rush to get it over with. I used to have a horrible temper; I was mad at Sam so much of the time that I couldn't enjoy myself. Now, I've really mellowed out. I love him; I love to touch him and have him touch me. If we lie in bed and just touch and stroke each other, that's just fine with me.

> *Sam:* Ten years ago when I couldn't get an erection, I had a difficult time dealing with it. But Eva was so patient with me. We just stayed in bed and held each other. I couldn't believe at first that that was okay with her but it really was. Now, since I'm retired, we have all the time in the world; I don't have the pressure to perform like I used to have at work.

> Our sex life is just another way of showing each other how much we love each other. It's not a separate act like

when I was younger. Don't get me wrong, I still enjoy sexual relations. It's just that it's not the only way my wife and I can express our love for each other.

On TV and in the movies, they're always showing young, vital people flirting and making sexual innuendoes to each other while us older folks are quietly going about our business. Eva and I flirt and make sexual innuendoes with each other, and I'll bet other couples our age do the same. Why don't they show that?

We remain sexual beings all our lives, and for the most part, our "sexual equipment" can continue to function throughout our lifetimes. The intensity may be lessened, but our enjoyment of touch, tenderness, and caressing can bring with it a whole new, wonderful experience.

Questions for Growth	**INTIMATE CONVERSATIONS**
	N ow more than ever, with all the physical and lifestyle changes you're undergoing, it's important to communicate your sexual needs, likes, and dislikes to your partner. Take turns sharing your answers to the following questions:
1.	What do you enjoy most?
2.	What do you enjoy least?
3.	What would you like to add?
4.	Which positions are the most comfortable?
5.	What time of day or night do you prefer?
6.	How often feels just right?

CHAPTER 19

The Seven Marital Themes and the Retirement Marriage

If we take care of the moments, the years will take care of themselves.

—Maria Edgeworth

TIME IS THE GREAT LEVELER. The major finding of my research into happily married retired couples was that their awareness of time running out influenced many of their attitudes, perceptions, and behaviors in relation to one another. In light of the "ticking clock," couples chose to be more tolerant, respectful, flexible, and caring in every area of their relationship. As one husband told me, "We have the time now, but we're aware that the clock is ticking . . . this is it!"

The couples dealt with the perception of diminished time by adopting more tolerant attitudes and behaviors, becoming more nurturing, reaching out to family and friends, sharing, being flexible, communicating openly, and managing conflict well. In all of this, they demonstrated a deep respect for one another.

These changes in attitude and behavior reflect the Seven Marital Themes we already encountered in the empty-nest marriage. We will now see how well they apply to the fulfilling retirement marriage. In patterning your lives after these themes, you too may enjoy a relationship in which you can say, as did one of my interviewees, "Retirement is the best thing that ever happened to us!"

Accept Each Other's Individual Differences

About 90 percent of the couples in my research expressed respect toward their partners' feelings. They avoided finding fault with, forcing their opinions on, or otherwise dominating, their mates. Instead, they practiced acceptance. As one wife said, "We each have unrestricted freedom and we don't find fault with everything."

This respect and acceptance also included the acknowledgment that one's partner had a different temperament. The diversity was not just tolerated. In many cases, it played a role in the success of the marriage.* For instance, one husband told me, "I'm the cockeyed optimist, and she's a pessimist. She has the understanding, love, and compassion, and I'm more logical, the don't-worry type. We counterbalance each other."

Take the Good with the Bad

Despite how fulfilling and vital their marriages were now, all of the couples I interviewed had experienced high and low points. Several had even contemplated divorce. My interviewees had also dealt with many losses along the way and with the burdens of ill health. Yet they were still together an average of forty-four years.

One couple, in particular, comes to mind in that regard. Fred and Linda had had a tumultuous relationship for many years. "We were opposites," Linda told me. "But it didn't make living together any easier. I'm intense and he acts like it's nothing—but that makes me even more intense. Three things held us together: our common goals for our children, our religion, and a good sex life. Everything else was a problem."

Then, several years ago, Fred took a forced retirement after he was

---

*Nevertheless, several couples acknowledged that the wife seemed to bend "for the sake of the marriage" more than the husband. Often, looking the other way was easier than facing an annoyance and arguing about it. But if the wife harbored any resentment about this, pride in her ability to be flexible in service of the marriage appeared to compensate.

diagnosed with lung cancer, and Linda had a mild stroke that impaired her ability to walk. Their illnesses made them more accepting of each other.

Linda: The tendency when everything is going good in your life is to focus on the things that aren't working. But when you have a major problem, you start looking at what you have to be thankful for in your marriage and how much you love and care for each other. Our priorities shifted to family and our relationship. In the last six months of Fred's forced retirement, we took out our love letters from when we were teens and in love, and we reread them. There were hundreds of them.

Fred: We both have often thought that if I didn't have this diagnosis, we wouldn't have worked on our marriage, and it wouldn't have been as successful as we now feel it is. Why don't all couples think like that? Think of all the wonderful things they have to be grateful for, all the things they appreciate about each other. We focus on all the good things instead of the bad.

Rehearsal	MARITAL DESSERTS
	When our children were growing up, we had a valentine box into which each of us would occasionally put poems or writings of different kinds explaining how much we cared for, admired, and respected each other. In effect, we wrote valentines to each other. Every few months after dinner, we would open the box and share the contents.
	Marital Desserts is an exercise the two of you can do to "focus on the good things instead of the bad."
1.	During the week, each of you will put at least five slips of paper into your valentine box. Each will enumerate a behavior that pleased you.
2.	At the end of the week, take turns reaching into the box and reading these statements of appreciation.

Give Up Unrealistic Expectations

"What a revelation to let go of unrealistic expectations!" a wife told me, and indeed she is right. One of the ways to accept your spouse and be happier in your marriage is to tear down obsolete and unrealistic expectations. Letting go of the notion of perfection is an important step toward acceptance. When you are clear and reasonable in your expectations, you respect your partner more. And if you don't always get what you want from him or her, you can also learn to accept that too.

However, when you accept your partner with all of his or her positive and negative traits, you are not throwing your hands in the air and saying, "I give up!" Rather, you are starting down a mature and productive road that has proved successful for many couples—especially those in long-term marriages—the road of *what is* instead of *what I wish*. The latter is mostly filled with *shoulds*—"He should help me more around the house." "She should know better than to go out with friends when I need her." You are who you are.

In fact, you may find that the more you attempt to change your partner, the more he or she will resist or retreat. Rather than trying to alter the behaviors, find ways to tolerate or even cherish them.

Rehearsal | **BECOMING MORE TOLERANT**

Reframing gives you the opportunity to become more tolerant. In Chapter 6, I asked you to imagine that you were sitting in a Victorian house, looking out of various windows. Each one offered a novel perspective on your child. Now go into this house again, but this time visualize your spouse with a quality that is difficult for you to accept. For instance, you may have a hard time with your wife's quietness when among friends. When you reframe, you could say to yourself, "I love talking, telling stories, and—let's face it—being the center of attention. Joan is very wise. She watches, observes, and really understands people. When we get home, she gives me a full rundown on what was going on. I enjoy her introspection and understanding."

Nurture Each Other

As I finished my interviews with the fulfilled couples in my study, I asked them what advice they would give to help others enjoy a successful adjustment to retirement. I wanted to know "what helped you most?"

The most frequent suggestion related to the importance of exhibiting caring, loving, and respectful behaviors toward one's spouse. For instance, one wife advised that women could "be understanding and sensitive to changes your husband could be experiencing. Caring overrides everything. Appreciate each other and each day." And a husband said, "I never let a day go by that I don't tell my wife that I love her. If you care for somebody, you have to let them know."

Nurturing and appreciation were especially important to these retired couples as they became more dependent on each other. At least 75 percent remarked that they relied more on their spouses physically and emotionally since retirement. One husband said, "I used to feel if my wife died I'd have this great bachelor life, but I don't feel that way now. I'm aware of how our lives are intertwined; we depend more and more on each other since retirement. This is natural. We realize that our whole existence is tied up with each of us doing certain things and that it will be different when one of us is gone."

Research speaks of husbands in late-stage marriages who have greater needs for nurturing and affiliation and who perceive their wives as indispensable pillars of strength; this was certainly the case with many of my interviewees. But this dependency can place more stress on a wife. She needs to take care of herself first and foremost.

And, as we have seen with Fred and Linda, compassion and nurturing become especially important when illness occurs. In fact, a spouse's illness can enhance the closeness of the relationship. The caregiver derives a sense of purpose and satisfaction, and the care receiver feels secure in being cared for.

Every relationship needs tender, loving care. However, you can get into a rut, take each other for granted, and even feel irritated by many things that each of you do, especially at retirement. What you need is an infusion of nurturing energy, a positive reconnection, a restoking of the fires that have burned low. This can come in the form of little behaviors that each of you do for each other.

Rehearsal | # APPRECIATION TIMES

The act of reinforcing each other's preferences is a positive step toward reconnection at retirement time. These simple acts—making the bed, bringing flowers, rubbing your partner's back—as small as they may seem, can increase the pleasure, caring, and commitment in your relationship. Do this easy exercise together.

1. Keep a pen and paper handy for one week.

2. Compile a list of all the little pleasing things that your partner can do for you. These pleasurable acts may center on leisure activities, household tasks, communicating, sensuality/sexuality, appearance, personal habits, and so forth.

3. At the end of the week, complete sentences such as, I feel appreciated and nurtured when you . . .

   ◆ help me cook dinner

   ◆ notice and comment on how I look when we go out

   ◆ hold my hand at times when we're with friends

4. Now, exchange lists with your spouse.

5. Set aside time each day for a week when both of you will do one of the listed acts. Do only those things you feel comfortable with. (It is important to feel good about this activity; demands will only undermine goodwill.) You can repeat those actions that you or your spouse particularly like.

6. At the end of the week set aside "talk time" to communicate your reactions to this exercise. What felt good? What didn't you like? What would you want more or less of?

7. Remember to reinforce positive behaviors with "I love it when you . . ." Showing appreciation further reinforces the positive effect of this exercise.

Reach Out to Family and Friends

Chapter 17 highlights the importance of family and friends to the retirement couple. Reaching out is part of successful aging. For one thing, when you reach beyond your marriage, it takes the pressure off your spouse to supply you with all of your "connection" needs. Grandchildren enrich your lives by providing connections and a sense of continuity. They bring meaning and joy. And, in a sense, they offer you the opportunity to refill your empty nest again.

However, because of the relational losses we incur as we age, it's important to add to our close relationships since they provide us with emotional, physical, spiritual, and financial support.

Share Values, Goals, and Marital Responsibilities

When the couples in my study explained why they had successful retirement marriages, sharing interests and holding similar values were cited as second-most in importance. And although not all couples had identical interests, there was still a willingness to accede to a partner's wishes for the sake of the relationship.

During our meetings, I gave my interviewees a list of twenty-one possible explanations for their happy, long-term marriages. I asked them to choose the ten most significant factors that contributed to their happiness and then, without seeing their partner's responses, rank them in order of importance. Interestingly, both husbands and wives agreed on eight of the ten factors. This is a remarkable consensus and suggests that these couples hold similar, shared views of their marriage.

These are the reasons husbands and wives offered, listed in order of the most frequently mentioned:

Wives	Husbands
1. My spouse is my best friend.	1. My spouse is my best friend.
2. My spouse shows a lot of respect for me.	2. I like my spouse as a person.
3. I like my spouse as a person.	3. We agree on a philosophy of life.
4. We agree on a philosophy of life.	4. We agree on aims and goals.

5. We agree on aims and goals.

6. We laugh together.

7. My spouse is very flexible in regard to our relationship.

8. I am proud of my spouse's achievements.

9. My spouse shows appreciation for things I do well.

10. We share outside hobbies and interests.

5. We laugh together.

6. I am proud of my spouse's achievements.

7. My spouse has a positive outlook on life.

8. My spouse shows a lot of respect for me.

9. I confide in my spouse.

10. My spouse shows appreciation for things I do well.

Clearly, these couples shared almost identical views of their marriage. This is different from what studies have shown occurs in the general population. For instance, in a study of fifty-six retired couples for whom marital satisfaction varied greatly, each partner articulated different perceptions regarding their marriage. Their responses were much more discordant than those given by my study subjects, who were all in satisfying late-stage marriages. Indeed, friendship consistently topped my interviewees' lists. There is a good reason for that. Marital friendship is one of the major underpinnings of enduring and fulfilling marriages. Aspects of friendship like respect, mutual admiration, acceptance, being there for each other, laughter, and shared values, worries, and enthusiasms add to this fulfillment.

Questions for Growth

TAKING YOUR MARITAL FRIENDSHIP PULSE

Together discuss the following:

1. Think of the qualities that make up a good friendship—trust, common values, empathy. Which do you think you have?

2. Which are lacking?

3. Brainstorm ways to bring missing qualities into your relationship.

Be Flexible

"Be flexible and keep everything simple, honey, then you don't get into too many complications," one wife told me. That's good advice. Rigidly adhering to old behaviors, insisting you're in the "right" no matter what, or becoming angry at the unexpected occurrences that bombard our lives each day will serve you poorly as an individual as well as in your retirement marriage. My study participants point out that one of the most, if not *the most important attribute* to possess as you age is flexibility—the ability to flow with life's events.

Again, their awareness of the finite number of years they had left together seemed to influence this attitude. One husband said, "Don't pick with the chickens and don't pick flyspecks out of the pepper. Realize that nothing is so important that it can't wait . . . roll with it and be good to each other."

This is especially true after retirement because there is so much togetherness. And as I mentioned earlier, more than a few spouses go along with activities to keep their partners company. Their flexibility in service of the relationship also added to the appreciation level of their partnership. One wife saw this as a source of growth. "I'm afraid of a lot of things," she told me, "but I overcome them to join my husband. I do it to make him happy and me happy, to be a part of what he does."

Flexibility can apply to one's psychological outlook as well. Thelma and Ed are happily married today, but that was not always so. "I admire my wife, her cooking, our sex life, and we share a tremendous number of interests," Ed told me. "But at our twenty-fifth anniversary, we were at loggerheads. We couldn't decide if we should throw a party or get divorced. We went to Marriage Encounter and had therapy that gave us some tools."

"We got wiser with the years," Thelma added. "I used to have a bad temper, but it's much, much better now, and he has learned how to deal with it. He is very bright and I admire him enormously. I think our life is ideal now. These are the happiest years of our lives."

Still, you may wish in your deepest selves that your lives will proceed just as you want, even though experience tells us that is unrealistic. So, if your children get divorced, a close friend moves away, or a medical condition is diagnosed, you become distressed. "How do we deal with this?" you may ask yourselves. But research supports the notion that the more flexible you are in regard to the roles you are playing in retirement and your approach to the many changes that you confront in your marital, home, social, and inner life, the more apt you are to live a long and satisfying life.

| Rehearsal | **GO WITH THE FLOW** |

Going into your deepest selves and engaging in self-talk regarding a readjustment of your expectations can put you on the road toward more flexibility.

Remember systematic desensitization? That's what you will be doing here, with a minor twist. In this activity you're systematically *resensitizing* yourself to the positive aspects of being more flexible.

1. Think about the statement: "Life is what happens every day. I'll work with what comes along and go with the flow."

2. For one week, spend a block of time (say from 6 P.M. to 8 P.M. each evening) carrying out the intention of the above statement. Work with what comes along and go with the flow during that period of time. (Your husband reports he banged up the car, or your wife confesses to having spent hundreds on a dress? Just go with the flow!)

3. Monitor your reactions. Do you feel more or less anxious? Did anything happen in a negative way because you were calmer about what happened and didn't overreact?

4. What was your partner's reaction to your new "go with the flow" attitude? If it was positive, that's useful information for you.

5. If this two-hour daily exercise in flexibility proves productive, stretch the time span to four hours, then eight. Think about doing it for two days. You are taking small steps toward new beginnings.

Communicate and Listen

In response to the question "What effect has retirement had on the communication in your relationship?" slightly more than half of my study couples commented on the improved communication in their marriage since the husband's retirement. In many cases, they attributed this improvement to the absence of stress since leaving work; increased caring, concern, and respect brought about by the "time factor"; and, to a lesser degree, the departure of children. "This has been a good marriage all along," one wife told me, "but since my husband retired, he is more outgoing; he talks more. It's probably due to having less tension here than he did at work."

Several couples remarked that they did not need to communicate verbally. In fact, patterns of interaction that other couples might perceive as problematic were not troubling to them. One wife said, "We're the least communicative couple in the world in terms of having discussions about things. Since his retirement, we communicate even less." Both husband and wife laughed at this. "He hears me on the phone and learns about what is happening by listening to me," she continued. "The fact that we're together is natural; we don't have to talk. It's a good feeling."

It seems that improvement in this area after retirement rests on your comfort level with a particular style of communication rather than on the amount of time you spend talking. You may choose to work at your interactions or you may just "let things happen." The laissez-faire couples in my study had established comfortable patterns of communication prior to retirement. Their postretirement interactions were just business as usual for them.

Practice Attentive Listening:
It's a Commitment and a Compliment

In an eye-opening exercise used in corporate workshops, a seminar leader begins by casually commenting on a newspaper article he will read to attendees. After he has read it aloud, most of the attendees seem bored and uninterested. The leader then offers five dollars to whoever can answer all of his questions related to the article. Most often, no one can do this. But if everyone heard the story, why couldn't at least a few answer the questions? If the leader had told them initially that they would receive a reward, would the participants have listened more carefully?

Attentive listening affects all areas of your lives but proves especially important in your marital relationship. Of all the communication skills that you use, listening is the most important in forming an intimate and loving bond. What better reward? No need to spend the five dollars.

Many couples in my study offered attentive listening as one of the major factors in their successful communication. When your partner listens, he or she makes a commitment to understanding and empathizing with you—an enormous compliment. This says, "You are important to me; I'm interested in knowing how you think and feel."

Empathic listening—really attending to your partner's emotions—is the highest form of listening. It is a learned skill that requires your focused attention and an attempt really to get into your spouse's shoes. In empathic listening you listen to your partner's words but also pay attention to his or her facial expressions, posture, and level of tension.

When you listen, you put self-interest on the back burner. Indeed, self-interest can be corrosive to effective listening when we interrupt, judge, advise, or daydream. Be aware of these obstacles.

Use the "As If" Solution

Unfortunately, not all of us do as well in the communication department as the couples in my study. At times you may argue, feel misunderstood, or become angry. You can find it difficult even to *like* your partner enough to want to listen, let alone empathize, when your stomach is churning and your heart is pounding. If this is the case in your marriage, try the "as if" solution.

When you spend so much time together, the little annoyances that you used to be able to ignore can affect your life. But if you act *as if* these irritations are less important, eventually your attitude will change as well. The truth is, these annoyances are insignificant when compared to your health and well-being. Besides, your anger and nagging won't change old habits. And by letting go, you might be able to have a more meaningful discussion about change.

Rehearsal	**JUST HEAR ME— PRACTICE IN EMPATHIC LISTENING**

Regardless of the level of communication in your marriage (she talks/he doesn't, he talks/she doesn't, you're both reticent or you both talk too much), this exercise allows you to know what it feels like to listen, be heard, and understood.

1. Find at least four pictures each from magazines—the more detailed, the better.

2. Sit down and face each other. Take turns.

3. *Talking partner:* Study your picture carefully for a few minutes. After noting its details and the feelings it evokes in you, lay it facedown and tell your partner, as specifically as possible, what you saw in the picture and the emotions it evoked in you.

4. *Listening partner:* Pay close attention to what your spouse is saying. Also note his or her facial expressions and general mood. Now tell your spouse what you heard him or her say and how he or she looked while speaking.

5. *Talking partner:* Correct and fill in noncritically where needed or, if you feel you were really heard, thank your partner for listening and understanding.

6. Trade places and repeat. Do as many of these pictures as you like. You need not do all eight at one sitting.

Negotiate. It's Another Form of Communicating

"My husband is considerate and understanding," one wife told me. "It's a two-way street; you have to consider your partner's feelings. I can't have my way all the time . . . we compromise." This couple understands the importance of compromise and negotiation. They know the pitfalls and appreciate how profoundly retirement caused them to restructure many elements in their relationship. Your successful adjustment will also depend on your ability to openly discuss your expectations and to negotiate and compromise on new patterns of living and working together.

Other research has shown that couples who successfully restructure the family unit after the children leave home and who enhance the commitment to their relationship during this transition enter retirement with a stronger basis for the major restructuring that is required at the retirement phase. But even if this recommitment and successful restructuring did not go on in your marriage, good negotiation skills can help.

It's never too late. Marriage is always a work in progress, and this progress continues through and beyond the retirement years.

You have been negotiating for years as you dealt with finances, relatives, and the kids but now in retirement you might need some structured, specific help in negotiating the many changes you may encounter.

Rehearsal	NEGOTIATING A WIN-WIN SITUATION

Ideally, both of you will learn and practice the following skills. But, even if just one of you practices them, it will benefit your marriage. In order to have a successful outcome, try to keep your emotions in check. Nothing disrupts the working through of a problem more than flying off the handle or stonewalling. Engage in this exercise with an open mind and a great store of flexibility. Most important, both of you need to experience benefits for the compromise to be successful. This must be a win-win situation.

1. **Set the stage.** Clarify the problem for the two of you.

2. **Tell the truth.** Get an honest dialogue going. Each of you should discuss your feelings regarding the problem. Remember not to blame or yell. Be empathic and ask questions when you don't understand. This also helps your partner express his or her feelings.

3. **Request the change.** One of you proposes a possible solution. If that is unacceptable, the other makes a counteroffer. Keep going back and forth until a workable compromise is reached.

4. **Agree on a win-win option.** Look for an option that to some degree, meets your needs. But remember you're never going to get it all—marriage is another word for compromise.

5. **Generate alternatives and agree to revisit the issue in the future.** Understand that your negotiation is not written in stone. It can be revised as your wants and needs change.

Anna was hurt and angry at Ben's refusal to visit their grandsons, aged 7 and 9. She went twice a week and enjoyed being with them—but she always went alone. When the boys asked where Grandpa was, she made up excuses. She had finally run out of patience. Here's how she and Ben negotiated a win-win solution to their problem.

Anna told Ben she wanted to talk about the situation with the grandchildren. She asked him if he would just listen to her feelings, and then she said she would like to hear his. "I'm really interested in knowing why you refuse to visit Jason and Zack," she stressed. She spoke about her own grandparents and the warm relationship she had with them—especially her grandfather. "I feel you're missing a golden opportunity to get to know your own grandsons and have them realize what a wonderful person you are."

Because Anna presented the problem nonthreateningly, Ben listened to her. "Well, I don't like young kids," he first told her. "They're too noisy, and I have nothing in common with them. They just irritate me." But then, reluctantly, he confided, "You know, I think it also has to do with my poor hearing. I'm afraid if I'm left alone with them even for a short time and something happened I wouldn't hear it, and I would feel so responsible. Besides, I didn't have any time with our kids, and I don't know what to do with young kids. I feel foolish around them."

Anna and Ben began to see the issue and how it felt through Ben's eyes—that's called empathy—and it got the ball rolling:

> *Anna:* How about if you just come once every two weeks at first? I promise I'll stay with you and the boys the whole time.
>
> *Ben:* I'm not ready yet. I'd like to just talk to them on the phone first. [Ben's receiver had an amplifier. He felt more comfortable on the phone than in person.]
>
> *Anna:* Okay, what if I call the kids on Wednesday, have a short conversation with them and then put you on the line?
>
> *Ben:* But I don't know what to say to them.
>
> *Anna:* I'll help you. A good beginning is to ask them questions about their day. Ask Jason about soccer and Zack about math. That shows you're interested.
>
> *Ben:* Wednesday it is, then!

Anna: Great! It's a beginning. I appreciate your talking with me about this instead of getting mad and thinking I'm nagging. This is just a trial. Let's review how we feel about this in a few weeks.

Ben: Good plan!

Anna didn't get all that she wanted in this negotiation, but she did begin to understand her husband's reluctance. When your partner makes a decision, he or she always has a reason for it, whether or not you agree with it. When you communicate and discover that reason, you can more easily move forward.

Ben had longed for connection with his grandsons but had hidden behind his fears. He often felt inadequate in social situations and relied on Anna to pave the way. Her offering to help him with the phone calls gave him the assurance he needed to take that first step.

Manage Conflicts

Couples in happy retirement marriages make a conscious effort to have fewer disagreements. They want to spend their remaining years in a more peaceful environment. In fact, 80 percent of the couples I studied chose not to engage in arguments or to keep them to a minimum. Still, these partners shared varying degrees of conflict in their relationships over the years. Some conflict is to be expected. One husband offered his view of its inevitability. "I see marriage like a cup," he told me. "Things get put into this cup as time goes on. These are little annoyances and things that disturb you. When these annoyances reach the top, the cup overflows and then . . . you fight. The fighting takes care of things until the cup overflows again!"

It's not the conflicts themselves, it's the way you deal with them that matters to the marriage. With the passage of time, you too may choose to lighten up. With the realization that you do not have infinite time left together, you can decide to spend your remaining years in increased tranquility. Life is too short to spend it arguing.

Previous studies show that late-stage married couples resolve their conflicts differently than at earlier periods in their marriage. They now use more humor, joking, and teasing as a defusing device. On many occasions during my interviews, I observed couples winking, nodding, smiling, and even ribbing each other. They also spoke, time and again, of how they accommodated and compromised, giving in when they felt the issue warranted little investment of time or emotion.

These couples sum up the prevailing view of what successful long-term married couples do—they mellow out. Indeed, the couples in my study offered the following suggestions for dealing with conflict:

- ◆ **Choose your fights carefully.** Remember the "don't pick with the chickens" comment? Couples "picked" only when the issues were non-negotiable.

- ◆ **Engage in an attitude adjustment.** Flex your flexibility muscles. If you have to give in once in a while, that's all right. The marriage benefits.

- ◆ **Practice humility.** Apologize when appropriate. Ask yourself: What's more important, being right or being happy?

- ◆ **Timing counts.** Know when to back off and when to deal with an issue.

- ◆ **Avoid personal attacks.** Remember, you're dealing with the problem, not the person; work on resolving the problem together.

- ◆ **Mellow out.** If your spouse is "hot," you can "chill out" or take a walk. You'll act as a circuit breaker to escalation of the conflict.

The last bit of advice about mellowing out seems especially important in light of recent findings regarding the negative health consequences of venting strong rage and hostility. Research no longer supports "letting it all hang out." Studies point to the risk of heart attack from overexpressed anger. Find a way to calm yourself or express your anger safely. The following exercise can help.

| Rehearsal | **MELLOW OUT** |

An old proverb says, "If you are patient in one moment of anger, you will escape a hundred days of sorrow." How true. Besides the health benefits, short-circuiting anger can also save your marriage from developing emotional scar tissue. But it's important to be willing to look at some of the reasons for your anger and to commit yourself to dealing with it. If your hot buttons are easy to push, try these suggestions to cool down:

1. *Be alert for red flags—issues, words, actions that set you off.* When you see or hear these, stop, take a deep breath, and refuse to react in the same old way. Become aware of your body. Is your stomach in knots? Are your fists clenched? Take more deep breaths, and as you exhale, count to ten. You do have some control.

2. *Work with your partner.* Together brainstorm signals your partner can give you to start the process of calming yourself down.

3. *Empathize.* Try breaking out of your usual perceptions by taking your partner's side. Consider how he or she sees the situation. That will slow your reaction.

4. *Do some self-searching.* Find the roots of your red flags. You might feel hurt, worried, unforgiving, or afraid you will not be heard. You may not know how to express feelings, or you may be concerned that you will not get your way. If you stop to think of these "reasons," you can slow your reaction. Use self-talk: "I'm feeling hurt, but I don't have to rage. I can use some control. It's not worth it to get angry and upset."

Release Your Angry Feelings Safely

Bernice was always under pressure from work, but since Alan's retirement, the tension had gotten worse, especially when she walked in the door at night. She usually came home stressed, but she felt a vise tightening around her head when he would ask, "What's for dinner?" This set her off and running with over-the-top anger.

Using the above exercise, Bernice became aware that she resented that she was working while Alan wasn't. She believed he was lolling away the day while she drove the two hours back and forth to a full-time position she was obligated to hold because of their financial burdens. However, she felt guilt at the prospect of confronting Alan because he had just undergone open-heart surgery and she didn't want to upset him any further. "The truth is," she told herself, "I feel trapped in expressing my feelings."

Driving home from work one night, Bernice started to see Alan's side of it. He helped clean the house and did the shopping. She had chosen the chore of making dinner every night, not him; she was responsible for creating the very thing that made her angry in the first place. This understanding took some of the wind out of her sails. When she got home, she discussed with Alan the possibility of changing the dinnertime routine. He happily agreed, since he was distressed with the shouting and the anger.

Having heard about the damaging effects of rage, Bernice decided to work on her overreaction. She vowed to check her usual response and asked Alan for a "good talk," telling him she was tired of the rage. He agreed to the meeting. Together they brainstormed ways he could alert her to when she would blow. His phrase "Be careful" was to be her cue. She agreed to listen for that if she couldn't monitor herself properly.

Bernice began to mellow out using the above guidelines. After realizing that the red flag was her ignorance of the source of her anger and the trapped feelings simmering beneath the surface, she decided to share her true feelings without jeopardizing Alan's health or their relationship further by writing a Love Letter, a technique popularized by author John Gray.

Rehearsal	**THE LOVE LETTER— RELEASE YOUR ANGRY FEELINGS SAFELY**
1.	***Express your anger.*** Write a short letter to the person you are angry with. Use appropriate phrases such as: "I don't like it when you . . . I get mad when you . . ."
	Bernice wrote: "Alan, I resent it when you ask for dinner the minute I come in the door and I'm so stressed out. Can't you wait? But what I really resent is that I have to work and you get to stay home and do whatever you want."
2.	***Express your hurt and sadness.*** "I feel disappointed at . . . I feel sad because . . . I feel awful when . . ."
	Bernice wrote: "I am disappointed in the way things turned out. It hurts to think you don't appreciate what I'm doing for us by working."
3.	***Express your fear and insecurities.*** "It frightens me to think . . ."

Bernice wrote: "It frightens me to think that I may have to work for another ten years. That's too much stress for me; I want some private and special time too."

4. ***Express your guilt and feelings of responsibility.*** "I didn't mean to . . . I'm so sorry I . . . I hope you can forgive me for . . ."

Bernice wrote: "I know you have health problems, and I don't mean to get so angry when I come home. I hope you understand my feelings now and that you can begin to forgive me."

5. ***Express gratitude.*** "I'm grateful that . . . You have been wonderful about . . ."

Bernice wrote: "You have been a wonderful husband and father. I'm grateful that you are in my life and for your kind and thoughtful ways. Actually, with your condition, I think you do more work than you should around the house."

6. ***Express love.*** "I now understand . . . I love you because . . . You are special to me because . . .

Bernice wrote: "You are so special to me. When I recall how much you pitched in when I was laid up after my back surgery, I love you more than ever."

7. ***Express your hopes for the two of you.*** "I'm looking forward to . . . I know in the future we . . ."

Bernice wrote: "Now that I'm in touch with why I'm angry as well as how special a person you are and how much I love you, I know that we can work this out. The future holds a lot of hope for us. I'm going to do some changing and make our lives better. We have too much of a good thing going."

Conflict was not over in Bernice and Alan's marriage. It never is. But through self-questioning and mellowing out on Bernice's part, and compromise for both, they engaged in what I would call "the good fight." By their actions, this couple emerged with enhanced understanding and moved toward resolving their problem.

Enriching Each Other's Lives

The couples who participated in my study were generous with their honest feelings and thoughts about their marriages. Perhaps these traits are best captured in a fiftieth-wedding-anniversary letter that one of the couples shared with me:

> Our once-upon-a-time began with our very first, very brief meeting. Only an introduction. From that moment, we both knew that our lives were to be linked forever. What we didn't know was how completely mismatched we were. Jake was a natural athlete and Type A from birth—always propelled by some innate force to move in triple time. I had always been a scholar, very, very quiet, and definitely not Type A. Almost all we had in common was our religious beliefs, but even there, the observances of our two families were quite dissimilar.
>
> However, it was such a different time. It was a time when grass was for cutting, Coke was for drinking, and pot was something used for cooking. It was a time when divorce was deemed a horror—second only to prostitution. So, despite the fact that in today's world no computer would have linked us, we had no alternative but to make our relationship work.
>
> As time has gone by, Jake has become more and more scholarly and on a one-to-ten Type A scale, he has slowed to about an eight and a half. As for myself, as any of you can testify, I am no longer very, very quiet. And, I have become a pseudo-athlete.

The letter went on to thank family and friends for their love and support. The reason Jake and Marie gave for the longevity and depth of their relationship? "It's simple," Jake said. "We each enrich each other's lives. That's the baseline. It's as simple as that."

Bring On Tomorrow— We're Ready!

I T WAS A HOT AND SMOGGY August morning. Bernie and I took a swim at our neighbor's pool in order to cool off, get a little exercise, and talk. The sparkling blue water was cool and inviting. We enjoyed total privacy since our neighbors were at work, and tall pines and flowering shrubs encircled the whole area. It was like a minivacation that we could achieve by walking just a hundred yards.

As I paddled around the pool, trying to increase my heart rate and shed a few fat cells, I started to consider some "deep thoughts." These had weighed on me for several days; they concerned how I see myself now and in the years to come. They were thoughts about who I am, the roles I want to play, the people in my life, and my general place in my family, my friendships, and my community.

I stopped paddling and turned to my husband, who was swimming laps at the other end of the pool. "Bernie!" I shouted over his splashing, waving my arms to get his attention. He picked his head up out of the water. "I'd like to share some thoughts and feelings with you," I continued, and he obligingly swam over.

"What's up?" he asked.

"I would appreciate it if you would just listen and not comment," I said as he looked at me quizzically. "I need a sounding board. If you want to talk when I'm finished, that's fine but I'm not really looking for answers."

"All right," Bernie said wiping the drops from his face. "I'm listening."

And so I began to share. I talked with him about my deepest concerns. I revealed my fears, rational and not, and what I hoped for and expected from my life. "This is a truly vulnerable time," I said. I had often shared my feelings throughout our thirty-five-year marriage, but I had never presented such a bottom-line depiction of my inner world.

Bernie listened without interrupting. He looked at me, and by the expression on his face I could tell that he was really listening to me.

I talked on for about ten minutes, maybe longer. When I finished, he stood in the pool quietly—an unusual occurrence. He often liked to provide solutions, as many husbands are apt to do.

"Hmm," he said. "I understand." And that was all he said. I believed him. I really believed that he understood how and why I felt the way I did. He accepted my view without questioning it. He seemed to be saying without actually uttering the words, "I understand and I accept and respect all that you have said."

I felt very calm, very understood, very good. Since my heart rate had slowed from all this understanding and calmness, I started to paddle some more.

After a few moments he swam over to me, put his hands on my shoulders, looked at me, and said softly, "I want to talk." This is not his usual way of starting a conversation, and to put it mildly, I was taken aback. But I liked this new approach.

"Just like I did when you talked, I would like you to listen to me without interrupting." (Something I do all too often.) He talked for ten minutes about how he perceives himself at his age, what he wants from life now and in the future, which people he envisions in his life, and his view of aging and his own mortality. He, like myself, was revealing very personal, private thoughts.

"I don't see myself the same way you see yourself and I don't have the same feelings about aging and the rest of my life like you do," he said. "That's okay, I know we're different." And he went on to talk some more.

When he finished, I was flabbergasted. Never in all of our years together, had we reached such a deep level of understanding, respect, and acceptance—not just of the familiar, but also of the unfamiliar, issues where we had differing views.

It is a profound experience to find that your partner listens to, understands, accepts, and respects you for just who you are. We had no Pygmalion schemes in mind. Both of us were different, and that was okay.

With Bernie's retirement and our daughter's wedding, we had been cast adrift in a sea of change. In fact, I would say that those two life events offered the biggest challenges to our relationship.

And we worked and worked and worked. We had endured many high and low points in the eight years since Bernie's retirement. On any page of this book you will find the footprints of some issue we had to work through. I have taken to heart the insights gleaned from my research, clinical practice, and personal life. A marriage is a work in progress that needs constant tending to remain alive and well. But as Leo Tolstoy wrote, "True life is lived when tiny changes occur."

And we are alive and well. Every day offers some other relationship challenge and life hurdle to surmount. I feel we have the tools and we have the willingness.

Bring on tomorrow—we're ready!

Notes

PART ONE: SUDDENLY THE ALGEBRA SHIFTS

7   *Time was*   Ken Dychtwald, *AgeWave: How the Most Important Trend of Our Time Will Change Your Future* (Los Angeles: Jeremy Tarcher, 1989).

Chapter 1: Scenes from a Midlife Marriage

17   *You hear over and over*   Winifred Gallagher, "Midlife Myths," *Atlantic Monthly* (May 1993): 51.

17   *You can look forward*   Ibid., 62. Behavioral scientist Bernice Neugarten has said that the hallmark of healthy middle age is "complexity"—a feeling of being in control of a crowded life while remaining involved in the world.

Chapter 2: Some Things Change; Others Never Will

24   *Those who do have a true psychological upheaval*   Dianne Hales, "The Joy of Midlife Sex," *American Health for Women* 16 (Jan.–Feb. 1997): 53.

24   *Apparently, the frequency*   Ibid., p. 54

27   *The Road*   This discussion is based on William Bridges's book *Transitions: Making Sense of Life's Changes* (Reading, Mass.: Addison-Wesley, 1980).

Chapter 3: The Growth Circle

34   *In a Growth Circle*   This is based on Virginia Satir's work.

35   *In fact, according to the latest research*   John Gottman interview in Thomas H. Maugh II, "Study's Advice to Husbands: Accept Wife's Influence," *Los Angeles Times*, Feb. 21, 1998, p. 1A.

35   *The transitions of empty nest*   Robert J. Havighurst, *Human Development and Education* (London: Longman's Green, 1953), p. 5.

Chapter 4: Empty-Nest Mothers and Midlife Concerns

45   *She will devote just 12 percent*   Based on the work of Alice Rossi, a highly respected sociologist at the University of Massachusetts. Cited in Naomi Golan, *Passing Through Transitions: A Guide for Practitioners* (New York: Free Press, 1981), p. 35.

47   *In many other cultures*   Pauline Bart, "The Loneliness of the Long-Distance Mother," in *The Anatomy of Loneliness,* Joseph Hartog, Ralph Audy, and Yehudi Cohen, eds. (New York: International University Press, 1980).

50   *My interviews highlighted*   This is partially based on the typology of Dawne Schoenholz, "Life Style Selection and Personal Satisfaction among Empty Nest Women" (Ph.D. diss., University of Southern California, 1980).

56   *In fact, by some estimates*   Bob Rosenblatt, "The New Age of Old Age," *Los Angeles Times,* May 11, 1998, p. S1.

56   *Statistics show that midlife adult children*   William H. Van Hoose, *Midlife Myths and Realities* (Atlanta: Humanics Limited, 1985), p. 69.

56   *They are more satisfied*   Gail Sheehy found this in her research with nearly 8,000 men and women who responded to a survey in *Family Circle.* Gail Sheehy, *New Passages: Mapping Your Life Across Time* (New York: Random House, 1995).

Chapter 5: Empty-Nest Fathers and Midlife Concerns

58   *A recent survey of middle-aged women*   Dianne Hales, "The Joy of Midlife Sex," *American Health for Women* 16 (Jan.–Feb. 1997): 78.

63   *Experience themselves as being*   Based on a study of 118 couples conducted by Craig Roberts and Robert Lewis.

63   *On the positive side*   Based on research by the Fatherhood Project in Corinne Nydegger and Linda Mitteness, "Midlife: The Prime of Fathers," in Carol D. Ryff and Marsha Mailick Seltzer, eds., *The Parental Experience in Midlife* (Chicago: University of Chicago Press, 1996).

64   *Children may be closest*   Also based on the Fatherhood Project research.

69   *Midlife isn't the first time*   Based on theme assignment in James E. Birren, *Guiding Autobiography Groups for Older Adults* (Baltimore: Johns Hopkins University Press, 1991).

Chapter 6: Letting Go and Finding Your PPQ

77   *You might have looked to your offspring*   Elinor Lenz, *Once My Child . . . Now My Friend* (New York: Warner Books, 1981).

78   Elinor Lenz warns about these perils in *Once My Child . . . Now My Friend.*

79   *Our attachments to others*   This is based on John Bowlby's work.

86   *And, without it, the transition*   Lillian Carson, *The Essential Grandparent* (Deerfield Beach, Fla.: Health Communications, Inc., 1996), p. 16.

86   *Sometimes rituals help us*   This discussion is based on Rabbi Debra Orenstein's book, *Lifecycles: Jewish Women on Life Passages and Personal Milestones* (Woodstock, Vt.: Jewish Lights Publishing, 1994).

Chapter 7: Replenishing Your "I" Account

94   *For instance, Jerome Kagan*   Jay S. Efran et al., "Lessons of the New Genetics," *Family Therapy Networker* (March–April 1998): 31.

94   *The following exercise*   This is partially based on an exercise in Susan Page's book *How One of You Can Bring the Two of You Together,* (New York: Broadway Books, 1998).

96   This discussion of assertiveness is partially based on Manuel Smith's book, *When I Say No, I Feel Guilty* (New York: Bantam Books, 1979).

98   *Men have not been paragons*   Will Courtenay, "Behavior Factors Associated with Male Disease, Injury, and Death," *American Journal of Preventive Medicine,* cited in Jed Diamond. *Male Menopause* (Naperville, Ill.: Sourcebooks, 1997).

99   *Consider your favorite hobby*   This discussion is based on Barbara Sher's book *Wishcraft: How to Get What You Really Want* (New York: Ballantine Books, 1979).

Chapter 8: Your "You" Account: Taking Care of Each Other

102   *Emotional Intelligence*   This is based on Daniel Goleman's book *Emotional Intelligence* (New York: Bantam Books, 1995).

105   *In most cases, working wives*   University of California, Berkeley, sociologist Arlie Hochschild made this clear in her now-classic book *The Second Shift: Working Parents and the Revolution at Home.* (New York: Viking, 1989).

105   *Unfortunately, the concept*   P. Blumstein, and P. Schwartz, *American Couples* (New York: William Morrow, 1983).

105   *Such unrealistic expectations*   According to Elaine Wethington of the Department of Human Development and Family Studies at New York State College.

Chapter 9: The Seven Marital Themes and the Empty-Nest Marriage: Tending to the "Us"

108   *When you stop labeling*   Based on a discussion in Susan Page's book *How One of You Can Bring the Two of You Together.*

114   *the average person dates only*   According to a recent study cited in Neil Jacobson, *Integrative Couple Therapy* (New York: W. W. Norton, 1996).

115   *Indeed, such community contacts*   This is based on Teresa Seeman's research at the University of Southern California and cited in Jane Brody's article "Good Habits Outweigh Genes as Key to Healthy Old Age," *New York Times,* Feb. 28, 1996.

118   *The Why Technique*   This is a cognitive therapy strategy outlined in Dr. Aaron Beck's book *Love Is Never Enough* (New York: Harper/Perennial, 1988).

120   *Men and women have differing expectations*   Neurolinguistic specialist Deborah Tannen in *You Just Don't Understand* (New York: William Morrow, 1990).

120   *One study found that 70 percent*   Cited in Harold H. Bloomfield and Robert K. Cooper, "Take 5 to Make Love Last," *Prevention* 47 (July 1995): 90.

121   *People often use*   This issue is discussed by Robert C. Solomon, a professor of psychology and philosophy at the University of Texas,

Austin, in his book *About Love: Reinventing Romance for Our Times* (New York: Simon & Schuster, 1988).

121 *To be an attentive, empathic listener* Michael P. Nichols, *The Lost Art of Listening* (New York: Guilford Press, 1995).

123 The discussion of flooding and stonewalling is based on John Gottman's article "What Makes Marriage Work?" *Psychology Today* 37 (March–April 1994): 38 and H. Marano, H. "The Reinvention of Marriage," *Psychology Today* (Jan.–Feb. 1992): 48.

123 *A woman doesn't take well to stonewalling* "Lingering Effects of Marital Arguments," *USA Today Magazine* 125 (Nov. 1996): 8.

Chapter 10: Use Relationship Reviews to Enhance Communication

128 *In fact, when successful marriages are studied* Society for the Advancement of Education.

Chapter 11: Sex and the Midlife Couple

138 *Their erections are more reliable* Judith Sachs, *The Healing Power of Sex* (Englewood Cliffs, N.J.: Prentice Hall, 1994).

140 *The Desire Discrepancy* This discussion is loosely based on Anthony Pietropinto, and Jacqueline Simenauer, *Not Tonight, Dear: How to Reawaken Your Sexual Desire* (New York: Doubleday, 1990).

141 *Moreover, interpersonal issues* Anthony Pietropinto, and Jacqueline Simenauer, *Not Tonight, Dear: How to Reawaken Your Sexual Desire* (New York: Doubleday, 1990).

142 *You might try these other strategies* Judith Sachs recommends them in *The Healing Power of Sex.*

142 *The naysayer should always* Dr. Peter Kilmann of the University of South Carolina, cited in *Not Tonight, Dear.*

145 *In fact, your spouse's character* Gallup, Love and Marriage I and II, cited in Andrew Greeley, *Faithful Attraction* (New York: Tor Books, 1991).

147 *The following sensual pleasuring exercises* William Masters and Virginia Johnson, *Human Sexual Response* (Boston: Little Brown, 1970).

147 *In addition, husbands and wives* This is based on Sonia Rhodes's book with Susan Schneider, *Second Honeymoon: A Pioneering Guide for Reviving the Mid-Life Marriage* (New York: William Morrow, 1992).

Part Four: The Retirement Years

151 *In a 1993 survey of retirees* This discussion is based on Gail Sheehy's book *New Passages: Mapping Your Life Across Time* (New York: Random House, 1995).

152 *Yet we rarely acknowledge* Jules Z. Willing, the former director of the Duke University Institute for Learning in Retirement, explains this in his book *The Reality of Retirement: The Inner Experience of Becoming a Retired Person* (New York: William Morrow, 1981).

152 *In the year 2000* Ken Dychtwald, *AgeWave.*

153 *In 1995, the average age of retirement was 60* Lewis R. Aiken, *An Introduction to Gerontology* (Newbury Park, Calif.: Sage Publications, 1995).

153 *Marriage is the context* Robert C. Atchley, the director of the Scripps Gerontology Center and professor of gerontology at Miami University, Oxford, Ohio, "Retirement and Marital Satisfaction," in M. Szinovacz, D. Ekerdt, B. H. Vinick, eds., *Families in Retirement* (Newbury Park, Calif.: Sage Publications, 1992).

Chapter 12: Retirement: For Better or Worse . . . but Not for Lunch

158 *Research has shown that* Gail S. Eisen, "Living in Harmony in the Retirement Years: Dimensions of Change in the Marital Relationship and Implications for Pre-Retirement Education" (Ph.D. diss., University of Michigan, 1989).

Chapter 13: What Work and Retirement Mean to Men

168 *My interviewees' lives echo* Based on a discussion in Robert S. Weiss's book *Staying the Course: The Emotional and Social Lives of Men Who Do Well at Work* (New York: Free Press, 1990).

169 *As another entrepreneur* Based on the article by Craig E. Aronoff and John L. Ward, "Facing Fears of Retirement. (Family Business)," *Nation's Business* 80 (Feb. 1992): 38.

169 This discussion of reminiscence and the film *Wild Strawberries* is based on Erik Erikson, ed., *Adulthood* (New York: W.W. Norton, 1978), p. 1.

172 This discussion of basic needs is based on Abraham Maslow's hierarchy of needs as elaborated in *Towards a Psychology of Being* (Princeton, N.J.: Van Nostrand, 1968).

173 This discussion on the stages of retirement is based on Robert Atchley's work, "Retirement and Marital Satisfaction."

178 *Anthropologist Joel Savishinsky* Joel Savishinsky, "The Unbearable Lightness of Retirement: Ritual and Support in Modern Life Passage," *Research on Aging* 17 (1995): 249.

178 *In a recent* Wall Street Journal *article* Tony Horwitz, "Home Alone 2: Some Who Lost Jobs in Early 90s Recession Find a Hard Road Back," *Wall Street Journal*, June 26, 1998, p. 1A.

179 *An interesting discussion of retiring policemen* Bill Rehm, "Retirement: A New Chapter, Not the End of the Story," *FBI Law Enforcement Bulletin* 65 (Sept. 1996): 6.

184 The discussion of shadow careers is based on "Your Shadow Career: Second Careers at a Later Stage," *Forbes Magazine* (June 16, 1997): 156.

184 *Overcoming the Myths and Stereotypes about Aging* J. Romaniuk, R. Wiggins, Jr., L. Flexer, R. Finley, and J. Priddy, *Assisting the Older Job Seeker: A Counselor Training Manual* The Virginia Center on Aging, Virginia Commonwealth University, Richmond, October 1980.

185 Strategies for getting back into the workforce are based on T. Harty, K. Kerkstra, and C. Hayes, "It's Never Too Late To Find a Job," *Black Enterprise* 26 (Feb. 1996): 125.

186 Advice on giving your partner support during the job search is based on Jill Jukes and Ruthann Rosenberg, *Surviving Your Partner's Job Loss: A Complete Guide to Rescuing Your Marriage and Family from Today's Economy* (Washington, D.C.: National Press Books, 1993).

Chapter 14: What Work and Retirement Mean to Women

187   *most married couples* Trudy B. Anderson, "Conjugal Support Among Working-Wife and Retired-Wife Couples," in M. Szinovacz, D. Ekerdt, and B. Vinick, eds., *Families in Retirement* (Newbury Park, Calif.: Sage Publications, 1992).

188   *Working women are usually more satisfied* Cary Kart and Charles Longino, "Comparing the Economically Advantaged and the Pension Elite: 1980 Census Profiles," *Gerontologist* 29 (1989): 745.

188   *Married professional women experience* Naomi Golan, *The Perilous Bridge* (New York: Free Press, 1986).

190   *Financial advantage can be one of them* Louis Uchitelle, "She's Wound Up in Her Career, but He's Ready to Wind Down," *New York Times*, Dec. 14, 1997.

191   *Another study found* Marie Haug and Linda Belgrave, "Partner's Health and Retirement Adaptation of Women and Their Husbands," *Journal of Women & Aging* 4 (1992).

191   *A University of Michigan study of 813 married women* Cited in Uchitelle, "She's Wound Up . . ."

192   *Research has shown that a husband's helping* Gary Lee, and Constance Shehan, "Retirement and Marital Satisfaction," *Journal of Gerontology* 44 (Nov. 1989).

PART FIVE: MANAGING SHIFTING NEEDS IN YOUR RETIREMENT MARRIAGE

193   The discussion of activity, diversity, and connection is based on Jules Z. Willing's work, *The Reality of Retirement.*

194   *Each marriage is, in fact, two marriages* Jesse Bernard, *The Future of Marriage* (New York: World Publishing, 1972).

Chapter 17: The Importance of Family and Friends during Retirement

214   *Many studies reaffirm the buffering effects* M. Okun, J. Melichar, and M. Hill, "Negative Daily Events, Positive and Negative Social Ties and Psychological Distress among Older Adults," *Gerontologist* 30 (1990).

214   *the MacArthur Foundation* Teresa Seeman, a participating researcher in the MacArthur Foundation study, cited by Jane Brody in "Good Habits Outweigh Genes as Key to Healthy Old Age," *New York Times*, Feb. 28, 1996.

216   *In 1970, Dr. Arthur Kornhaber* Arthur Kornhaber, *Contemporary Grandparenting* (Thousand Oaks, Calif.: Sage Publications, 1996).

217   *Moreover, today one quarter of all grandparents* This is from the Yankelovich Partners, a research firm. "Grand Tradition," *Modern Maturity* (Sept.–Oct. 1998): 24.

217   *According to recent research* Ibid.

217   *Our children and grandchildren* As Erik Erikson put it so well, it is often through involvement with grandchildren that the seventh and eighth stages of the adult developmental cycle—Generativity vs. Stagnation and Integrity vs. Despair—can be resolved.

218   *Boys and young men need*   Robert Bly, *Iron John*, quoted in L. Carson, *The Essential Grandparent* (Deerfield Beach, Fla.: Health Communications, 1996).

218   *Fifty-seven percent of grandparents*   Yankelovich Partners, "Grand Tradition," 24.

218   *Advice on baby-sitting guidelines* adapted from Kornhaber, *Contemporary Grandparenting.*

220   *Friends can stand you in good stead*   G. Lee and M. Ishii-Kuntz, "Social Interaction, Loneliness and Emotional Well-Being Among the Elderly," *Research on Aging* 9 (1987).

221   *Constructing a Relationship*   This is partially based on an exercise in Elwood N. Chapman's book *Comfort Zones* (Los Angeles: Crisp Publishing, 1990).

Chapter 18: Sex and the Retirement Couple

224   *Sexual activity is the aerobic equivalent*   T. Walz,, and N. Blum, *Sexual Health in Later Life* (Lexington, Mass.: Lexington Books, 1987).

224   *In relation to attitudes regarding sex*   Andrew Greeley reports on these results of a two-part Love and Marriage Gallup Study conducted in 1989 and 1990 that was the first full-scale national examination of sexuality and fidelity in marriage. Andrew Greeley, *Faithful Attraction.*

225   *the body's release of cortisone*   Walz and Blum, *Sexual Health in Later Life.*

225   *more than two hundred medicines*   Deborah Haffner, "Love and Sex after 60," *Geriatrics* 49 (Sept. 1994): 20.

Chapter 19: The Seven Marital Themes and the Retirement Marriage

234   *I asked them to choose*   Approximately half of the twenty-one factors submitted were utilized from a study conducted by Jeanette C. Lauer and Robert H. Lauer, *Til Death Do Us Part* (New York: Harrington Park Press, 1986).

235   *For instance, in a study of fifty-six*   Gail S. Eisen, "Living in Harmony."

238   *an eye-opening exercise*   J. Newstrom and E. Scannell, *Games Trainers Play* (New York: McGraw-Hill, 1980), p. 209.

239   *When your partner listens*   M. McKay, P. Fanning, and K. Paleg, *Couple Skills* (Oakland, Calif.: New Harbinger Publications, 1994).

240   *Other research has shown*   C. Swensen and G. Trahaug, "Commitment and the Late-Stage Marriage Relationship," *Journal of Marriage and the Family* (Nov. 1985): 939–45.

244   *Research no longer supports*   Jamie Talan, "The Anger Factor," *Los Angeles Times*, Sept. 19, 1995, sec. E.

References

Aiken, Lewis, R. *An Introduction to Gerontology.* Thousand Oaks, Calif.: Sage Publications, 1995.

Anderson, Trudy B. "Conjugal Support Among Working-Wife and Retired-Wife Couples." In M. Szinovacz, D. Ekerdt, and B. Vinick, eds., *Families in Retirement.* Newbury Park, Calif.: Sage Publications, 1992.

Angier, Natalie. "For Men, Better Wed than Dead." *New York Times Syndicate,* 1990.

Anson, Ofra, A. Antonovsky, S. Sagy, and I. Adler. "Family, Gender and Attitudes Toward Retirement." *Sex Roles* 20 (1989): 355.

Aronoff, Craig E., and John L. Ward. "Facing Fears of Retirement. (Family Business)." *Nation's Business* 80 (Feb. 1992): 38.

Atchley, Robert C. "Retirement and Marital Satisfaction." In M. Szinovacz, D. Ekerdt, B. H. Vinick, eds., *Families in Retirement.* Newbury Park, Calif.: Sage Publications, 1992.

Barber, Clifton E. "Gender Differences in Experiencing the Transition to the Empty Nest: Reports of Middle-Aged and Older Men and Women." *Family Perspective* 14 (1980): 87–95.

Barry, Dave. *Dave Barry Turns Forty.* New York: Fawcett, 1990.

Bart, Pauline. "The Loneliness of the Long-Distance Mother." In *The Anatomy of Loneliness,* Joseph Hartog, Ralph Audy, and Yehudi Cohen, eds. New York: International University Press, 1980.

Baruch, Grace, Rosalind Barnett, and C. Rivers. *Lifeprints: New Patterns of Love and Work for Today's Woman.* New York: New American Library, 1984.

Beck, Aaron T. *Love Is Never Enough.* New York: Harper Perennial, 1988.

Bernard, Jesse. *The Future of Marriage.* New York: World Publishing, 1972.

Blaker, Karen. *Celebrating 50: Women Share Their Experiences, Challenges, and Insights on Becoming 50.* Chicago, Ill.: Contemporary Books, 1990.

Bloomfield, Harold H., and Robert K. Cooper. "Take 5 to Make Love Last." *Prevention* 47 (July, 1995): 90.

Bloomfield, Harold, with poetry by Natasha Josefowitz. *Love Secrets for a Lasting Relationship.* New York: Bantam Books, 1992, p. 129.

Blumstein, P., and P. Schwartz. *American Couples.* New York: William Morrow, 1983.

Bly, Robert. *Iron John* quoted in L. Carson, *The Essential Grandparent.* Deerfield Beach, Fla.: Health Communications, Inc., 1996.

Bowen, Murray, and M. E. Kerr. *Family Evaluation: An Approach Based on Bowen's Theory.* New York: Norton, 1988.

Bowlby, J. Holan, "The Nature of the Child's Tie to His Mother." *International Journal of Psychoanalysis* 39 (1958): 350–373.

Bradford, L., and M. Bradford. *Retirement: Coping with Emotional Upheavals.* Chicago: Nelson-Hall, 1979.

Bridges, William. *Transitions: Making Sense of Life's Changes.* Reading, Mass.: Addison-Wesley, 1980.

Brody, Jane. "Good Habits Outweigh Genes as Key to Healthy Old Age." *New York Times,* Feb. 28, 1996.

Buber, Martin. *I and Thou.* Translated by W. Kaufman. New York: Scribner's, 1970.

Butler, Robert. "Age: The Life Review." *Psychology Today* (Dec. 1971).

Carson, Lillian. *The Essential Grandparent.* Deerfield Beach, Fla.: Health Communications, Inc., 1996.

Carter, Jimmy, and Rosalynn Carter. *Everything to Gain: Making the Most of the Rest of Your Life.* New York: Times Books, 1987.

Carter, Rosalynn, with Susan K. Golant. *Helping Yourself Help Others.* New York: Times Books, 1994.

Chapman, Elwood N. *Comfort Zones.* Los Angeles: Crisp Publications, 1990.

Chernin, Kim. *The Obsession.* New York: Harper & Row, 1981.

Conaway, James. "Reinventing The Good Life." *Fortune* (Aug. 19, 1996): 110.

Courtenay, Will. "Behavior Factors Associated with Male Disease, Injury, and Death." *American Journal of Preventive Medicine.* Cited in Jed Diamond, *Male Menopause.* Naperville, Ill.: Sourcebooks, 1997.

Covey, Stephen. *The Seven Habits of Highly Effective People.* New York: Simon & Schuster, 1989.

Cuber, J., and Harroff, P. *The Significant Americans: A Study of Sexual Behavior Among the Affluent.* New York: Appleton-Century-Crofts, 1965.

Diamond, Jed. *Male Menopause.* Naperville, Ill.: Sourcebooks, 1997.

Dreyfus, Nancy. *Flashcards for Real Life.* Berkeley, Calif.: Celestial Arts, 1993.

Dumaine, Brian. "Why Do We Work?" *Fortune* (Dec. 26, 1994): 196.

Dychtwald, Kenneth, and Joe Flower. *Age Wave: The Challenges and Opportunities of an Aging America.* Los Angeles: Jeremy Tarcher, 1989.

Efran, Jay S., Mitchell A. Greene, and Don E. Gordon. "Lessons of the New Genetics." *Family Therapy Networker* (March/April 1998).

Eisen, Gail S. "Living in Harmony in the Retirement Years: Dimensions of

Change in the Marital Relationship and Implications for Pre-Retirement Education." Ph.D. diss. University of Michigan, 1989.

Erikson, Erik. *Childhood and Society,* 2nd ed. New York: W. W. Norton, 1963.

Erikson, Erik, ed. *Adulthood,* New York: W. W. Norton, 1978.

Farrell, Michael, and S. Rosenberg. *Men at Midlife.* Boston: Auburn House, 1981.

Fengler, Alfred P. "Attitudinal Orientations of Wives Toward Their Husbands' Retirement." *International Journal of Aging and Human Development* 6 (1975): 139.

Ferraro, K., and T. Wan. "Marital Contributions to Well-Being in Later Life." *American Behavioral Scientist* 29 (March/April 1986): 423–37.

Gallagher, Winifred. "Midlife Myths." *Atlantic Monthly* (May, 1993): 51.

Gallup, *Love and Marriage I and II,* cited in Andrew Greeley, *Faithful Attraction.* New York: Tor Books, 1991.

Golan, Naomi. *Passing Through Transitions: A Guide for Practitioners.* New York: The Free Press, 1981.

———. *The Perilous Bridge.* New York: The Free Press, 1986.

Golant, Mitch, and Susan Golant. *Finding Time for Fathering.* New York: Ballantine Books, 1992.

Goleman, Daniel. *Emotional Intelligence.* New York: Bantam Books, 1995.

Gordon, Suzanne. "The Fundamental Meaning of Choice." *Los Angeles Times,* June 21, 1991, p. B7.

Gottman, John. "What Makes Marriage Work?" *Psychology Today* 37 (March/April 1994) 38.

Gould, Roger. *Transformations.* New York: Simon & Schuster, 1978.

Gradman, Theodore, J. "Masculine Identity from Work to Retirement." In *Older Men's Lives,* Edward H. Thompson, ed. Newbury Park, Calif.: Sage Publications, 1994.

"Grand Tradition," *Modern Maturity* (Sept./Oct. 1998): 24.

Gray, John. *Men Are from Mars, Women Are from Venus.* New York: Harper-Collins, 1992.

Greeley, Andrew. *Faithful Attraction: Discovering Intimacy, Love and Fidelity in American Marriage.* New York: Tom Doherty Books, 1991.

"Grumpy Old Men," *MacLean's* 109 (April 22, 1996): 31.

Hales, Dianne. "The Joy of Midlife Sex." *American Health for Women,* 16(Jan./Feb. 1997): 78.

Harder, Arlene. *Letting Go.* Holbrook, Mass.: Bob Adams, 1994.

Harty, T. K., K. Kerkstra, and C. Hayes. "It's Never Too Late to Find a Job." *Black Enterprise* 26 (Feb. 1996): 125.

Havighurst, Robert J. *Human Development and Education.* London: Longman's Green, 1953.

Hochschild, Arlie, and Anne Machung. *The Second Shift: Working Parents and the Revolution at Home.* New York: Viking, 1989.

Horwitz, Tony. "Home Alone 2: Some Who Lost Jobs in Early 90s Recession Find a Hard Road Back." *Wall Street Journal,* June 26, 1998, p. 1A.

Jacobson, Neil, and Andrew Christensen. *Integrative Couple Therapy.* New York: W. W. Norton, 1996.

Johnson, Sue. "The Biology of Love." *Networker* (Sept./Oct. 1997): 37.

Jong, Erica. *Fear of Fifty.* New York: HarperCollins, 1995.

Jukes, Jill, and Ruthann Rosenberg. *Surviving Your Partner's Job Loss: A Complete Guide to Rescuing Your Marriage and Family from Today's Economy.* Washington D.C.: National Press Books, 1993.

Jung, Carl. *Development of Personality.* London: Routledge, 1954.

Haffner, Deborah. "Love and Sex after 60." *Geriatrics* 49 (Sept. 1994) 20.

Haug, Marie, and Linda Belgrave. "Partner's Health and Retirement Adaptation of Women and Their Husbands." *Journal of Women & Aging* 4 (1992): 5.

Hogan, Mary Ann. "The Good Marriage." *Mother Jones* 20 (July/Aug. 1995): 18.

Karp, David A. "The Social Construction of Retirement among Professionals 50 to 60 Years Old." *Gerontologist* 29 (1989): 750

Kart, Cary, and Charles Longino. "Comparing the Economically Advantaged and the Pension Elite: 1980 Census Profiles." *Gerontologist* 29 (1989): 745.

Kasindorf, Martin. "Divining the George Bush Ex-Presidency." *Los Angeles Times Magazine,* July 23, 1995, p. 6.

Kornhaber, Arthur. *Contemporary Grandparenting;* Thousand Oaks, Calif.: Sage Publications, 1996.

Lauer, Jeanette C., and Robert H. Lauer. *Til Death Do Us Part.* New York: Harrington Park Press, 1986.

Lee, Gary, and Constance Shehan. "Retirement and Marital Satisfaction." *Journal of Gerontology* 44 (Nov. 1989): 226–30.

Lee, G., and M. Ishii-Kuntz. "Social Interaction, Loneliness and Emotional Well-Being Among the Elderly." *Research on Aging* 9 (1987): 459–82.

Lenz, Elinor. *Once My Child . . . Now My Friend.* New York: Warner Books, 1981.

Lerner, Harriet. *The Dance of Anger.* New York: Harper & Row, 1985.

Levinson, Daniel. *Seasons of a Woman's Life.* New York: Knopf, 1996.

Louden, Jennifer. *Couples' Comfort Book.* San Francisco: Harper San Francisco, 1994.

Macklin, Jeanne. "Women, Stress, and Midlife." *Human Ecology Forum* 23 (Fall 1995), 20.

Manheimer, R. J. "The Changing Meaning of Retirement." *Creative Retirement* (1994): 44–49, quoted in, Joel Shavishinsky "The Unbearable

Lightness of Retirement: Ritual and Support in Modern Life Passage." *Research on Aging* 17 (1995): 243–59.

Marano, H. "The Reinvention of Marriage." *Psychology Today* (Jan./Feb. 1992): 48.

Maslow, Abraham. *Towards a Psychology of Being.* Princeton, N.J.: Van Nostrand, 1968.

Mason, Bobbie Ann. *Feather Crowns.* New York: Harper Perennial, 1993.

Masters, William, and Virginia Johnson. *Human Sexual Response.* Boston: Little, Brown, 1970.

Maugh, Thomas H, II. "Study's Advice to Husbands: Accept Wife's Influence." *Los Angeles Times,* Feb. 21, 1998, p. 1A

McKay, M., P. Fanning, and K. Paleg. *Couple Skills.* Oakland, Calif.: New Harbinger Publications, 1994.

Neugarten, Bernice. "Dynamics of Transition of Middle Age to Old Age." *Journal of Geriatric Psychiatry* 4 (1970): 82.

Newstrom, J., and E. Scannell. *Games Trainers Play.* New York: McGraw-Hill, 1980.

Nichols, Michael P. *The Lost Art of Listening.* New York: Guilford Press, 1995

Nydegger, Corinne, and Linda Mitteness. "Midlife: The Prime of Fathers." In Carol D. Ryff and Marsha Mailick Seltzer, eds., *The Parental Experience in Midlife.* Chicago, Ill.: University of Chicago Press, 1996.

Okun, M., J. Melichar, and M. Hill. "Negative Daily Events, Positive and Negative Social Ties and Psychological Distress among Older Adults." *Gerontologist* 30 (1990): 193.

O'Neil, J. M., and R. W. Stillson. "Predictions of Adult Men's Gender-Role Conflicts: Race, Class, Unemployment, Age, Instrumentality, Expressiveness, and Personal Strain." *Journal of Counseling Psychology* 38 (1991): 458.

Orenstein, Debra. *Lifecycles: Jewish Women on Life Passages and Personal Milestones.* Vermont: Jewish Lights Publishing, 1994.

Page, Susan. *The 8 Essential Traits of Couples Who Thrive.* New York: Dell, 1994.

——— *How One of You Can Bring the Two of You Together.* New York: Broadway Books, 1998.

Peterson, Karen S. "Viagra Treats Male Fear of Facing Midlife." *USA Today,* April 28, 1998, p. 4D.

Pietropinto, Anthony, and Jacqueline Simenauer. *Not Tonight Dear: How to Reawaken Your Sexual Desire.* New York: Doubleday, 1990.

Pineo, P. "Disenchantment in the Latter Years of Marriage." *Marriage and Family Living* 23 (1961): 3–11.

Polston, Betty L. "Creative Marriage in the Retirement Years: A Qualitative Investigation of Those Strategies That Contribute to a Fulfilling Marriage After Retirement." Ph.D. diss., Pacific Western University, 1995.

———. "The Search for a 'Model for Success' in Retirement Marriage."

Perspectives on Retirement: Newsletter of the International Society for Retirement Planning (Spring 1995).

Proffitt, Steve. "His Defining Moment." *Los Angeles Times Magazine*, Dec. 7, 1997.

Pruchno, Rachel A., Norah D. Peters, and Christopher Burant. "Child Life Events, Parent-Child Disagreements, and Parent Well-Being: Model Development and Testing." In Carol D. Ryff, and Marsha Mailick Seltzer, eds. *The Parental Experience in Midlife*. Chicago: University of Chicago Press, 1996, p. 564.

Rehm, Bill. "Retirement: A New Chapter, Not the End of the Story." *FBI Law Enforcement Bulletin* 65 (Sept. 1996): 6.

Reichard, S. F. Livson, and P. G. Peterson. *Aging and Personality*, New York: John Wiley, 1962.

Rhodes, Sonya, with Susan Schneider. *Second Honeymoon: A Pioneering Guide for Reviving the Mid-Life Marriage*. New York: William Morrow, 1992.

Romaniuk, J., R. Wiggins, Jr., L. Flexer, R. Finley, and J. Priddy. *Assisting the Older Job Seeker: A Counselor Training Manual*. Richmond, Va.: The Virginia Center on Aging, Virginia Commonwealth University, October 1980.

Rosenblatt, Bob. "The New Age of Old Age." *Los Angeles Times*, May 11, 1998, p. S1.

Rubin, Lillian. *Women of a Certain Age*. New York: Harper & Row, 1979.

Ryff, Carol D., and Marsha Mailick Seltzer, eds., *The Parental Experience in Midlife*. Chicago: University of Chicago Press, 1996.

Sachs, Judith. *The Healing Power of Sex*. Englewood Cliffs, N.J.: Prentice Hall, 1994.

Satir, Virginia. *Peoplemaking*. Palo Alto, Calif.: Science and Behavior Books, 1972.

Scarf, Maggie. *Unfinished Business: Pressure Points in the Lives of Women*. New York: Doubleday, 1980.

Schlossberg, Nancy K. *Counseling Adults in Transition: Linking Practice with Theory*. New York: Springer, 1984.

Schoenholz, Dawne R. "Life Style Selections and Personal Satisfaction among Empty Nest Women." Ph.D. diss., University of Southern California, 1980.

Scileppi, Kenneth. *Caring for the Parents Who Cared for You*. New York: Insight Books, 1992.

Shavishinsky, Joel. "The Unbearable Lightness of Retirement: Ritual and Support in Modern Life Passage." *Research on Aging* 17 (1995): 243–59.

Sheehy, Gail. *New Passages: Mapping Your Life Across Time*. New York: Random House, 1995.

Sher, Barbara. *Wishcraft: How to Get What You Really Want*. New York: Ballantine Books, 1979.

Silverberg, Susan B. "Parents' Well-Being at Their Children's Transition to Adolescence." In Carol D Ryff, and Marsha Mailick Seltzer, eds., *The Parental Experience in Midlife*. Chicago: University of Chicago Press, 1996.

Smith, Manuel. *When I Say No, I Feel Guilty*. New York: Bantam Books, 1979.

Solomon, Kenneth, and Peggy Szwabo. "The Work Oriented Culture." In *Older Men's Lives*, Edward H. Thompson, ed. Newbury Park, Calif.: Sage Publications, 1994.

Solomon, Robert C. *About Love: Reinventing Romance for Our Times*. New York: Simon & Schuster, 1988.

Sontag, Susan. "The Double Standard of Aging." *Saturday Review* (1972), cited in Maggie Scarf, *Unfinished Business: Pressure Points in the Lives of Women*. New York: Doubleday, 1980.

Strindberg, August. *The Father*. Adapted by Richard Nelson. New York: Broadway Play Publishing, Inc., 1996.

Swensen, C., and G. Trahaug. "Commitment and the Late-Stage Marriage Relationship." *Journal of Marriage and the Family* (Nov. 1985): 939–45.

Talan, Jamie. "The Anger Factor." *Los Angeles Times*, September 19, 1995, sec. E.

Tannen, Deborah. *You Just Don't Understand*. New York: William Morrow, 1990.

Thompson, Edward H. "Older Men as Invisible Men in Contemporary Society." In *Older Men's Lives*, Edward H. Thompson, ed. Thousand Oaks, Calif.: Sage Publications, 1994.

Uchitelle, Louis. "She's Wound Up in Her Career, but He's Ready to Wind Down." *New York Times*, December 14, 1997.

Van Hoose, William H. *Midlife Myths and Realities*. Atlanta: Humanics Limited, 1985.

Viorst, Judith. *Necessary Losses*. New York: Simon & Schuster, 1986.

Wallerstein, Judith, and Sandra Blakeslee. *The Good Marriage: How and Why Love Lasts*. Boston: Houghton Mifflin, 1995.

Walz, T., and N. Blum. *Sexual Health in Later Life*. Lexington, Mass.: Lexington Books, 1987.

Weishaus, Sylvia, and D. Fields. "A Half-Century of Marriage: Continuity or Change?" *Journal of Marriage and the Family*, Aug. 1988, 763–774.

Weiss, Robert S. *Staying the Course: The Emotional and Social Lives of Men Who Do Well at Work*. New York: Free Press, 1990.

Willing, Jules Z. *The Reality of Retirement: The Inner Experience of Becoming a Retired Person*. New York: William Morrow, 1981.

"Your Shadow Career: Second Careers at a Later Stage." *Forbes Magazine* (June 16, 1997): 156.

Index